THE GRASS ROOTS FUNDRAISING BOOK

How to Raise Money in Your Community

By
Joan Flanagan
For
The Youth Project

THE **SWALLOW PRESS** INC.

CHICAGO

The Youth Project

The Youth Project is a non-profit, tax-exempt organization designed to assist citizens in the building of local community organizations. It was founded in 1970 and operates with field offices in Atlanta, San Francisco and Washington, D.C. Utilizing support from foundations, church groups and individual contributors, The Youth Project provides modest seed funding and substantial technical assistance to new and growing citizen action organizations staffed by young people.

Specific contributions for this book came from:

> Edward Hazen Foundation
> Norman Foundation
> Veatch Program, North Shore Unitarian Society
> Playboy Foundation
> Max and Anna Levinson Foundation
> McDonald's Corporation

The Youth Project
1000 Wisconsin Avenue, N.W.
Washington, D.C. 20007

Author's Acknowledgments

Grass roots fundraising is a team sport. "I couldn't have done it without you" is always true, and it should never go unsaid.

This book is also a team effort. It represents thousands of hours and mountains of advice shared by hundreds of people. Although there are too many to list here, I deeply appreciate each and every one of you, and wish you continuing success on your fundraising efforts. It also represents the work of dozens of volunteers who read through the manuscript to clarify the final draft.

It represents the vision and concern of The Youth Project staff and board. They were my best advisors throughout the project. Everyone deserves special recognition for their creativity—from Margie Tabankin who launched the project to Lenny Conway who guided it to completion, and Chuck Savitt who read through reams of drafts, The Youth Project field staff who recommended the top fundraisers around the country, and Darlene Kovarik who taught me about bookkeeping.

I especially want to thank my hard-working typists Phyllis Fox, Eunice Militante, and Barbara Hughes, and my brilliant, considerate editors, Andra Medea and Ron Dorfman.

Special thanks go to the Business and Professional People for the Public Interest (BPI) who gave me an office and encouragement as well as many, many good examples.

Most of all, thanks to my family and friends for two years of moral support and optimism. I couldn't have done it without you.

JMF

Preface

Six years of working with hundreds of grass roots groups in urban and rural America has taught The Youth Project that the best source of funding for an organization is its own constituents. Accordingly, one of our primary objectives when helping to build local citizen organizations is to move them towards financial self-sufficiency. We commissioned *The Grass Roots Fundraising Book* to assist this process.

Through membership drives, raffles, ad books, bake sales, bingo games, door-to-door solicitations and a variety of other local fundraising events, many local groups have, after a few years, been able to raise all or most of their operating budgets. In addition to generating income, good grass roots fundraising is good organizing. Such activities increase community participation, develop leadership skills and help give the local membership a greater sense of identity with the organization.

Most people, however, have not had any experience in planning local fundraisers and need assistance to determine what events would be appropriate for their situation. Therefore, this book provides a compilation of how-to information which includes a detailed analysis on choosing the event most profitable for the organization; what steps should be taken and who should do it.

To maximize the book's impact in communities, The Youth Project now is designing a series of grass roots fundraising training institutes. During the next two years, the institutes will be conducted by Joan Flanagan and others in locations across the country. Our hope is that citizen groups will utilize both the book and this followup training to pave the way for organizational self-sufficiency.

Lenny Conway
Executive Director
The Youth Project

Washington, D.C.
June, 1977

ABOUT THE AUTHOR

Like most Americans, Joan Flanagan learned about fundraising by doing it: carrying her membership dues to Brownies, selling American Field Service travelog tickets, and washing cars for the church youth group. She sold concessions at the high school football games, buttons for political candidates, and the most Girl Scout cookies in her troop.

Joan joined the Citizens Action Program (CAP) as a volunteer in 1970, and was hired as office manager in 1971. This Chicago action organization ran up an impressive list of victories: reducing air and water pollution, exposing property tax scandals, stopping the Crosstown Expressway, and improving conditions for senior citizens. At the same time, CAP leaders and staff were teaching Joan about fundraising: dances, ad books, raffles, rummage sales, theatre parties, Bingo, and door-to-door solicitation.

In 1975, Joan was hired by The Youth Project to research grass roots fundraising. To prepare this book, she visited more than twenty-five urban and rural communities and 150 organizations, attended sixty benefits, and read all of the current fundraising literature. In addition, she volunteered on twelve fundraising events, including a senior citizens dinner, a discotheque party, and a symphony concert. She also taught at eleven fundraising workshops to make sure that the information was clear, correct and could be copied.

A native Chicagoan, Joan graduated from Homewood-Flossmoor High School and Denison University. In the coming months she will be presenting a series of training workshops with other grass roots fundraising experts. The Youth Project is sponsoring these workshops to help membership organizations improve their fundraising skills and gain greater financial self-sufficiency.

Contents

INTRODUCTION 11

1. WHY DO IT? 15

2. HOW TO DO IT 21
   Ethics 31

3. FUNDRAISING IS SELLING 34
   How to conquer fear 38

4. BENEFITS 44
   How to shop for supplies (chart) 47
   How to estimate the income (chart) 50
   How to price the tickets 51
   Basic arithmetic 53
   Checklists—assets, goals, basics for any event 57

5. BENEFITS FOR BEGINNERS 60
   Bibliography 60

   BOOK/PLANT SALE 63

   COFFEE 65

   HAUNTED HOUSE 68
      Holidays 70

   MEMBERSHIP CANVASS 73

   MOVIES 74

   POT LUCK SUPPER 86
      International food feast 88
      Taste and Tell 88

RAFFLE 89
    50/50 monthly raffle 91

6. INTERMEDIATE FUNDRAISERS 93

AUCTION 93
    Auctioneer's Auction 97
    Dutch Auction 97
    Memorabilia Auction 97

BAZAAR 98
    All-Day Raffle 103
    Silent Auction 103

CELEBRITY LECTURES 105

COCKTAIL PARTY 110
    How to find a rich person 111
    Do-it-yourself cocktail party 115

COOKBOOK 116
    Retail marketing 118
    Wholesale marketing 119

DANCE 121

HOUSE TOUR 126
    Christmas Sale House Tour 127
    Bus Tour 127
    Showcase House 129

LUNCHEON 130
    Invitations 131

THEATRE PARTY 132
    Patron tickets 134

7. THE BIG TIME 137
   AD BOOK 138
   ANTIQUE OR ART FAIR 139
   CARNIVAL 140
   CONCERT 141
   DINNER 143
   LAS VEGAS CASINO NIGHT 144
   MARATHONS 145
   MOVIE PREMIER 146
   TELETHON & RADIO MARATHON 147
   TENNIS TOURNAMENT 147

8. FUNDRAISING FOREVER 148
   DUES 148
   BINGO 151
   BUSINESSES 153
   CORPORATE GIVING 156
   DEFERRED GIVING 159
   DIRECT MAIL 160
      Small local mailing 162
   DOOR TO DOOR CANVASSING 164
   NEWSLETTER 165
   SERVICES 166
   SPEAKERS BUREAU 168

9. PUBLICITY 172
How to promote an event 177
Bibliography 178

10. MAKING BOOK 181
Legal and taxes 181
How to handle the money, or ideas from a
    non-accountant 182
Bibliography 186

11. APPENDIX 190
How to plan an annual fundraising calendar 191
How to schedule a rummage sale 194
How to prepare a donor card 199
Where to get advice 200
Exercise to make fundraising more familiar 202
Bibliography 204
The Foundation Center Regional Libraries 209
How to rebound from a fund-loser 216
Training Schools for Organizers and Leaders 219

The Youth Project
1000 Wisconsin Avenue, N.W.
Washington, D.C. 20007

Introduction

You have a vision of how the world could be better, and you have a plan to make it happen. You have an organization to achieve the plan and it has members willing to do the work to win the victories. What else do you need?

Money.

This book will tell you how to use your own common sense and energy to raise the money you need. You can create your own fundraising plan using the members and resources you have right now, so that you can pay the bills and build your organization at the same time.

It's not easy. But if you do it right, you'll get the good feeling that you can be sure of all the money you need this year, and in the years to come. You will have a stronger organization that can win bigger victories. You will get more members and better leaders. And you'll make a lot of friends and share good times together.

Grass roots fundraising will open doors to discover new people and new experiences. Each person can grow and stretch and learn something new every day. You will make memories to cherish for the rest of your life.

This book is a distillation of the advice of more than 600 people in the United States and Canada who have done successful fundraising. Most of them learned to do it by using their own good sense and imagination. They were all very generous in sharing their stories, their triumphs, and their occasional disappointments. All of them were eager to learn more. From all of them to all of you, here is the best current advice on grass roots fundraising. Use it, add to it, and share it with your friends.

This book is written for everyone from the loyal member who bakes a cake for the bake booth to the chairperson of the fundraising committee, the treasurer, and the president. It is written for the staff person responsible for raising money as well as for the Board that hires the staff. It is written for brand new groups that have a handful of people with a vision but no budget, and it is written for established organizations that have hundreds of members but need more money for expansion.

It is different from other fundraising books in two ways. I assume you already have some active members (even if there are only a few) and leaders elected by them. So there is no chapter on "Board Development," which is what professional big-money fundraisers call recruiting rich people to be on the Board. Grass roots fundraising respects the integrity of home grown leaders and loyal members. This is "do it yourself" fundraising, using the people you already have to make the money you want.

I also assume that you have a program *you* want to accomplish. This book is written for the doers, the action people, the get-up-and-go folks. I assume your members are clear-sighted, level-headed people who can choose challenging goals and make a plan to achieve those goals. So there is no chapter on how to design a project that some bureaucrat outside the community will want to fund—"program planning" in development jargon. Grass roots fundraising gives everyone who benefits from your program the chance to support it, so that you can do what your members want to do.

Grass roots fundraising is primarily raising money from other individuals, although you will also learn how to get big donations from institutions, churches, and corporations. Is it possible to raise a significant amount of money from individuals? Of course. In 1975, individuals gave more than $21 *billion* to not-for-profit organizations in America. This was 80 per cent of *all* money given for philanthropy in the U.S. Churches and religious causes get virtually all of their money from individuals, and always have. If they can do it, you can too.

The greatest resource you can have in grass roots fundraising is the creativity and energy of your own members. You can make use of this talent right now to launch an exciting, profitable fundraising program or to improve and expand the one you already have. It doesn't matter if your organization is small or inexperienced. All you have to do is decide to do it.

You can take what you have and make anything happen. For example, Kate Bradley had lived all her life in Petros, in Morgan County, Tennessee. She and her neighbors were thirty-five miles from the nearest hospital, and there was one 86-year-old doctor to treat the whole county. When Vanderbilt University medical students set up a health fair in Morgan County in 1972, they discovered most of the people who came out for the free check-up needed and wanted medical care. They tested and treated 1,200 people the first year and 1,000 the second, most of whom had never had a physical or even the most basic tests.

Kate decided it was time Morgan County had a health clinic. She started from scratch, in a community with an average income of $5,000, among people who had no history of giving to anything except their churches, and at a time when 160 men were on strike. In two years, she and her neighbors raised $25,000 to build their own clinic. They had rummage sales every Saturday, showed movies at the school, ran quilt raffles, and sponsored turkey dinners, cake walks, a Halloween carnival, gospel singings, and craft sales to raise the money. They even sponsored the first puppet show ever held in Petros, Tennessee. Local men worked nights and weekends to do the construction, wiring, plumbing, panelling, and painting.

Today they have their own clinic, their own doctor and nurse practitioner, a special program for diagnosing and treating the black lung disease common among miners, and they're preparing an office for a dentist. Fees are low, but everyone pays for each visit, even if it is only $1.00. As Kate says, "It gives them pride. This is their clinic, not a charity." Kate has hosted visitors from all over Appalachia and travelled as far away as New Mexico to tell other isolated, low-income groups how they too can get their own clinics.

The Morgan County clinic got built because the people did what they knew best to raise the money. Everyone who put up a jar of jam or nailed up a piece of panelling has an investment in the clinic and the community. Each is proud of what he or she contributed for the good of all.

You can do it too. I hope next year you can tell the story of how you achieved your success, how you made your dream come true.

Chapter 1
Why Do It?

Grass roots fundraising includes all the ways to raise money using your own members and your own resources. Ad books and auctions, bake sales and barn dances, carnivals and cake walks, all are grass roots fundraisers.

"Grass roots" has nothing to do with gardening. You can be a tenants' club in a big city skyscraper and still be grass roots. You can be a national environmental organization with a goal of one million dollars, or a high school ecology club with a goal of $100. You can be a brand new block club that has just won its first stop sign, or a state-wide action league working on six issues in fourteen counties. "Grass roots" simply means you are ordinary people. You don't have to be a professional fundraiser, or have a lot of money yourself, or know a lot of important people to raise money for your group. To do grass roots fundraising you need only a basic understanding of money and people.

You already know a lot about money. Everybody works, pays taxes, buys things, and would like to buy more. When you outfit the kids for school, or plan a vacation, you are managing money.

You already know a lot about people too. Any group activity—throwing a party, singing in the choir, belonging to the PTA, working for a political candidate, going to school, playing on the company softball team—has taught you about how people like to do things together.

Now you are going to be the fundraiser for your group. As an active member of an ambitious organization, you know it takes money to run your program. You can use what you know about money and what you know about people to do grass roots fundraising. What's more, you can intentionally strengthen the group at the same time that you raise the money.

The dual goal of grass roots fundraising is to pay the bills and to build the organization. Your fundraising program should fit natural-

15

ly with the strategy and goals of the members. Every new block club that joins a city-wide program should increase the income and the strength of the group. Just as you set goals for your chapter, such as setting up a women's credit task force, working for property tax reforms, or remodeling the church kitchen, you should set specific goals for your fundraising program. When you choose to do grass roots fundraising, you can set your own financial goals and organizational goals.

The Financial Goals

There are a lot of benefits from doing your own fundraising besides the cold, hard cash. When you map out your fundraising strategy, consider all that you can gain from raising your own budget by your own work.

You gain self-sufficiency. A well-planned, long-range fundraising campaign will guarantee that you can pay your staff, buy your supplies, and run your program. It's a good feeling to know you can take care of yourself, whether you are a not-for-profit corporation or an individual.

You gain independence. When you have an income from a wide variety of fundraising events, you know you have the talent and the techniques to raise money. No one can threaten to cut off your funds. You are free to plan and run whatever programs the members choose.

You gain peace of mind. Knowing you can plan and control your income will take away the anxiety of the leaky roof, or the horror of a missed payroll. You can use your energies to make things happen, rather than worry about which creditor to put off. As any coach will tell you, "Winners decide what they want to do. Losers worry about what they don't want to have happen to them."

You gain pride. Remember how proud you felt when you got your own first paycheck? The pride of raising your own money, and sharing the success, will boost the morale of your group in the same way. Grass roots money is honest money. Everyone in the group can be proud of his or her part in raising the money. You can answer any questions from a new member, a donor, or the press honestly and easily from your own open, up-to-date reports. Raising your money from a variety of sources will also reduce the temptation to accept money from any single donor who could compromise the organization.

Never underestimate the moral advantage of raising your own money. Be proud of your independence and the support of your neighbors. When Kate Bradley was raising money for the Petros, Tennessee, health clinic, she learned the railroad was going to sell the land around its unused tracks. She wrote the president of the railroad and asked for the first option to buy the land for the clinic building. Then the politicians in Morgan County learned the land was for sale and tried to outbid her. It was clear they could double or triple her offer. Coal companies in Tennessee are used to getting their own way by using county and state politicians. Kate drove 175 miles to Nashville to meet with the railroad president and the representatives of the coal companies. When she walked into the meeting she saw she was the only woman in the room.

The president said, "You must be Mrs. Bradley."

"I am," she said, looking him straight in the eye. Without waiting to be asked, Kate Bradley spoke her piece to the older man:

"Sir, I know you are going to honor your letter giving the health clinic the right to buy your land in Petros. I know these politicians can give you a lot more money. But I just want you to know that our money comes from cupcakes. We've had a rummage sale every Saturday, and held dinners and bake sales. Everyone in the community has given me a quilt, or a jar of beans, or put up some preserves to sell for the clinic. That's where my bid comes from."

The railroad president sold her the land, and adjourned the meeting.

Grass roots fundraising proves you have a lot of people who support your work. If most of your neighbors will help you sell tickets, you know, and the people outside of your group will know, that your people want the program enough to work for it.

This gives you a boost with other funding sources. Ironically, successful grass roots fundraising makes it easier for you to raise money from institutions. Foundations and national church giving programs that hand out grants are interested in groups that can show their own people will support them. Corporations and United Way executives want to choose the best outfits from a flood of applications, and they need some way of judging your effectiveness. If you can go to foundation executives and show them that you signed up 60 new members last month, or had 500 people at your dance, or that you raise 75 per cent of your budget yourself, they can feel confident that their money will be well spent if they give it to you. Since most big-money funders have little or no staff support, the depth and breadth of your grass roots fundraising is their only concrete evidence that the people in your community *want* your program.

Many foundations today make what they call a matching grant or a challenge grant. They will give you a set amount of money if you will raise a specified amount in a given time period. For example, in 1976, Virginia Citizens for Better Reclamation could get $1,000 from The Youth Project if they were able to raise $200. They did it with membership dues, a barn dance and a quilt raffle. Then they got another $1,000 because they were able to raise $600. Altogether, in the first year they raised more than $3,500 themselves, recruited more than 200 members, and launched a promising campaign to preserve the mountains in Virginia.

The foundations can test the strength of local support and a program's willingness and capacity to raise money in this way. They do not want to invest money in a group that may become dependent on them year after year. The grass roots group gets the benefit of knowing that every dollar it raises is doubled. People don't always like "charity" from the outside; matching grants are joint efforts and help work toward local independence.

Wily old Ben Franklin was the first person in America to use the matching grant. In 1750, he lobbied the Pennsylvania Assembly to create the first government matching grant—for his favorite project, the Pennsylvania Hospital. The assemblymen agreed to appropriate £2,000 if Franklin's volunteers could raise £2,000. As Franklin wrote in his autobiography:

". . . the members [of the Assembly] now conceiv'd they might have the credit of being charitable without the expense . . . ; and then, in soliciting subscriptions among the people, we urg'd the conditional promise of the law as an additional motive to give, since every man's donation would be doubled; thus the clause work'd both ways."

The Organizational Goals

You should plan to use your grass roots fundraising to improve three major parts of the organization: the program, the membership, and the publicity.

PROGRAM GOALS:

Grass roots fundraising proves the popularity of your program. Your program is your product, it is what you "sell" to everyone, members and non-members alike. If people give you money to run a sports program, or fight an expressway, or support the symphony, you know they support your goals. If they won't pay for it, they don't want it. This gives you a way to compare the popularity of different programs. If people support your campaign against the highway, but don't contribute to the recycling center, you know which one to put first.

If contributions to a program have dropped off, it may be time to change the program or let someone else try it. For example, a civic club may be very enthusiastic about raising the money to set up a recycling center, but then lose interest in running it every Saturday. It is time to turn it over to the Scouts or the local environmental club and move on to something new.

MEMBERSHIP GOALS

Grass roots fundraising can be a magnet to bring in new members. People are naturally more eager to join a group of people they met at a party in their own neighborhood at which they got a personal introduction to the president. After they have had a chance to meet the folks, they will feel more comfortable at a business meeting or an action. Everyone feels shy in a new group and afraid they will be different from the old members. The more controversial your program is, the more potential members may be timid about joining unless they know a current member. The hoopla and fun of fundraising events gives the new people a chance to learn who you really are in the most pleasant surroundings.

Fundraising work will deepen the commitment of the members who do it. If they go out to "sell" their club to their neighbors or local business people, they must learn more about their group, its structure, and its goals. They must also be proud of the booty they bring back. Besides getting credit for their important work in supporting the organization, they should also get a bigger voice in how it is spent.

Grass roots fundraising is the most democratic way to raise money. For those of us who spend a great deal of our lives in meetings, democracy can be an irritatingly laborious way to make decisions. But it is also the fairest, the most reasonable, and the most productive way for groups to make workable, popular decisions.

The enthusiasm created by successfully raising your own budget will be reflected in all your meetings and events. You can tell the minute you walk in the room if a group has the vitality and confidence of members who raise their own money; you can see the sparkle in their eyes. Which leads us to the most important point: people who raise their own money will control their own organization. They can hire and fire their staff, they can expand, and they can make choices. He who pays the piper, picks the tune; it may be a cliche, but it is also true.

Plan fundraisers that are fun for everyone. It is important to share good times together, to make your own fun, to sing your own songs, and to have an occasion to look forward to. The jokes, the food, the prizes at a good party build the friendships which are the glue of the organization. Even putting up posters or cleaning the gym can be fun when you do it with people you like. Throw a party for every victory, celebrate holidays, and install your new officers with a flourish. Some organizations hold birthday parties for themselves every year to bring together all their members and staff, publicize themselves to friends, and let their supporters know it is time to send in another donation. The clever entertainment and good spirits turn a pot luck supper in a church basement into one of the most enjoyable, and profitable, events of the year.

PUBLICITY GOALS

Good fundraising creates good publicity. Your event gives you many chances to tell your story to new people. If you are selling your cookbook in the bank lobby, or raffling chances at your club, you are an ambassador for the group. When you run a hay auction you will reach all the farmers in the area; when you run a flea market in the town square you will reach all the shoppers. As you sell ads for the ad book to business executives, you are teaching the corporations about the importance of your work. So *all* of your efforts are productive. Even if you do not make a sale, you have made every person you talk to more aware of your organization.

Good publicity helps introduce you to others who would like to help. The Runaway House in Washington, D.C. gave a reception for *Washington Post* columnist Art Buchwald as "Runaway of the Year, 1943." They invited society and news media stars, and as a result of the good publicity and new friends they made, the Runaway House was chosen as the recipient of the profits from the 1976 annual pet show at Mrs. Ethel Kennedy's home in McLean, Virginia—a tidy $10,000.

Fundraising can also produce publicity to improve your image. The leaders of the gay community and the police department run a charity softball game each year in San Francisco. The profits go to send poor kids to summer camp or provide meals on wheels for shut-ins. More than 3,500 people come to see the game and it always gets great press coverage. Both the gays and the cops get a better image.

A comprehensive grass roots fundraising plan produces a solid financial base, enthusiastic members, and colorful publicity. Created with care and imagination it will get better every year, and generate more money from less work.

Chapter 2
How To Do It

How do you turn the dreaming into doing? Where do you start? You start with the members you have, get them moving and keep them going. Apply the physics of fundraising: take your members' potential energy—all their ideas and talents—and turn it into kinetic energy—planning events and asking for money. Then keep up the momentum. You know it takes more energy to bring a pan of water to the boil than it does to keep it boiling. The same is true with people. It takes an extra push at the beginning but gets easier once you're rolling.

The grass roots fundraiser's goal is to use the members' energy most efficiently. Try to get the greatest dollar return for each member's hour of work. Copy the people who are best at making money and making people work together efficiently: good business people and good organizers.

Good fundraising is good business. The best business executives have the best program skills—in preparation, execution and follow-through. The same professionalism will increase the productivity of any organizational fundraising program.

At the same time, good fundraising is good organizing, caring about people on a personal level. The best organizers learn the best "people" skills—teaching, motivating, and understanding others as individuals and as groups. The same clarity and consideration will improve both the quantity of volunteers and the quality of their work.

Good fundraising also involves good manners. The best business leaders and the best organizers both work at being thoughtful to others: they are always on time, they remember names, and they follow-through promptly on their promises. These are the skills that make every meeting more pleasant—and make everyone look forward to the next meeting.

These skills will make all of your fund-raising activities more profitable and more pleasant. Most involve simple common sense, while some take a little extra discipline. Figure out how they apply to

21

your own situation, then start to use them regularly—for your own fun and profit.

Good Fundraising Is Good Business

The idea behind good business practices is that you will make the most money by providing the best product most efficiently. Your product is your program—staffing ranchers' anti-strip mining organization, lowering homeowners' utility rates, or keeping the art museum open. The more efficiently you sell your program, the more money you will make.

Successful grass roots fundraisers choose good business practices because they work. Recently, many of the organizations opposing the worst of the big corporations have foolishly rejected what is good about business along with what is bad. Making money is not wrong, evil, unsavory, or something to be ashamed of. Money itself is neutral—it is neither good nor bad. Only one's choices in getting and spending money have values attached. The difference between a healthy grass-roots organization and a greedy multi-national corporation is in how they make their choices. When people who share common values make their choices by an open, democratic vote, they are going to make moral choices about how they raise and how they spend their money.

You choose to spend your money on staff, supplies, and program to achieve the goals of the group. The more money you have, the more good you can do. Obviously, it would be wise to copy those business practices which have evolved over centuries to produce the highest profits. These include preparing long-range plans, making the most money in the least time, and keeping clear records.

MAXIMIZE THE PROFIT

One of the goals of grass roots fundraising is to make the most money in the least time. You want to make a lot of money quickly, so that the members can spend more of their time on the program, cleaning up the parks or fighting the nuclear power plant.

Always consider which fundraising events will be most economical in terms of the volunteers' time. It is much easier and quicker to sell one $100 ad page than it is to sell twenty $5 dance tickets or 400 raffle chances for a quarter each. The time of your skilled members is your most valuable asset—don't waste it.

Respect your members' time and also respect your customers' time. If your volunteer goes to the bank and asks for $100 when she could get $1,000, it means it will take that member ten times as long to make the same $1,000. This volunteer would use her time better doing her homework to pinpoint the highest possible donation she could get from the bank. Then when she goes to the bank and asks for $1,000 in a lump sum she gets her $1,000 in one-tenth of the time. Also, asking for the higher figure tells the bank: 1) she's done her research on the community's resources; 2) she respects the bank; and 3) she is serious about her program and serious about raising money.

It takes thorough research to calculate what will be the highest amount you can get from each giver, and it takes real courage to ask for it. Boldness pays off. The more money you can get from each meeting, the more time you will have left to prepare your testimony for the city housing committee.

Another tool to increase the profit per member hour is a detailed schedule to help you get control of your time. (See sample schedule in the Appendix.) Parkinson's observation (which can be proved whenever you have to do housework or filing) is that work expands to fill the time available. I think people are attracted to political campaigns because they know it will be an exciting, high-publicity, *short* effort with a definite deadline. Win or lose, after election day, you're *through*.

You can also attract more workers to your fundraising program, and increase each one's profits, by preparing a complete timetable with specific deadlines for each stage of the project. The more efficiently you pre-plan and publicize the event, the more you can shorten the actual work time. When Bob Russell took over the Montgomery County, Indiana, United Fund, he inherited a corps of workers who usually took months to collect funds from local residents. In 1970, Bob did a brilliant pre-campaign promotion including a contest for all the school children to design MUFFY (*M*ontgomery *U*nited *F*unds *F*or *Y*ou) and a kick-off parade with all the county high school bands and baton twirlers. The actual solicitation and collection of money was compressed into a fourteen-day blitz. The same corps of workers collected $84,000 in just two weeks, almost double the take from the previous year's twelve week campaign.

MAKE LONG RANGE PLANS

Serious business persons work systematically, set goals, and know where they are going. They make long range plans, assume they will be in business for a long time, and try to make more money every year.

The most efficient way to boost your profits is to schedule your big fundraisers so they can become annual events. Then you don't have to start from scratch every blessed year. There is no reason to re-invent the wheel every year for your big fundraiser, especially when you can make more money each year improving the wheel you have. The first time you do an event is really training time—you are learning how to do it. Every following year you should make more money as you gain expertise.

The Women Employed Ad Book made $3,500 its first year, 1972. In 1975, it netted almost $9,000. The WE leaders had four years of trained salespeople and staff who were able to pinpoint the best targets, reduce costs, increase incentives, and streamline the sales procedure.

When you hit on an exceptionally good idea, the jump can be even more dramatic. Leaders of eight women's groups in Baltimore pulled together a "Women's Fair" to provide a setting for all local women's groups to explain their programs, present information, and recruit members. The first fair in 1973 made $525, and was jammed all day with visitors eager to sample this tempting smorgasbord of organizations. The second fair was held at the Pimlico Race Track to kick off International Women's Year in January, 1975. It netted $2,500—nearly five times as much!

You can always find something extra to add new life to a proven winner. The Coyote Point Museum Auxiliary in San Mateo has presented a Decorator's Show House each spring for twenty-one years to raise money for the children's natural history museum. They get the area's outstanding interior decorators to transform a vacant mansion and then run tours through the house. (See Chapter 6.) In addition to the regular tours, over the years they have added an art gallery, an antique shop, a luncheon room, a tea room, and a wine tasting! Repeating and improving the Show House program increases the attendance, publicity and profit each year. Careful work on the mailing list makes the increase cumulative, so that the attendance has grown from 3,000 in 1958 to 27,500 in 1976.

This sort of predictable, business-like fundraising plan will also allow you to work with regular for-profit businesses to your mutual benefit. In the San Mateo Show House, the Auxiliary provides the setting and the businesses get the exposure. Each decorator presents his or her best work and each tourist gets a program listing the decorators' names and addresses. Both the Coyote Point Museum fund and the decorators' businesses benefit.

The reverse happens in Viroqua, Wisconsin, where the bank provides the setting and the charities provide the attraction: the best baked goodies in Vernon County.

The bank lets a different civic group run a bake sale in its lobby each Saturday. When the farmers and shoppers come to town, they know they can get mouth-watering goodies like krumkake, rosettes, and doughnuts, using their good Wisconsin butter in Norwegian family recipes. The bank gets more traffic because of the bake sale, and each organization gets a bigger market without having to worry about publicity or the weather, while knowing well ahead of time which will be its Saturday. By cooperating, both the bank and the local charities make more money.

Just as repetition of an annual event increases each year's profits, repeating events throughout the year will also boost profits. Try to regularize your fund-raising calendar. A thrift shop is a regularized rummage sale; house-to-house solicitation is a regularized membership drive. The CIA (Community Improvement Association of Calumet Park) runs a raffle that dependably produces $250 a month. In addition, the drawing is shrewdly scheduled for the CIA's monthly meeting so the optimistic gamblers swell the audience.

KEEP ACCURATE RECORDS

Clear, complete records are the best tools to use to regularize your fundraising efforts and increase your profits. You will get the most customers for this year's County Fair if your invitations are compiled from last year's receipts and mailing list. You can be a better shopper and make more money if you know the expenses and profit from each part of last year's fish fry.

In fundraising, as in any serious business, it is essential to keep complete records of all transactions. You need to know exactly where you stand today and to be able to predict how well you will do next month. In a healthy grass roots organization it is doubly important to have clear, complete, up-to-date records. First, you need specific data to prepare budgets, plans, and schedules. Second, since the group's decisions are made democratically, delegates can cast sensible votes only when they have accurate information on current income and expenses.

Clarity is desirable in all fundraising efforts; it is indispensable in your record keeping. A democratic organization must have clear records that anyone can understand. Reports that only the treasurer can decode or records written on the back of last week's agenda are confusing in the short run and lead to disaster in the long run. People invented numbers to communicate precise amounts. "It costs $9.00 to print 1,000 tickets" is specific and informative. "A lot of tickets don't cost much" is ambiguous and inadequate.

Your records are your recipe for future successes—make them

as precise as possible. Uncertainty causes wasteful guess-work and discouragement. It's like trying to cook with your grandmother's recipe: "Add enough milk to make liquid, stir for a little while, cook until almost golden, add some of the sauce, and cook til done." Clear reports, exact numbers, and current records will make all your fundraising more manageable.

Good Fundraising Is Good Organizing

The goal of grass roots fundraising is to raise money and to build a strong organization at the same time. Just as it is profitable to copy successful business people who are the best at raising money, it is also fruitful to copy successful professional organizers who are the best at building organizations. Talented organizers succeed because they work hard to understand and motivate people, both as individuals and as groups.

The first step is understanding that you must work with the world as it really is. The world is made up of people who come prepackaged with ideas, emotions, and values. To make your fundraising plan succeed, you have to do your homework and take the time to think about what makes people tick.

Since you want people to give you money, the first facet of human nature you need to consider is the reason people give money when they are asked. Fundraising is simply asking people to give you money to support a program. What makes fundraising exciting is that each person gives for a different reason. The challenge is to figure out *why* they give. What do they want in return? What is their self-interest? Do they want their names in the newsletter or do they want to be asked to join the finance committee, or more directly, do they want to raise funds that improve neighborhood schools? The key to any successful request is discovering beforehand what will make the donor take action—give.

There are no formulas to provide an easy answer. You can't say all Democratic lawyers under 40 in Connecticut will give to ACLU. People are like snowflakes—each one is different. Each one will act —give—only if he or she believes there is a reason which is personally important.

MAKE IT PERSONAL

So *make* it personally important. Individualize everything as much as you can. Make each donor feel as though he or she were your most intelligent and most important supporter. If I have my choice between responding to letters addressed "Dear friend," "Dear sister," "Dear concerned American," "Dear fellow Republican," or "Dear Joan," I am going to respond to the Dear Joan letter.

Add a personal note whenever you send an invitation or make a call. "Will you sit at my table?" or "Can I give you a ride?" is much better than "I hope I'll see you there." The personal touch helps the shy people feel welcome and comfortable, and makes everyone feel like you want them to become part of the group as well as give money.

Put the donors first and you will understand more about them and why they support you. If you want to find a prospective donor's self-interest, all you really need to do is ask. Then listen. A good listener is more rare than the golden eagle. Besides learning a lot, you'll find there is nothing more flattering than sincere interest in someone's comments. Direct mail professionals tell you to literally count the number of "you's" and the number of "I's" in a letter, and if the "I's" outnumber the "you's," do it over. This is also an excellent rule when you ask for money person-to-person.

Asking *in person* is the best way to individualize a request for money. It is more pleasant and more profitable to discuss the program live than over the phone or in a letter. When you are a live, in-person human being, you can get a donation this year, and lay a strong foundation for next year. The American Friends Service Committee does *all* of its fundraising through person-to-person visits—and they have a 100 per cent renewal every year.

Grass roots fundraising rule Number One is "People give to people." Every successful fundraiser, professional or volunteer, when asked what advice to give someone just starting to raise money, answered, "Tell them 'People give to people.' " Everyone appreciates individual attention.

An extra advantage of asking in person is that the people who ask not only become better fundraisers, but they usually become better givers themselves. Since they know what it takes to ask for money, they will respond better to a fund request than someone who has never raised money. Thus grass roots fundraising produces more members who are both better fundraisers and better givers.

SET GOALS

A grass roots fundraiser plans a program with three goals: 1) Each person will feel good about his or her work; 2) each event is a success; and 3) the whole organization is stronger and more unified. Like a professional organizer, the experienced fundraiser knows *nothing* happens strictly by accident. The profit, in terms of both dollars and satisfaction of the workers, has to be planned. Just as the business person sets goals to make more money, the fundraiser sets goals to make measurable improvements in the group: more members, stronger committees, and better leaders.

Begin at the beginning: start raising money at the very earliest opportunity. Passing the hat at the first public meeting helps the audience realize that *someone* had to pay to print the agenda, rent the room, and make the coffee. Asking for volunteers for the finance committee helps them realize that this will be a serious campaign which will need an office, professional staff, and lots of supplies. If you are trying to get a stop-sign on a dangerous corner, you may be able to win the stop sign quickly with few expenses. If your goal is to win 24-hour free public transportation for senior citizens, it is going to be a long, expensive campaign. When you launch the fundraising immediately, everyone in the first meeting knows you are serious about winning and will work harder to bring more people to the next meeting.

Since one of your goals is to expand the core of volunteers, actively recruit and involve everyone you can in the fundraising. Never turn down a volunteer. Use your imagination to think of a job for everyone. Senior citizens can be your official hosts and hostesses. Housebound parents can bake for the bake sale. Teenagers can put up posters, park cars, and run the check-room. Even smaller children can help with decorations—they *like* to cut out leaves for the Harvest Moon Ball.

Each new volunteer gives you access to another family, another group of friends, new businesses, clubs and churches. The potential of every member is multiplied by all his friends and acquaintances. In the late Mayor Richard J. Daley's new math, each city job was worth seven votes. I think each volunteer is worth more than seven new contacts. Clearly, the more volunteers you attract, the more potential givers you can reach. Professional fundraisers call this "donor acquisition," organizers call it "building the base," and preachers call it "evangelism."

To guarantee bringing more people into the action, set goals and then break them into manageable pieces. For example, you set a goal of finding 100 new members during the six weeks you work on the nuclear moratorium dance "Atom Eve." Break this goal into parts for each person. If you have 10 people on the planning committee, then each planner needs to find 10 new members, or 2 a week for five weeks. Asking each leader to find two new members each week for five weeks is a manageable task with competition built in. A goal of 100 new members with no assignments or timetable will never be reached.

PLAN THE FUN

Last, but certainly not least, decide to have fun while you raise the money. Plan the fun just like you plan the work. Make up your mind to have a good time, and your volunteers will be chomping at the bit to start the next project. In 1975 Lois Weisberg and Juanita Banez from BPI pulled together 125 people to produce and sell a concert with Antonia Brico conducting the Chicago Symphony Orchestra and the women of the William Ferris Chorale. The fifteen-member organizing committee crowded into the tiny BPI conference room every Monday morning, did the work, and planned the fun. In three months they scheduled a brunch, a cocktail party, a champagne picnic, and a "sold-out celebration luncheon" as well as forty-nine film showings. Starting from scratch to produce BPI's first special event, they sold out all 4,000 seats in the Auditorium Theatre and netted $25,000.

Most important, they decided to make many new friends for BPI and they succeeded. They produced such an overwhelming feeling of good will that, like the five minute ovation at the end of the concert, no one wanted the project to end. At the wrap-up meeting of the organizing committee, each one asked "What can we do next?" and "Who should we get for next year?"

Everybody wants to feel like a winner in a winning organization. The beauty of grass roots fundraising is that every member can improve his or her own skills and increase the budget at the same time. Each person should feel more and more self-confident, closer to the other members, and prouder of the organization as the fundraising campaign goes on.

Good Fundraising Is Good Manners

Grass roots fundraising is no more than members asking for money to support their organization. The fundraiser's job is to arrange matters so that both the asker and the askee enjoy the experience and will want to do it again. Good manners are a basic tool to make any transaction go more smoothly.

Respect the expectations of the people you meet. Everything is easier when you both play by familiar rules. Courtesy is not to be confused with hypocrisy. Courtesy is caring enough about the other person to learn how they want to be treated, and then making the extra effort to act the way they expect.

Good manners are simply common sense and respect for others. Respect the time of busy people: make an appointment, be on time, get to the point, and do not stay too long. Treat other people as you would like them to treat you, and try to see things from their point of view. Address their mail correctly, and if you are not sure, take the time to look it up. Even if you think a letter to "Dr. Marcus Welby, M.D." looks all right, Dr. Welby knows that it should be either "Marcus Welby, M.D.," or "Dr. Marcus Welby."*

A good impression may not always bring immediate results, but it will pay off in the long run. You will discover many people who are very interested in your work, but have already spent this year's budget. Though they may not give money themselves, they may be willing to introduce you to other givers. If the potential donors remember you favorably as the serious, courteous representative of an exciting project, they may well make allowances to contribute next year. It is imperative to treat each person as an important, intelligent individual. If you slight someone even unintentionally, you are not going to be welcomed back.

Give a personal touch to your fundraising by sending prompt, individual thank-you notes. When Sally Berger and her partner called on Chicago executives to raise money for the Michael Reese Hospital Research Institute, each sent every exec a hand-written thank-you note for meeting with them. Then they each sent a hand-written thank-you note for the donation. The hospital staff also sent an official thank-you letter and receipt. Thus each donor received *five* thank-you notes. Sally got writer's cramp writing more than 700 notes—and increased the annual research budget from $260,000 to $1,400,000.

Be sure to thank your own workers too. Cleveland Women Working, which organizes clerical workers in downtown Cleveland, ran a raffle as its first fundraiser and netted $950 in only three weeks. More than 80 women successfully sold raffle chances—and each got a hand-written thank-you from the leaders.

Thank the people who do not expect to be thanked. Remember the workers who are doing their jobs, but who do something extra for you. If policemen re-route the traffic, or a janitor comes in early to let you in the building, or secretaries stay late to get the mailing out, let them know, in writing, that you noticed and appreciated their work. Let their boss know too.

Good manners make every meeting easier for you and for the other person. Remember fundraising rule #1: People give to people. Since each transaction requires at least one meeting, make it easy on

---

My favorite name blunder came in 1971 when I was selling ads for CAP. I went into a pub named "Brian Boru's" and arrogantly insisted on speaking to Mr. Boru. The bartender said, "That will be a little difficult, darlin'. Brian Boru was the king of Ireland who defeated the Vikings at the Battle of Clontarf in 1014. Would you perhaps rather see the manager, who is still alive?"

yourself and make each one a pleasure. Learn—and use—good manners and decide to enjoy every encounter. You will.

Ethics

The values of the members form the foundation of the organization; shake their faith and the entire organization will crumble. In the same way, an honest grass roots fundraising campaign must be run with standards of behavior built on the members' values. Being clear about your standards and maintaining them is critical to building a long-term trusting relationship between the people who give money and the members who spend it.

Your first responsibility is to see that you are raising money for an honest, ethical organization. This means one that has open access for any person who wants to join, open democratic decision-making, clear, complete, up-to-date reports, frequent reporting to all representatives, and sensible financial controls. An ethical organization makes sure that the people who raise the money have a say in how it is spent. Think of the photo of the president of the "Women's Board" presenting a check to the male president of the "Board of Directors" so the all-male board can decide how to spend the money. If volunteers are asked to raise money, but are denied a voice in spending it, that is simple exploitation. Never waste your talents on any group which will not allow you to help prepare the budget and vote on expenditures. If the staff or entrenched leadership refuses you access to the decision-making, the real action, join a different group. There is simply no way you can honestly ask anyone to give their money to support an organization which wants their money but not their ideas.

Be sure the board which runs the organization is democratically elected and representative of the members. There is a professional fundraising theory that the board should always be made up of the richest and most powerful people to be found. But a grass roots fundraiser respects the integrity of the members. Put your own people first. If you have a group of welfare mothers who want to build an after-school center for your kids, never deny one of your own members a place on the board so you can include the wife of the bank president. Although you must be pragmatic about the self-interest of the rich and powerful people, do not fall into the lure of finding the "right people" to "do it for you." It is immature to depend on even well-intentioned people outside the organization, and it is unethical to let anyone who does not have a real following in the membership make decisions for the group.

Your standards must include a genuine curiosity and concern about all the people involved. Consciously work to treat each person as an individual. Stereotypes are confusing, unprofitable, and often just wrong. It is a common mistake to exclude or ignore people as volunteers or donors because they have been labeled. We all do it. She won't help because she's "a limousine liberal" or "a suburban socialite" or "not a feminist." He won't give to us because he's "a rockbed Republican" or "a male chauvinist" or "a culture vulture." It's unfair for you to make someone else's decision by not asking for help in the first place because of your own stereotypes. It is also 100 per cent unprofitable. Include everyone—you will be pleasantly surprised at the number and variety of allies you really have.

Set your own standards and be accountable to your own membership. Make specific, clear, and public criteria for donors that feel comfortable to the whole group. The Chicago NOW chapter sold the centerfold of its 1973 ad book to *Playboy* because it would be a humorous turn-about and the group would use the money well to fight for women's rights in Chicago. That was all right with the majority of the membership. On the other hand, Women Employed's ad book committee voted to refuse ads from any employment agency they knew exploited women. WE decided that a clear distinction between the good agencies and the bad agencies was more important than the money.

No one else can set your standards for you. Each group decides for itself what is proper. For example, Roman Catholics raise money from Las Vegas nights, liquor, and lasagna. Episcopalians think the gambling is wrong, but will sell mulled wine next to the bratwurst booth. Methodists abstain from Bingo and booze, but sponsor lavish dinners. What you decide is less important than *how* you decide. The Board must openly and democratically vote on where to draw the line, based on public organizational policy. It is better to return a donation than to lose members because it offends their values.

Never accept or pursue a donation which would restrict the choices of the organization. It is a common tactic of industry to try to buy off trouble before it arrives. Business people know when they're guilty, and they know you're smart enough to find out when they're guilty too. They also know bribery has worked with other groups, and they may hope it will work with you.

Does this mean you can never accept money from the "enemy"? Again, this has to be openly and democratically decided by the leaders. When the Citizens Action Program (CAP) did its first ad book, Father Leonard Dubi sold a full-page ad to Valentine Janicki, colorful trustee of the scandal-ridden Metropolitan Sanitary District and proprietor of a religious novelties store. Dubi was completely clear that CAP would continue its campaign to force the Sanitary District to stop polluting the Southwest Side. CAP took Janicki's money, continued the campaign, and won without breaking stride.

Blackmail is the other side of bribery. It is just as wrong to tell a polluter your group will ignore his polluting plant if he agrees to underwrite the dance as it is to accept his bribe to leave him alone. If you choose to take money from a person or corporation you are attacking, make sure you both understand this donation will in no way affect your adversary relationship.

The goal of grass roots fundraising is to build an adult, self-sufficient organization. A mature organization is like a mature person. It has learned to set its own standards, it respects the integrity of its own members and the individuality of those outside the organization, and it is proud of its own principles.

Chapter 3
Fundraising Is Selling

All fundraising is really selling. You are selling your program —renovating Symphony Hall or counseling ex-convicts. Like a salesperson, you have to understand the psychology of your customers. You have to figure out who your customers are and how to reach them most effectively.

There is a psychological advantage to selling the positives of the program: You get away from the feeling that you are begging. Be proud to offer an opportunity to support the most exciting program in town. Instead of saying, "Give me money because I think ecology is important," you can say, "Give me $500 and we will bring 200 kids who have never seen a bluebird or a chipmunk to the wildlife center for a day." It is an honor to raise funds for an innovative and important project.

Any sales campaign begins by defining the market for the product. Your market is everyone who will benefit from your program. If your goal is to reduce pollution in Pittsburgh, everyone in Pittsburgh will benefit from your success and everyone should support it. If your goal is to improve women's working conditions, your market is all women who work, as well as all people who care about women who work.

Accentuate the Positive

Always sell the program creatively and forcefully. A basic sales technique is to present any feature of the sales item as a "benefit"; that is, take the basic package and highlight each element as attractive and special. Copy the best sales techniques used by professional sales people and advertisers.

Think positively. Always sell the best parts of your program and brag about your accomplishments. Never assume that everyone knows you built the playground because the story was in the newspaper. Clip the story to show them what you've done, then tell them about your new idea to build two more playgrounds and run a coordinated sports program after school.

Break down the costs of the program, and tell people exactly what their money will buy. For example, the American Friends Service Committee Midwest Office's 1975 Christmas letter set out examples of what each donation could provide. They ranged from $5 to $1,000 to give an idea of the scope and variety of AFSC projects, while appealing directly to the donors:

$5 supplies sufficient yarn for sweaters for 5 Vietnamese children.

$9 provides a month's supplemental feeding for a child in a Santiago shantytown.

$15 enables a mother in prison to stay in touch with her children and arrange for their care.

$25 gives information and materials to a labor group wanting to know about the B-1 bomber and other military spending.

$50 provides counseling to senior citizens on Social Security income, food stamps or Medicare.

$75 allows educators and parents to work together on teaching non-violence or on the problems of suspensions in schools.

$120 enables an Arab and Israeli to meet for dialogue and join in a common search for better understanding.

$300 helps defray the costs of an international seminar to promote peace among nations.

$1000 gives 5 ex-offenders room, board and the loving counseling they need for a lasting re-entry into society.

This gives the potential donor a picture of what his or her money will buy: sweaters, food, counseling. The donation seems much more important and tangible than if the AFSC had said something vague like: "Help us relieve suffering."

Always ask for a specific amount. I discovered when doing house-to-house solicitation that if I said "Any donation will help," I got contributions in the range of 25¢ to $1.50. When I asked for "ten to twenty-five dollars" I got an average donation of $12.50. When I said, "For a donation of $5.00 or more you can receive the newsletter," I got $5.00.

Asking for a specific amount can also justify a high price for a simple event. The Democratic National Committee sponsored a barbecue fundraiser for Jimmy Carter with a "51.3%" theme, the percentage of women in the U.S. population. Four hundred women paid $51.30 for an ordinary barbecue plus a new version of a Southern classic: "Fritz's Grits", named in honor of candidate Walter "Fritz" Mondale.

Although you should always try to ask for a specific amount for a specific program, you should also appeal to the broader vision of the donor. For example, when you ask Father Reilly for $250 for scholarships for ten ghetto girls to take a self-defense course in their public housing project, the immediate program is the course. The intermediate goal is trained self-defense teachers to teach the rest of the women in the project to protect themselves. The ultimate goal is for every woman to be safe and confident wherever she goes and whatever she does. You should make it clear to Father Reilly that you are asking him to contribute both because he understands the immediate dangers in the housing project and because he shares the vision of a world where all can live with dignity and control their own lives.

One final note: Never ask anyone to pay off your deficit or make a donation because you "need" the money. Everyone wants to back a winner. Political fundraisers have proven the importance of having their candidates seem to be the front runner in the first poll; it increases the donations. In fact, you will notice that if it is a close race, the second place candidate will often produce his own poll to "prove" *he* is really in first place. People want to back a winner, to pay for successful programs. In politics, it is an investment which they hope will be repaid with political responsiveness when their candidate wins. If they donate to the Community Congress Fair Tax Program, they hope their property taxes will be reduced when CCFTP wins. Remember, everyone wants to be part of a winning team, even if their part is only giving money. Sell your "most likely to succeed" program and donors will give out of their own desire to share your success.

Be Prepared

Make the most of every opportunity. Be prepared to meet with potential donors at their convenience. If Mrs. Gotrocks is leaving for Nairobi for three months and the only time she can see you is tomorrow for breakfast at 7:30 a.m., be enthusiastic and prepared to see her at breakfast. She may be a lark who has already been up for two hours, jogged her mile, and done her paperwork, whereas you may be an owl who is a total zombie in the morning. So what? A professional will be up and ready to go. Even if you're like me and think that morning is only for farming and fishing, get up, drink coffee, run around the block, and be there—bright, alert and *on time*. The same is true if you're a lark and have to meet Frank Sinatra after the last show at 2:30 a.m. Take a nap, stay hungry, don't drink, do whatever you have to, but be at your best when you meet him. A real professional makes the special effort to overcome her biological clock and be at her best. Remember, you are asking *him* to do *you* a favor—to meet with you. Then you are going to ask him to commit himself to the organization with a large donation. Anyone with any money gets lots of these requests. You may get only one chance, so make the most of it.

Get control of your time. Own and use a watch and a calendar; start and end all meetings on time, and pay all your bills when due. Send your own invoices promptly. Respect the busy schedules of your volunteers and, especially, your donors. The best way to get more out of your time is to talk less and listen more. Read *Get Control of Your Time and Your Life,* by Allen Lakein.

Do your homework. Then you will be ready for any short-notice meeting. If you are to sell donors on your project, you need to know all about your organization, why it needs money, and how it spends money.

As you do your homework on the immediate needs and final goals, also keep track of where the money goes. It is good promotion to keep a donor informed through the year with news—especially good news: we saved the park, or we got the mayor to give us permanent space in City Hall to do free blood pressure testing. While Nancy Klimley raised $900,000 for the Chicago Heart Assn., she sat through lengthy (low cholesterol) lunches with doctors discussing their research. Each time she went out to ask for money, she could explain the current status of each research project, and whom the Heart Assn. hoped to fund next.

When you know your facts and figures, practice talking about the group's work *and* asking for money. Be sure to practice both parts. Some people can give a beautiful talk on the importance of their organization, but can never bring themselves to ask for the money. Most potential donors will wait for you to ask for the money. If you don't ask they have nothing to respond to. Don't leave it to implication—say exactly what you want.

Since that is the hardest part, practice it first and most often. Then you'll be more comfortable with "closing"—asking for the sum you want. Ask someone else to pretend to be the banker. Then the two of you can rehearse presenting your case and asking for his donation. The one playing banker should ask logical questions, and you should practice complete but short answers. The banker should also try to divert you to other subjects—the state of the economy, the World Series, the renovation across the street—and you should practice gracefully but firmly returning the conversation to your topic—a donation for your organization. Never go in and ask for any donation without having practiced first. Jason Robards is better because he rehearses; so am I; so will you be.

A real professional always tries to get good advice. Solicit as much advice as possible. As Yuri Rasovsky, who produces original radio plays, says, "If I talk to two people I get confused; if I talk to six or seven I get enlightened." Your own membership is always the best place to start; ask questions and listen—you'll be surprised how clever they are. (See the Appendix for more sources of advice and a bibliography of materials written by successful fundraisers.)

Don't be afraid to ask other volunteer or professional fund-raisers and sales people to brainstorm on your project. This book is the result of 600 people sharing their ideas with me. I found that the most successful people were the most generous with their time and encouragement, and I'm sure the best people in your community will be tickled to help you.

How to Conquer Fear

Money is like sex. Everyone thinks about it, but no one is supposed to discuss it in polite company. Everyone has a lot of inhibitions about money, especially asking for money; think of all the cartoons of the office worker afraid to ask for a raise. In our society fears about money are *normal*.

Most people are afraid to ask someone else for money. They are afraid they will fail and afraid they will lose face. A few admit they are afraid, but others will give a lot of excuses: I can't make calls at the office; I don't know anyone rich, I can't get a baby-sitter. Or they postpone forever: I can't do it until after the kids are back in school, the holidays, the election, the tennis season, the vacation, the promotion. Volunteers often make asking for money sound like a bothersome chore, like taking out the garbage. It is not a chore; it is a challenge. Asking for money is like going out to beat up a bear. The larger the amount, the more frightening it becomes, because you have to beat up a bigger bear.

One of the jobs of a good fundraiser is to teach volunteers how to conquer their fear of the unknown. The first step is understanding that each person comes complete with his or her own set of fears and hang-ups, and the package of inhibitions usually includes a fear of asking for money. The second step is realizing this is normal and nothing to be ashamed of. The third step is working with the volunteers so they can get control of their own fears.

It is imperative that you understand and appreciate your volunteers' real feelings, because when members succeed at fundraising they do more than bring in money for the organization. They have also overcome their own fear. When they raise money, they have won a personal victory, they have conquered the bear. When people can raise money, they can do anything.

WHY PEOPLE GIVE

Asking for money is actually a common transaction that happens all the time. Each of us is asked for money much more often than we ask others. Just think of how many fund appeals you get in the mail every day; how many do you send? We have all been in touch with fundraising since the days we carried our dime dues to Scouts or saved our allowance to subject our tummies to junk food and death-defying rides at the county fair and the parish carnival.

To get over the feeling that fundraising is intimidating, make it familiar to each member. First ask everyone to think about why they themselves give. Have them write down on paper every contribution they remember, who asked for it, and why they gave. Cover everything: the Girl Scout cookies from your niece, your dues to the block club, the T-shirt from your alderman, the bumper sticker from the high school football team, the tickets to the fireman's ball. Figure out why you gave to each one. Most of the time, you give for one of two reasons. Either someone is selling something you want anyway, or it is in your own self-interest to give. Once you understand why you give to people, you will understand why others will want to give to you.

For example, the easiest way to raise money is to sell something people want to buy anyway. For example, what happened when you bought your niece's Girl Scout cookies? She was happy; it pleased her parents; it helped her troop; it reminded you of the fun you had as a Scout; and you got all those tasty cookies. When you sell something people want to buy, they too will get good feelings as well as a good product.

The other impulse is contributing to something that will clearly pay off in your own interest. When you bought the tickets to the fireman's ball, you not only had fun at the ball, you knew you were supporting your volunteer fire department, which you want to be well-prepared if you ever need it. A lively grass roots program provides something that is just as much in the citizens' self-interest— more power to influence the government, or decent housing or innovative arts.

While buying something like the cookies gives you a product you want, contributing to a cause in your self-interest gives you a program you want: a better block club, halfway house, or museum. Either way you are making an investment to please yourself. The seller is neither begging nor bullying. He or she is simply giving others an opportunity to get what they want. Just as people look forward to getting a good product each year, like Girl Scout cookies or UNICEF Christmas cards, they will look forward to getting the good news about your program.

Fear is very expensive. Remember Flanagan's Fear Formula:

Fear is the parent of procrastination.
Procrastination is the thief of time.
Time is money.

Fear causes inertia which is the prime cause of low morale and low income. The biggest fear of taking any new action—whether it is selling the cover of the ad book to the bank president or leading 200 people to confront the mayor—is the fear of losing face. This is why most people would rather be followers than be leaders. They think, "How can I volunteer to sell the bank president? If I fail, everyone will know. I'll feel like a fool."

STRATEGY FOR SUCCESS

Get together in a group before and after each major sales effort. Frankly discuss the work, share the funny stories, applaud the successes, and strategize on the hard cases. Remember, fundraising is always more imposing for the new members, so give them an extra boost. Even Jesus sent the Apostles out in pairs when they were starting their mission (Mark 6:7). Pair a new volunteer with a veteran and give them a sure-sell ad to renew from last year. Build on success. Let them sell a $10 ad to the hot dog stand and a $50 ad to the funeral home before you send them to the savings and loan for a $100 ad. Prepare attractive sales kits and give simple instructions. Above all, plan enough time so you can be available to answer questions, give advice, and listen.

To take control of fear, make it concrete. If you just let it spin around in your head, all you think about is the fear and not its consequences. Put it on paper, and put down what you stand to lose and what you stand to gain. If you fail, you don't get the ad. However, you still get 1) experience, 2) the knowledge that you were brave enough to try, and 3) an introduction to make it easier next time.

Focus on your strategy rather than your fear. Instead of sitting home being afraid, get out and do some research. Find out everything you can and use it to succeed. Maybe you will find out that the bank president is a graduate of the University of North Carolina. Then you can invite your group's treasurer, who just happens to be a former Tarheel football hero, to go with you. When you go in well backgrounded, you will feel more confident and give a better presentation.

Divide the difficulties instead of taking them all at once. First decide to call today to make the appointment. Tomorrow you can send a confirming letter with clippings about your group. The next day go to the library and do some research on the bank president.

Then practice your sales pitch. If you lay out a schedule to make each part manageable, then you will have your homework finished and feel more secure when you do meet to make your pitch.

See if you can find some allies to put in a good word for you. If you know the bank president is unfamiliar with your group or uncertain about your goals, seek support from someone you know he respects. Ask the pastor of the biggest church or the most popular local politician to write a letter recommending you.

As a last resort, take the situation and turn it around. Think what will happen if you *don't* call to make the appointment. First, you are 100 per cent guaranteed you won't make the sale. What's more, Frank is an usher at the bank president's church, and may ask him if he has talked to you when they usher on Sunday. Soon everyone will know you never called. So it turns out the only way to really lose face is by being afraid to take a chance!

There are other fears besides the fear of losing face. One is the fear that the donor will dislike you personally or dislike your organization. Remember the two reasons people want to give, and learn to sell them something they want anyway. If they buy, it doesn't make any difference whether they like you. If they don't buy, you've learned something useful about your program, yourself, and/or your opposition in the community.

Let's say that Mark Twain, a volunteer for the Hannibal Day Care Center, goes to ask W. C. Fields for the premier of his next film. He knows that Fields has a legendary dislike of small children. Although Twain wants to get the premier, he is scared to death that Fields will attack him.

The author gets an appointment to see the great actor, who lets him get as far as, "Hello, I'm Mark Twain and I'm here to ask you if you would donate the premier of your next movie for the Hannibal Day Care Center." Fields says he hates kids and does not want to have anything to do with it. The point of Twain's visit is *not* to make Fields like kids. The point *is* to get the premier. So Twain says, "I'm so sorry you feel that way. You should consider that the Day Care Center provides 200 children with quality care and education at a price working parents can afford. But what will interest you, as star of the film and chief executive officer of Fields Films, Inc., is that the Hannibal Day Care Center has run the biggest and best film festival in Missouri for the last five years. We can guarantee you the biggest audience and the best press in the Midwest."

He is not asking Fields to like him, or to like the Hannibal Day Care Center, or to like kids at all. He is asking Fields to take advantage of a real opportunity to promote his film.

Selling a product the donor wants is one way to overcome a fear of his disliking you, because you can leave your personal feelings out of it altogether. The other way involves discovering and using his self-interest. This usually takes a lot more subtlety and practicality.

In 1975 a statewide women's political organization held its first convention in a small university town. The local chapter planned an ad book to underwrite its expenses as host of the convention. They managed to sell ads quickly in some smaller towns nearby, but couldn't sell any ads in their own town because it was run by one man who hated women. He owned literally half the town, the only TV station and the only newspaper. When even as well-established a women's group as the League of Women Voters wanted to announce a meeting, they had to *buy* an ad in his paper—he gave no free publicity to any women's group. He was also head of the chamber of commerce.

But they had to raise the money. Frustration led to anger and anger led to strategy. They said, "He hates us. Whom does he like? Other men. And power." So they went to the center of male power— the local chamber of commerce meeting. Ten women marched into the meeting and insisted on speaking. They asked Mr. Big in front of the men he wanted to impress to set the standard, endorse their ad book and buy an ad. His self-interest made him do it. After he bought, all the rest of them bought. Anger and intelligence made the fundraisers overcome their fear. They made the first inroads to power and raised $4,000.

Many of the best people have the deepest convictions about the importance of their group's work but have inhibitions about raising money. For example, public interest and civil rights activists especially, who, with others, believe strongly in the virtue of their own cause, still feel uncomfortable about asking for money for fear of presenting an impression of moral superiority. As public interest lawyer Mary James says, "I have an inhibition about fundraising because I'm afraid I'll be viewed as suggesting a moral superiority. I'm afraid I'm suggesting that the donor is lacking morally because he hasn't supported our virtuous cause yet. How can I ask without seeming self-righteous?" Lawyers, and others, should use the most basic concept of American law: that everyone is innocent until proven guilty. Instead of thinking that the donor will feel you are being self-righteous, assume, if anything, he or she is *more* moral and virtuous than you. When you go to ask for help in winning justice and freedom for all Americans, say "I came to you *first*, because I know you share the same values and prize these rights even more than we do."

When you wonder "How can I presume to tell X what he should do?" and "What if he thinks I think I'm better than he is?" remember: 1) Since your cause is really just, he should be flattered to be asked to support it; 2) If you don't ask him, you can't get a positive response. All you are doing is giving him the *opportunity* to support your cause. If he doesn't want to, he will say no, or not now. When you don't ask you are making his decision for him and guaranteeing the support is zero; 3) You are not telling him what to do. You are informing him of an exciting program and offering him a chance to help support it. The choice is his.

Reward Your Fundraisers

The whole organization should understand and appreciate the achievements of the fundraisers. Successful fundraising takes intelligence, concern, hard work and courage. Fundraisers deserve a lot of applause and appreciation.

Reward each person who succeeds in raising money. In the business world, the payoff is high salaries and special rewards like trips to Europe for the top salespeople. Maybe you can't offer that, but that's not what your people are working for, anyway. Spotlight the top fundraisers in your organization. Offer them public recognition. The Broadmoor Improvement Association in New Orleans puts the names of the ad sellers in its ad book for the annual Home Improvement Show. Women Organized for Employment in San Francisco gives its top salespeople flowers and applause at the theatre party where the ad book is distributed. Wilmington United Neighborhoods (WUN) in Delaware calls the top salesperson up to the stage at their annual convention to receive a framed certificate of appreciation in front of 600 delegates.

Clearly it is no small achievement to raise money. It requires overcoming deep fears and inhibitions about money, seriousness about the need for money, belief in the future of the organization, and an appreciation of human values. Money is the oxygen of the organization's actions—it keeps the group moving. Fundraisers are vital to the life of the organization and must be appreciated and applauded to keep the group alive and growing every year.

Chapter 4
Benefits

Benefits or special events are simply occasions which allow your members to ask other people for money. Many people prefer selling a ticket to a dinner or a dance to just asking someone for a donation. Other advantages of benefits are that they give everyone a chance to get together doing something fun, they publicize the group, they bring in new members, and they give many people a chance to learn new skills. Benefits produce both money and a sense of accomplishment.

The ideal event is one which raises money, conveys a message about your program, and offers something for the spirit. The first goal, raising money, can be set by doing your arithmetic first. Make it a challenge.

The second goal is to get across a message about your program. When the Prison Reform Task Force sponsored the first major show of prisoners' art in New York City, they raised $10,000 in ten days. Just as important, they raised the public's awareness of problems in New York and New Jersey prisons. The show-goers thought it was clever of the artists to include pieces of ticking, blankets and pillow cases in their works. Then they learned the prisoners had to use their bedding. They had to because the prisons had insufficient art supplies. The publicity and pressure from the task force resulted in increasing supplies to most New York state prisons.

The third goal is to offer something for the spirit. Appeal to the best in the members. If you have a women's political organization, offer an interesting speaker rather than a fashion show. If you have a peace group, offer an international dinner highlighting the diversity of different cultures, rather than a John Wayne film festival. If you have an ecology club, offer a garden walk rather than a car rally. If you are serious about improving the world, run events for intelligent, caring human beings. Never sell short the idealism of your own members just so you can sell tickets. In the long run, you

44

will bankrupt their faith in the group, and that faith is the real currency you need to be successful.

Every event needs a plan, a timetable and a deadline. The deadline is the date you choose for the event and print on the tickets and posters. Your timetable is a schedule of everything that needs to happen. Work out your timetable by planning backwards from the deadline date to the present date. See the Appendix, p. 194, for a sample timetable for a rummage sale. Note especially that you must plan in the beginning for a week of work *after* the event. This is the time to send the thank-you notes, write the reports, and complete your records.

The plan is a written description of who does each job for the event. After everyone has volunteered or accepted an appointment for a job, be sure each one knows exactly what needs to be done, and when. *Never assume anything.* Make sure that Clara knows she is supposed to bring the extra chairs because she has a station wagon. Double check that Fred will play the piano even if you know he has the music and can't wait. Not only is it dangerous to take anything for granted, it is also unpleasant to take any*one* for granted. Even if Harvey has run the ticket booth for the last twenty years, *ask* him *early* if he wants to do it again, and ask him if he needs any help.

The Shopper

It is much more efficient and usually more economical to have one person volunteer to be the shopper. His or her job is to get everything needed for the event at the lowest possible price. The shopper finds out first exactly what the costs of the event will be.

The shopper is really a researcher and dispatcher. It must be someone who likes to talk on the telephone, has plenty of time, and will keep precise records. It is good for the shopper to be persuasive, and great to be miserly as Scrooge. The shopper may not have to actually buy or pick up all the supplies, but must discover the best price available on each item and assign someone to pick it up.

The shopper answers these questions:

1) What does the group already have? For example, receipt books, ticket rolls, cash boxes. No reason to buy doubles.

2) Who can get what free? Record each donation and the name of the person who will arrange for it. For example, door prizes, or a hall.

3) What can we borrow? For example, a raffle drum for the door prize drawing.

4) What should we rent? For example, a sound system.

5) What can we buy on consignment? This means you pay for more than you need, then return the balance for a refund. Many liquor stores sell this way, allowing you to return unopened bottles. This way you are sure you won't run out, but don't have too much money tied up in supplies.

6) What will we have to buy for use only at this event? For example, ice, paper products, coffee.

7) What will we buy that we will keep after the event? If you can buy it and keep it to use again, it is an asset. For example, a coffee maker, trays, a flag.

Obviously, the shopper needs to pay more attention to items in category 7—things you will use over and over like a coffee maker— than items in category 6. There is very little difference in quality in plastic cups or paper napkins, but a great deal in appliances.

Basic rules for the shopper:

Always get at least three bids for any asset you buy or for any purchase over $25.00. Record other advantages besides price—guarantees, repair or maintenance service, delivery, or payment plans.

Never guess.

Always assume it costs more today than it did the last time you bought one. Since the shopper's job is to get *accurate* prices and costs, he or she should always call and ask the price *now*.

Don't be shy. Always ask for special consideration. Your organization is doing important work that no one else in the community can do. Since the merchants will also benefit from your work, they ought to support you too. Always ask for a contribution, then a discount, or a bulk rate, or deferred payment, or at the very least a door prize contribution.

Patronize local businesses. Especially if you are a neighborhood community group, they have the most to gain from your successes, so they have the best reason to give you a deal.

Thank everyone who gives you a contribution or a special deal. Be sure they are introduced if they attend the event. Send them copies of the program with their names in it. Be grateful and they will be glad to help you again next time.

SAMPLE CHART FOR GETTING SUPPLIES

SHOPPER'S NAME: E. Scrooge PHONE: 787-1000 EVENT: Christmas Party DATE: December 18, 1977

ITEM	ALREADY HAVE	STORE	PRICE	ADVANTAGES	WHO CAN DONATE	WHO CAN LEND	WHO CAN PICK UP & **RETURN**
Receipts	500						Bob
Hall					American Legion		
Door Prize					J's Jewelry Store		Fred
Raffle Drum						St. Bastion's	Sister Margaret
Sound System		S Sound	$15 Rent	will bill			Ralph
Liquor		A	$40	will deliver			
(all on consignment)		B	$45	free ice			Mike
		C	$50	closest; open til 4 am			Mike
Coffee Maker		D	$30				Sallie
		E	$30	Repair in store			Sallie

Do the Arithmetic First

For early planning you will have to estimate costs. For your final arithmetic get the exact figures for expenses in each category from your shopper. Write down everything you will have to pay for, including every purchase, rental or fee. The total is your costs. Although you have to estimate your costs at the beginning to set a ticket price, try to get accurate figures as soon as possible to know exactly what you have to make to reach your profit goal.

Things to consider are:

Place (room rental)

Printing—Tickets
          Invitations
          Posters
          Program

Postage
Insurance
Advertising

Entertainment—Band(s)
          Theatre group
          Guest speaker
          Rental fees—sound system

Refreshments—Food
          Beverages
          Supplies—cups, napkins

Supplies—Decorations
          Prizes
          Cash boxes
          Extension cords

If this is the first time you have held an event, ask someone who has held a similar event how much they spent in each category. If you are planning something original you will just have to start from scratch and figure it out yourself.

If you are repeating an event from last year be sure to recheck *every* cost. Everything goes up each year, but it never goes up by the same amount every year. For example, one year paper costs doubled, but the next year they went up only 10 percent. Also you may not get last year's special price if the supplier is having a bad year, or you may get a *better* price if the supplier is having a good year. It never hurts to put the suppliers on your newsletter list either. If someone has been following your work for a year they will appreciate what you have accomplished. This year they may contribute more because they know you and your work.

Income

Although you can determine your costs accurately, you will have to estimate the income at the beginning. After you know the members' abilities, enthusiasm, and spending patterns, you will be able to predict the income very closely.

Write down all the ways you can get money from each event. To estimate your income before the event, multiply the number of workers by their quotas for each part: ticket sales, donations, etc. For income at the event, multiply the number of people there times their expected expenditure for each item, For example, if there are 200 people at the dance and half of them (100) buy a raffle chance for 50¢, you can estimate you will get $50.

Write down how much you anticipate to earn from each part. Count on what you get in *before* the event, and consider what you make *at* the event as a bonus. You can never control the weather or flu epidemics or traffic jams, so don't depend on revenue from the party itself to pay your bills.

Obviously this will be a lot easier the second time around. That makes it especially important that you produce accurate and complete reports after the first event. In order to make the most helpful report for the next time, you need to record what the income was from each part of the event *this* time. Try to have separate cash boxes for each thing you sell. (You can use shoe boxes or cigar boxes if you don't have real cash boxes.) Write down how much change was in each cash box when you start. After the event, add up all the money in each box. Then subtract the amount you started with, and you know the amount from each item. You now know that you sold fifteen newsletter subscriptions but only four T-shirts, or fifty sandwiches but only ten cakes. Next year you will know in advance what your crowd wants, and you won't be stuck with left-overs.

HOW TO ANTICIPATE WHAT THE INCOME WILL BE—GROSS

BEFORE THE EVENT

PEOPLE WORKING	ITEM	PRICE PER ITEM	QUOTA/PERSON	GROSS/PERSON	TOTAL GROSS
10	Tickets	$ 2.50	20 tickets	$ 50	$500
2	Patron Tickets	$25.00	5 tickets	$125	$250
5	Senior Tickets	$ 1.00	10 tickets	$ 10	$ 50
TOTAL: 17					$800

AT THE EVENT

PEOPLE ATTENDING	ITEM	GROSS/ITEM	PURCHASES PER PERSON	PURCHASED BY % OF CROWD	GROSS
200	Raffle	$.50/ticket	1	½ = 100 people	$ 50
200	Bar	$.50/drink	2	100% = 200 people	$200
200	Sandwiches	$1.00	1	¼ = 50 people	$ 50
TOTAL: 200					$300

How to Price the Tickets

One of the questions that always seems most perplexing for new benefit committees is how much to charge for tickets. After you have done a few benefits you will know which price range works best for your group. For your first time you have to combine common sense and luck.

There are eight things to consider when you price the tickets. Discuss all of these questions in your committee to get the best advice from everyone who will actually be selling the tickets.

1. How much do we want to make on this event? Let's say you are going to do a costume party dance at a church hall. All of your costs add up to $300. You would like to make $500. So you need to gross $800. Divide $800 by each possible price to find out how many tickets you need to sell to reach your goal. If you charge $10 you have to sell 80 tickets. If you charge $2 you have to sell 400 tickets. Then if the members say $10 is too high, but they can't sell 400 tickets, you may settle on $4 so you have to sell 200 tickets, which they can do.

Costs $300
Profit   + $500

Gross Income $800   Goal for the event
Ticket price $4 x 200 ticket sales — $800 Goal (Gross)

2. How much do others usually charge for this event? If other groups usually charge $5 in your area for a party, and your members are used to paying $5, then maybe you can charge $5 too. On the other hand, if no one ever charges more than $1.50 for an event in your area, you will have to do a super sales job, lower your profit goal, or add in other ways to make money besides the ticket price.

3. What is the *real cost* to our members to attend? If each couple has to buy two $4 tickets that will cost them $8. If they also have to hire a babysitter, pay to park their car, and buy a couple of drinks, their total bill could be as high as $20! Be sure that your people will be willing to pay that much. It may be better, and more profitable, to have a day-time, free-parking, family event.

4. What other income can we count on? For example, if you run a cash bar for a hall full of people who like to drink, you can make a dollar a person. For our dance example, this would mean if you have 200 thirsty people, you would make $200 on the bar. (Double salt the popcorn.) Thus you now have to make only $600 on the tickets to cover costs and make your $500 profit goal. So you

can price the tickets at $3 each. At first you have to guess what this income will be; later on you will be able to predict it fairly accurately.

Gross income goal	$800
Estimated bar receipts	−$200
Revised ticket goal	$600

	$ 3 New ticket price
Possible ticket sales 200	÷ $600-new ticket goal

5. Can we have more than one ticket price? You can always have more than one ticket price to assure that everyone can attend, and also to insure that those most able to pay do so. For example, you may have 50 members who are senior citizens on fixed incomes who would like to come to the dance. So set a senior citizen price at $1. You also know the local politicians will want to make an appearance and "say a few words." If you're lucky you will be in a district with several hotly contested races. Even if the politicians do not attend they should buy tickets in advance. Charge the politicians and other people with more money than time a special "patron" price, say $25 a ticket. If you sell ten patron tickets you get $250.

If you sell ten patron tickets and fifty senior citizen tickets, you will get $300. Now your 200 regular customers can pay only $2.50 to make the last $500.

10 patrons at $25 each		$250
50 seniors at $1 each	+	50
200 members at $2.50 each	+	500
Goal		$800

6. How will the price affect our image? A lower price will make tickets easier to sell so you will get a bigger crowd and reach people at all income levels. On the other hand, you may decide you want to give the impression of prosperity and success by sponsoring a classy, high-priced, downtown event. Consider how the price will affect everyone's impression of the group and the event.

7. Do we want to give any tickets away for free? This can be a useful public relations device. Many groups give free tickets to the press, clergy or the staff. Sometimes the sponsor gives tickets away to a good cause. For example, when BPI sponsored a concert with Antonia Brico conducting members of the Chicago Symphony Orchestra, all the tickets for seats behind pillars (which the theatre usually sells) were given to blind students. BPI also gave blocs of

tickets to inner city students who might otherwise never have a chance to hear the Orchestra. The group also gave its copy of the movie "Antonia: A Portrait of the Woman" to the Chicago Public Library. All of which added to BPI's image as an organization concerned about quality of life for Chicagoans.

The other reason for giving away tickets is to create an illusion of popularity. Theater people call this "papering the house." Especially for politicians, it is much better to give away lots of tickets and have a full house, than undersell and have empty seats. Of course the ideal is to sell every possible ticket, but if the night comes and you have to make a good impression, hand out all the unsold tickets as "rewards" for the workers to give their friends.

8. What is the members' feeling about the importance of making money right now? Enthusiasm is contagious, so a vigorous action campaign will spark a vigorous fundraising campaign. If the members feel they are in an exciting campaign, and they know they need the $500 to send forty members to the state capital for the key vote on crucial legislation next week, they will probably be eager to get out and sell tickets. A successful action campaign creates a feeling of camaraderie among the members. If victory is in sight they will be willing to dig deep for a higher price than usual.

As long as the members feel that what they are doing is important and that they have a chance for success, they will work harder and contribute more to the group. If they have been inactive, or think someone else is doing everything, or that there is little hope for success, they may attend out of loyalty but will not make a special effort to sell or to give. Success breeds success. (Stitch this into your sampler under "people give to people.") You can charge more when you are winning than when you are in a holding pattern or have suffered a recent set-back.

KEEPING SCORE

The only way to get control of your fundraising event is to *do the arithmetic first.* This is simple adding, subtracting, multiplying and dividing. Go through these steps with the correct figures for your event:

Costs: $300

1. How much will it cost us to do what we want? (See p. 48 for how to figure costs.)

Net profit goal: $500

2. How much do we want to make from this event? This is the money you will have left to spend, called the "net profit."

Costs $300
  +   +
net $500
Gross $800
Gross = event goal

One ticket: $4.00

                200 tickets
Single $4 ÷$800 Gross
ticket
price
200 tickets = goal

                 75 tickets
Single $4 ÷$300 costs
ticket
price
75 tickets = break-even
                point
                (costs)

Ticket   20 tickets
sellers 10 ÷200 tickets
20 tickets = quota for
                each
                seller

              5 tickets per week
Weeks   4 ÷20 tickets
until   (Seller
dance   quota)
5 tickets = weekly goal

3. How much do we have to make all together to cover our costs and make our goal net profit? The total you need to make is called the gross. Add the costs #1 and your goal net profit #2 and you get the gross #3. This is the goal for the event.

4. When you know the gross, you use it to decide how much to charge for each ticket. See "How to price the tickets," p. 51. Let's say you choose to charge $4 for each ticket.

5. How many tickets do we have to sell to make the gross? The gross divided by the ticket price gives the number of tickets you have to sell to make your goal.

6. What is the break-even point in terms of ticket sales? Break-even is when your sales equal your costs. Divide your costs $300 by the ticket price $4, and you see you have to sell 75 tickets to break even. Every ticket sold after the first 75 is profit.

7. How many tickets can each person sell? What should be an individual goal or quota? Divide your ticket goal, 200 tickets, by the number of ticket sellers and you get each person's quota. If you have 10 people on the ticket committee each one has to sell, or get sold, 20 tickets.

    In real life it never comes out exactly even. One will sell 30 and another will sell 10 tickets. But everyone works better when they know exactly what is expected of them.

8. How many tickets does each seller have to sell to make his or her quota? If each seller's quota is 20 tickets and the dance is four weeks away, each one should try to sell 5 tickets a week. Week-

ly figures seem more reasonable and do-able than a vague total, plus they are an incentive to get started right away.

9. What is the percentage profit on this event? This shows you how much of the total income, the gross, is profit, or money you can spend later. Do this again after the event so you know what the real profit percentage was. To find the percentage profit divide the net profit, $500, by the gross, $800. This gives you a percent profit of 63%. Let's say you sell all your 200 tickets, and make an extra $100 from the refreshments and another $50 from a raffle. So the gross profit after the event turns out to be $800 + $100 + $50 or $950. Gross $950 minus the costs $300 leaves a net profit of $650. Divide the real net of $650 by the real gross of $950 and you see the actual percentage profit was 68%.

Gross   63%
$800 ÷ $500.00 Net
Percentage profit = 63%
This is based on
your calculations
before the event.

Using real figures
after the successful
event:

Gross   68%
$950 ÷ $650.00 Net
Real percentage
profit = 68%

PERCENTAGE PROFIT

          90%
$200 ÷ $180.00

          40%
$5000 ÷ $2000.00

Knowing the percentage profit on each event allows you to compare the efficiency of different fundraisers.

For example: A pot luck dinner draws 100 people at $2 each. The gross is $200. The costs are only $20 because almost everything is donated. Gross $200 minus costs $20 equals net profit of $180. Net $180 divided by the Gross $200 equals percent profit of 90%.

A hotel luncheon with a paid speaker draws 200 people at $25 each. The gross is $5,000. The costs are $3,000 because you have to pay for everything. Gross $5,000 minus the costs $3,000 equals net profit of $2,000. Net $2,000 divided by the Gross $5,000 equals percent profit of 40%.

Your goal is to increase the percentage profit on every event. You can do this by either lowering the costs or raising the gross income. Or you can adjust both.

Making a list—and checking it twice

Remember the best people to ask for money are people who have already given you money. So be sure to always *get* a list of the people attending an event, and *keep* it so you can invite them next time. You can give a receipt for every contribution; make a carbon copy at the same time and keep the copy. If you are doing something with a lot of traffic and impatient people, offer a door prize. Keep all the door prize slips with names and addresses. That will become your invitation list next time. You can simply ask people to sign a list when they come in, but this may look too business-like for a formal affair or a festive occasion.

Some people will ask you *not* to put them on your list; you must always honor such requests. Mark their receipt or door prize slip clearly "Do not mail" or "Do not include on invitation list." But most people like to be notified of fun events, so they will be pleased to give you their names.

Be very cautious about making a list from addresses on checks. Most people do not want to receive personal mail at the office. Many wives use checks printed with only the husband's name. If Martha Washington gives you a donation, be sure you record her name even if George's name is on the check. If someone doesn't want a receipt, *ask* if you can put him or her on the mailing list, and if so, how the mail should be addressed.

Always number the tickets and keep track of who has which numbers. At the end of the sales, each seller must turn in enough tickets and money to match the number of tickets he or she started with. For example, if you give Cliff twenty $4 tickets he must return either twenty tickets or $80 dollars or some combination that adds up to $80. If he sells fifteen tickets, he turns in five tickets and $60. More than one fundraiser has turned into a fund-loser because this simple step was *not* done.

The last thing to do is to mentally walk through the event as though you were the customer. What would make you more comfortable, especially if you were new? There are several things you can do to make newcomers feel welcome. Use name tags to help everyone learn names. Have several outgoing people serve as hosts and hostesses to make sure each new person is introduced to a veteran member. Put up a display of photographs or recent clippings to serve as a conversation starter. Station a few pleasant young people to help the oldsters with stairs and coats. Recruit an enthusiastic master of ceremonies to make frequent announcements and introductions. Print a simple program so everyone knows what happens when. Mark an area for lost and found. If you are selling anything, be sure you have enough bags. Double-check to make sure the washrooms are well stocked and clean. Anything you can do to make people feel wanted will make everyone have a better time, spend more money, and guarantee they will return next time.

Checklist for Assets

What do we already have in the organization to make this fund-raising project a success? What factors should we consider in choosing an event?

PEOPLE

A. Leaders—their time and talents.

B. Members with experience with this kind of event.

C. Total number of members who will *work*.

D. Total number of members who will attend or contribute.

E. Possible allies and new members who will get involved.

F. Staff.

MONEY

A. Seed money available for the event—from treasury, loan, advance sales.

B. When will we have to spend the money? When will the money come in? What is our break-even point (income=expenses)?

C. Who will handle the money coming in? Who will control money going out?

D. Bank—will we need a separate account? Do we need any special arrangements to handle lots of cash?

TIME

A. How much time does the organization want to spend fund-raising? Is there any way to shorten it?

B. Are there any major conflicts in the organization's calendar? The community calendar?

C. How much staff time do we want to allocate to this project?

D. If this event is to be repeated annually, is this the best time of the year for it?

E. What consideration should we make for bad weather? E.g., an alternative snow/rain date, inside location, or insurance.

Checklist for Goals—What do we want to achieve from this project?

A. Amount of money. NET. Percent of annual budget.
B. Number of people involved. Where and how.
C. Number of leadership roles possible.
D. Number of new members brought in.
E. Experience. Which new skills will be learned? What do we want to know for the next event, and for this event next year?
F. Who will take the leadership positions?
G. How will it challenge the elected leaders?
H. What will be the publicity generated? How much, what kind, where?
I. What will be the psychological effect of the event:
    a. Within the organization
    b. Outside the organization to people you want to join
    c. To the enemy
    d. To the staff
J. Can it be repeated—in six months, one year? What is the probable increase next time?
K. Which new sources of income will we reach?
    a. New members
    b. Non-member individuals
    c. Institutions—businesses, churches
    d. Foundations
L. Organizational advantages—morale, new people, new area, new style event.
M. Fun

Basics for All Events:

A. Notification of the police
B. Proper insurance
C. Cash boxes
D. Cash in proper denominations for each cash box
E. Receipts
F. Literature on your organization
      Current newsletter or fact sheet
      Written notice of next meeting or event(s)
      Membership cards
      Sale merchandise—buttons, cookbooks, research, etc.
G. Sign-up list (Can be accomplished simply with door prize)
H. Name tags for committee or everyone
I. Emergency numbers for police and fire
J. Cash for emergencies; coins for pay phone
K. First aid kit
L. Pens
M. Tape
N. Poster board and black markers
O. Errand runner for emergencies and forgotten things
P. Watch
Q. Aspirin
R. Comfortable shoes
S. All necessary phone numbers—band, host, speakers, ice
T. Name of doctor or nurse who will be present
U. Sense of humor, tact, patience and imagination
If location does not provide, also bring:
A. Fire extinguisher (know how to operate)
B. Sound system

Chapter 5
Benefits For Beginners

There are an infinite number of things you can do to raise money. Here are some examples of benefits that have worked well for their grass roots organizations in recent years. There are seven small events which need few workers and little seed money, nine medium-sized events which need more time, money and labor, and ten biggies which need the largest investment of time, talent and money.

Of course you are not limited to these samples. Your local talent can always dream up something better using your own resources. A poor rural group in Kentucky invented the "Sorghum Stir-off" and raised $6,000 for their group. They planted four acres of sorghum cane for molasses, harvested it, refined it into 600 gallons of sorghum, bottled and sold it. An affluent urban group in Arizona ran a "Stock-a-rama" where people bought play money to "play" the stock market for a month. Forty volunteer stockbrokers kept track of each person's transactions. At the end of the month, the person who hypothetically "made" the most money got a prize, and the person who "lost" the most got his money back. This group netted $4,000. Each event worked well because it was created by and for a specific group. You, too, can take a chance and pioneer a new event for your area.

The best way to collect new ideas is to ask the members what they would like to try. Check the section "Where to get advice" in the Appendix for more suggestions for getting fresh ideas. There are also several good books available on an assortment of events and how to do them best.

Lots of Examples and Advice

BEST ALL AROUND

"101 Surefire Fund-Raising Ideas," by JoAnne Alter, October 1976 *Family Circle* Magazine. It is printed on beige paper and pulls-out to save. Covers 101 super ideas from all over the United States.

including bazaars, auctions, shows, tours, dances, and sports. Includes five children's events and 14 "Easy Money-makers," plus a page of advice. Reprints are available from the Reprint Department, *Family Circle,* 488 Madison Avenue, New York, NY 10022. 8 pp. 35¢.

Ways and Means Handbook—A Chairman's Guide to Money Making Projects. The Sperry and Hutchinson Co., Consumer Relations, 2900 W. Seminary Dr., Fort Worth, TX 76133. 1964. 32 pp. 25¢. This is the best "how to" on events—food fairs, carnivals, tours, sales, and services. Includes checklists and a sample annual calendar for a one-day, once-a-year county-wide event.

BEST FOR SMALL GROUPS
LITTLE OR NO SEED MONEY

Good Cents—Every Kid's Guide to Making Money. The Amazing Life Games Co. and Friends. Boston, MA. Houghton Mifflin Co. 1974. 128 pp. $5.00. 44 projects for kids, which are adaptable to anyone with little seed money, less time, but lots of energy. (This is my favorite.) Includes thirteen holiday-linked events.

Shaking the Money Tree. League of Women Voters Education Fund, 1730 M St., N.W., Washington, D.C. 20036. 1969. 24 pp. 35¢. Explains twenty-nine simple but fun projects which need little or no seed money, such as the "Stay at Home Tea."

MINORITIES

How to Raise Money for Community Action. Scholarship, Education and Defense Fund for Racial Equality (SEDFRE), One Penn Plaza, New York, NY 10001. 1970. $1. 23 pp. Excellent, concise, nononsense guide written especially for small minority organizations.

WOMEN'S CLUBS AND CIVIC BOOSTER GROUPS

Fundraising for the Small Organization. Philip G. Sheridan. Distributed by J.B. Lippincott Co., Philadelphia, PA. 1968. $5.95. 240 pp. 56 events good for small and medium sized groups. Features good old fashioned hometown examples like the "Greatest-Mom-in-the-World" and the "Good Neighbor" contests.

How to Succeed in Fund-Raising Today. Helen Knowles, The Bond Wheelwright Co., Porter's Landing, Freeport, ME 04032. 1976. 250 pp. $7.65. Written for women's clubs and small or medium town booster clubs. Many clever ways to raise money, especially good on thrift shops, fashion shows and decorator's show houses.

FEMINISTS

The Not-So-Helpless Female. Tish Sommers. David McKay & Co., 1973. 240 pp. Out of print but you can get a copy FREE with a donation of $10 or more to: Alliance for Displaced Homemakers, 3800 Harrison, Oakland, CA 94611. Sensible how-to plus "35 Ways to Raise Money" with a special feminist and/or ecological twist. Also chapter on "Grantswomanship."

ALUMNI GROUPS

It's For Your Benefit. Abby Evarts Mandel. Alumni Office. Smith College. Northhampton, Mass. 01063. 1975. 7 pp. $2.00. How to prepare and present most profitable benefit using resources of college alumni. Based on author's successful benefit cooking classes starring Smith alumna Julia Child.

MOSTLY FOR MEN

Money Raising Ideas for Exchange Clubs. The National Exchange Club. 3050 Central Ave., Toledo, OH 43606. 32 pp. 35¢. Basic guidelines plus several suggestions that have worked well for the all-male exchange clubs in the past. Includes best section on sports events, covering everything from bowling to rodeos and tennis to turkey shoots.

SPECIFIC EVENTS NOT COVERED HERE

The Flea Market and Garage Sale Handbook. Irene Copeland. Popular Library, New York. 1977. 224 pp. $1.75. Good, thorough advice, books and periodicals, and state laws.

Getting It Together: Handbook on How to Run a Fair. Shoshana Cardin and Jo-Ann Orlinsky. Women Together. Order from: Jo-Ann Orlinsky, 1530 Bolton St., Baltimore, MD 21217. 1974. 79 pp. $2.00. Planning and execution with specific examples of how they did the 1973 Women's Fair.

Large Card Parties and Tournaments—How to Organize. Choose from: Bridge, Canasta, Cribbage, Euchre, Gin Rummy, Pinochle, or Poker. (Specify Game.) The United States Playing Card Co., Cincinnati, OH 45212. Free.

DINNERS

Cooking for Small Groups. U.S. Department of Agriculture, Bulletin No. 370, Superintendent of Documents, U.S. Government Printing Office, Washington, D.C. 20402. 1974. 22 pp. 35¢. Planning menus, formula to adjust menu size for fifteen to fifty people, and recipes.

Keeping Food Safe To Eat. Home and Garden Bulletin 162, Office of Information, U.S. Department of Agriculture, Washington, D.C. 20250. Free. 10 pp. 1975.

Church and Club Suppers. Good Housekeeping Magazine Bulletin Service, 959 Eighth Avenue, New York, NY 10019. 1965. 8 pp. 15¢. How to organize a dinner, recipes for groups, and qauntities to prepare.

THE BOOK/PLANT SALE

The used book and plant sale is a good warm weather fundraiser. Everyone seems to have extra books they would be glad to donate to a good cause. City folks especially love to buy bargain plants. Plants are the ideal pet for apartment dwellers because God delivers their sunlight, the city delivers their water, and they never need a walk when it is 10° below zero.

Preparation. Put a notice in the newsletter and add a note to every agenda instructing members to start collecting their old books and bring them to a central collection point. If there is a storage room in the building where you regularly meet, ask members to bring their books each time they come to a meeting. Suggest they also ask their neighbors to clean out their old books and donate them to the sale.

About two months before the sale ask the plant growers to make cuttings from their best plants. Your library has several books on house plants that can tell you how to do it. An expert member or a guest speaker from a local plant store or garden club can give a short demonstration at a meeting too. New plants can be started in bottles, cans, or yogurt or cottage cheese cartons.

Make arrangements for a busy sidewalk location on what you expect will be a sunny weekend. If you can tie-in with another event that will attract crowds it is even better. Many big city neighborhood groups sponsor garden walks, antique fairs and art shows that draw thousands of people. Merchants' associations also sponsor sidewalk sales, craft sales and art shows as well as parades. Ask the owner of a bar, restaurant, or shop with a wide sidewalk or patio if you can use the area in front of the establishment. You can also use a section of a busy parking lot or the lawn of a church. Be sure to get permission in writing so you are guaranteed space.

Put a notice in the newsletter notifying everyone of the final date, time and place. Include a rain date. Recruit a committee to transport the books and plants from your storage location to the sale area the night before the sale.

PRICING. If you are having a two-day sale, price the hard

cover books at $1.00 and the paperbacks at 25¢ the first day, then mark them down to 50¢ and 10¢ the second day. Don't try to put a price on each book. Just put up two large signs for hardback and paperback books.

Price the baby plants at ½ what the local plant stores are charging. Plant nuts will know they are getting a bargain and buy a lot. If anyone has contributed mature plants, price them at ¾ the local plant store price.

If you have any special items, for instance a complete set of encyclopedias or a large fern in a macrame hanger, price them separately and put them in a special area.

Just separate the books by hard cover and paperback. Some groups have tried sorting by fiction and non-fiction, or by author, but one of the attractions of book sales for the bargain book buyer is browsing through all of the titles. They *like* to look through everything, so save yourself the work of sorting and let them hunt to their heart's desire.

You can sort plants by their ideal environment: sunny, semi-sunlight, or shady home preference. Or sort them by their care requirements: needs lots of care, needs some care, or can get along by itself. Then naive shoppers will know which plant to buy.

Sale Day. Get there early and get all your wares out. Have your cash box and receipts ready to go. Line up teams of salespeople to help the customers. Be sure you have lots of bags with handles and boxes for people to collect and carry home their purchases. If you have members who like to talk about books or plants, station them as free advice givers. Enthusiasm is contagious, and they will have everyone believing they can grow plants or read the entire *Great Books of the Western World*. Follow the timetable for the rummage sale in the Appendix.

Afterward. Be sure to send the owner of the sale location a thank-you note and give him or her a nice mention in the newsletter. Then you'll be likely to get their good space again next year. Thank all the workers. Sell any left-over books to a second-hand book buyer, then give any the buyer won't buy to a charity resale shop. Give any left-over plants to the loyal workers.

VARIATIONS. You can sell almost any used or free merchandise in this kind of sale. Choral groups and student clubs often have a lot of old records they can sell, and any group can run a bake sale. If you know skilled craftspeople, ask them to contribute their weaving, macrame, woodcarving, quilts, pottery, prints, paintings, photographs, or jewelry for sale. Either ask them to donate their work or to sell it to you on consignment, in which case the group might get 25 per cent while the artist gets 75 per cent.

PROFIT FORMULA. Your profit is 100 per cent of the sales, since everything is donated. If you also take craft items on consignment, your profit is your percentage of the sale price of consignment items. The key to success is getting a good space in connection with a busy event like a successful art fair, so you can get lots of shoppers. Another hint: Do not pre-judge your merchandise according to your own tastes. Even if you cannot imagine anyone who would ever want the complete works of Edgar Guest, or the anthology of maudlin Christmas stories or "Irish Recipes from A to B," put them out for sale. Almost inevitably the books you hate will be the first to go and the ones you like will be left. However, you should delete any pornographic books in order to stay respectable and legal. It won't do for the mayor's daughter to go home and announce she got "The Porn Potpourri" at *your* sale!

THE COFFEE

A coffee is simply an occasion to get neighbors together in a home, tell them about your program and ask them for money. Although it is called a "coffee" here, you can serve tea or any other kind of simple non-alcoholic beverage. You can do just one coffee or a multiplying series where each coffee produces money and new coffee hostesses. This lends itself well to political campaigns to introduce the candidate, church stewardship campaigns to launch new drives, and community campaigns to focus on local problems.

Preparation: Find someone to be the host or hostess for the coffee—to provide a place for the coffee, contribute the refreshments, and invite the neighbors. Print up invitations with the date, time and place. The host or hostess can distribute them in the neighborhood, at the club or church, and mail a few to other friends farther away. The written invitations should be distributed about one week before the coffee and then followed up with as many phone calls as possible. You can expect about a ten per cent turn-out from strangers and about thirty per cent from people you know. Thus, if you are the host for a coffee in your precinct for a political candidate and you have invited 200 people in the precinct, expect twenty to show up. If you are the hostess for a coffee to discuss the pledges and program for your church and invite ninety people from your church, expect about thirty to show up.

The host or hostess prepares simple refreshments. It does not have to be coffee. You could serve lemonade, Kool-Aid or iced tea in the summer or hot cider or hot chocolate in the winter, plus cookies or snacks. Feel free to use paper cups. If you are doing a series of coffees and want to get more volunteer hosts, simple refreshments will make it easier to recruit new people. Do not serve alcoholic beverages.

At the Coffee. Use name tags so people get to know each other. One reason people like coffees, especially in big cities, is that they give everyone a chance to meet some neighbors. The host should make sure everyone is introduced and that everyone understands the purpose of the coffee. Be sure to have plenty of literature on the group available for the newcomers.

THE SPEAKER. The first choice for a speaker is an officer of the group, or the candidate at a political coffee, or the pastor at a church gathering. The speaker explains what the group is doing, how it affects the people in the room, and exactly why the group needs money. For example, the president of a block club could outline the history and goals of the block club, explain that it has received permission from the city to make the adjacent vacant lot a playground, and that $2,000 is needed for equipment. The speaker then asks for questions and answers them briefly. Keep everyone on the topic. If someone asks why the block club hasn't done anything yet about the parking problem, agree that it is a serious issue, refer the questioner to the head of that committee, and return to the playground.

THE STING. Someone besides the speaker or the host should actually ask for the money. Since the speaker is your president or candidate he or she must keep open communications with the whole community. It's poor etiquette for the host to ask his guests for money. So choose another person who is poised, convincing, and persuasive to be the coffee chairperson and ask for the money.

You can pass out pre-printed "pledge cards" which have spaces for the donor's name, address and phone numbers, plus boxes to check for the amount he or she wishes to contribute. For example, you could have boxes marked $10, $5, $2 and "other." Indicate on the card to whom checks should be made payable. The chairperson explains exactly what the money will go for: $200 for bulldozing, $300 for swing sets, $300 for benches, $500 for fencing, $500 for landscaping, and $200 for signs. Then the chairperson asks for a specific amount with a reason why that amount was chosen. "There are 200 families who signed the petition for this playground. If each one gives $10 we can get the work done and have the park ready before school gets out." The chairperson makes the need urgent and adds a specific time limit, like "before school gets out." This helps prevent people from saying, "I can't give now. I'll send something in." The chairperson should also honestly say, "I think this is long overdue in our neighborhood, and I have given my $10 already." Do not ask for questions—they have already been asked, and answered by the speaker. Ask people to fill out their pledge cards or their checks now, and say you will collect their cards and the money. Now comes the hardest moment of the coffee. The chairperson has to keep quiet and just wait. This will induce the audience to fill out the cards or write checks. Since the American school system is designed to make people acquiescent about filling out forms, they will do it when everyone else does. After they feel awkward long enough in the silence they will write out the check.

PRIMING THE PUMP. Be sure you know a few people who are coming and ask them in advance to give so they will get things moving. They become the "floor team." They are the first ones to hand in their cards and checks and encourage the others to follow suit. They also help during the discussion if anyone in the audience has an ax to grind or wants to tell a long story about why they hate playgrounds because they fell off the swings when they were seven. The floor team makes sure the discussion always gets back to the playground, why it is a good idea, and why money is needed *now*.

COLLECTING THE CARDS. You can apply fundraising "triage" to the group. Triage is a battlefield term for dividing the wounded into those who will live without any care, those who will die no matter what the doctors do, and those who will live only with immediate care. The doctors work on the last group. In the same way, you can divide any fundraising audience into groups for the best return on your efforts.

There will be some who will give no matter what. Even if the speaker is late, the coffee is terrible, and they don't get a seat, they are going to give because they have already decided the playground is a good idea and their kids will love it.

Then there are those who will never give. They come only for the refreshments and to be seen looking concerned about the community. They won't give to you and they probably don't give to anyone else either. After a while you will get to know the deadbeats and just send them to the cookies. You need to be careful not to waste your time trying to get money out of a hopeless case while missing someone who would like to give.

This is the middle category and the focus for the chairperson. These are people who have not made up their minds and want more information. Take the time to explain any details they want to know —insurance, security, or supervision. The chairperson's job is to get their donations *now*. If they say they want to think about it, or have to ask the wife or husband, or that they will mail it in, try to convince them to decide right away. If you don't get the money that night, you will most likely never get it. Less than two per cent of the people who say they will put it in the mail really do.

Afterwards. Be sure to send the host/hostess a thank-you note from the president plus a report on the total. Record each donation on a donor's card. Send thank-you notes to the donors.

> PROFIT FORMULA. *Costs:* Printing annd mailing invitations and printing donation cards. Refreshments and place are donated by host/hostess.
> *Income:* Donations.
> *Profit* = Donations less costs.

For more information, get *Winning Elections: A Handbook in Participatory Politics,* by Dick Simpson. The Swallow Press, 811 W. Junior Terrace, Chicago, IL. 1972. 200 pp. $3.95. Best explanation on coffees as people- and money-producers with samples of materials used in successful independent political campaigns.

THE HAUNTED HOUSE & OTHER HOLIDAY FAVORITES

The Haunted House is an example of a holiday fundraiser. It is really amateur theatrics, used to entertain and to deliver shoppers to your fall bazaar. The whole thing is tied to Hallowe'en, October 31. Other holiday examples are listed at the end of this section.

Preparation. Obviously the first thing you need for a Haunted House is an old spooky-looking house. The ideal house has a scary exterior, lots of rooms inside, and a floor plan that will allow you to run people in one door and out another. Old homes often have front and back staircases, so this will work nicely. The house must be structurally sound; you cannot use anything dangerously dilapidated.

Although a house is preferable, you can also "haunt" a smaller area. Scout Groups and 4-H Clubs have run the haunted basement, the haunted attic, the haunted schoolroom and even the haunted barn. Church groups have also run the haunted tent and the haunted choir loft.

An ideal set-up would be an old rectory next to a church where you can also run a small sale and serve refreshments. Since many old rectories qualify as haunted house architecture, this makes a good fundraiser for church groups.

Arrange to use the house the week-end before Hallowe'en, or two week-ends before. If a family is living in the house you will have to close off certain rooms and offer them another place to live while their house is being "haunted."

INSURANCE. You must have adequate insurance for crowds going through a house. If you are using a rectory it should already be covered on the church policy. Otherwise you may have to get special short-term liability coverage for the fundraiser to cover any accidents that may occur or any damage to the house. Ask your local insurance salesperson or broker for the least expensive policy. Also ask if the salesperson or the company can donate the coverage. DECORATION AND SCENARIO. Get a committee to decorate the house. Set skeletons and black cats around the house and tape a huge King Kong face over a second story window. Find someone who is good with electricity to rig up scary lighting and sound effects. Plan a theme for each room: catacombs, mad scientist's lab, vampire's crypt, wolfman's lair, witches' kitchen, Dracula's den, or outer space "2001" science fiction room. Ask for volunteers to play Halloween roles in each room: witches in the kitchen brewing up some fiendish broth, a vampire to sit up in the coffin when the tour comes by, a pair of mad scientists building Frankenstein's monster, a cuckoo astronaut for the outer space room. Each character is responsible for his or her own costume and props. Have the characters in each room work out a little business to do when the tour comes by.

The tour. Have a few people who are good with children serve as the tour guides. They lead the kids in groups of five or six through the house and introduce each act. For example, when the group approaches the vampire's crypt the guide tells the kids they have to be very quiet since it is daytime and the vampire is sleeping in his coffin. Then the guide opens the door on a sinister room with a coffin in it. The "vampire" sits up and says something scary to the kids.

CHARGES. Charge each kid a quarter (25¢) to go through the house. Many kids will go through more than once, especially if you run a good show and are open more than one day. Teenagers love the haunted house routines too and adults will love to go through just to see their friends perform. If you are open from 10 am to 5 pm you can run several hundred people through the house.

PROFIT FORMULA. Your profit is all the 25¢ tickets you sell minus the cost for the insurance. If you get the insurance donated it is all profit. You can also set out a plastic pumpkin for donations so adults can put in a dollar or more if they want.

The profits from the haunted house are relatively low, but the people involved will have a ball. There are almost no costs involved and you will be providing a service to the community by offering good safe recreation for the kids.

The way to make money is to take the kids and their parents through the house and into the church basement for a small harvest bazaar. Set up the fool-proof bake sale featuring autumn favorites like pumpkin pie and home-made preserves. Especially if you are in a big city, dried fall flowers and vegetables like gourds, pumpkins, dried weeds, cat-tails and Indian corn are great money makers. Ask someone with a station wagon to make a trip to the country to collect the produce. Mark it at one-half what the florists are charging and you will easily sell out. Sell apple cider and doughnuts and run a small rummage booth. You can also run a raffle for favorite fall prizes like tickets to an important football game, a turkey with all the trimmings, or a turkey dinner for four at a good restaurant.

ANOTHER SPIN-OFF: Sponsor a Hallowe'en costume party for the adults in the evening. Characters from the Haunted House can do their "bits" for extra entertainment during the band's breaks. You can have "The Monster Mash" and ask everyone to come as monsters. You can have a "Harvest Home" barn dance with square dances and reels, or choose a theme like "Gay '90's," "Roaring Twenties" or "Wild West." In an election year you can ask everyone to come as their most or least favorite politicians. Teen-agers like a "Happy Days" fifties' sock hop.

Holidays: Other holidays that lend themselves to fundraisers include:

NEW YEAR'S EVE (DECEMBER 31). Have a dress-up party or dance. It is possible to run your regular event with extra prizes and razzle-dazzle. One organization in Buffalo, New York runs its Bingo on New Year's Eve. They make over $1,000 because they make it *the* place to be on New Year's Eve. After the Bingo the members and workers go out to celebrate another great year.

TWELFTH NIGHT—JANUARY 6 (THE TWELFTH DAY OF CHRISTMAS). Sponsor a night of Elizabethan revelry complete with Renaissance costumes, a feast, dances, jugglers and fools. In the Middle Ages the serfs got the twelve days of Christmas off from their drudgery at the manor, so they really whooped it up on the last night. Ask the library for a book for costume and menu ideas.

LINCOLN'S BIRTHDAY (FEBRUARY 12) OR WASHINGTON'S BIRTHDAY (FEBRUARY 22). Have a patriotic birthday party with American foods and revolutionary costumes. If you saved all your Bicentennial hand-outs you should also have good colonial recipes and games to use.

VALENTINE'S DAY (FEBRUARY 14). Good for a dance or a ladies' luncheon. Natural opportunity also for a press event to expose the current "sweetheart deal" between local politicians and road/dam/development builders.

ST. PATRICK'S DAY (MARCH 17). Perfect for a corned beef and cabbage dinner or a beer blast. You can also join or start your local parade. Casey Kelly, publicity chair for Chicago NOW, organized a delegation to march in the St. Patrick's Day parade as the "Chicago Irish Feminists for E.R.A."

APRIL FOOL'S DAY (APRIL 1). Connecticut ACLU organized 48 "April No-Fools Day Parties" across the state. They mailed an invitation that read:

On the eve of a traditionally humorous date, at parties statewide, we will seriously dramatize our determination to REFUSE TO BE FOOLED by government—to protect our civil liberties—and to raise funds to carry out the heaviest legal commitment ever."

They asked for a minimum of $5 and raised a total of $7,600.

MAY DAY (MAY 1). Celebrate the coming of spring with May baskets and a maypole dance. This is also Law Day, by Presidential proclamation, and Solidarity Day for unionists and socialists.

INDEPENDENCE DAY, (July 4). Perfect for parades, sack races, barbecues, picnics, ice cream socials, and any other All-American festivities.

HALLOWE'EN (OCTOBER 31). Costume parties, haunted houses and fall bazaars.

SEASONS

Christmas Season: Now commercially defined as the day after Thanksgiving (fourth Thursday in November) until Christmas, December 25. Time for Christmas craft sales, caroling, dinners and bake sales.

Spring. Spring bazaars, plant sales, garden walks.

Summer. Any kind of outdoor sports or contests, picnics and barbecues.

Fall. Fall bazaars, harvest celebrations, hayrides.

Winter. Winter sports like ice-skating, sledding and tobogganing, Christmas or Hanukkah food and craft sales, indoor events like speakers and movies.

DATES TO AVOID: Mother's Day, Father's Day, Thanksgiving and Christmas are reserved for family affairs. Memorial Day and Labor Day are often used by labor unions or corporations for picnics or sports. Check your calendar to avoid Ash Wednesday, Good Friday, Easter, Passover, Rosh Hashanah, and Yom Kippur, which change dates each year.

OTHER HOLIDAYS

Friday the 13th. Have a "Festival of Fate" party starting at 8:13 pm. Book a fortune teller and a palm reader to tell people's fortunes and serve Chinese fortune cookies. Sell patron tickets for $13.13. Put on a skit about the good luck the organization will have next year.

Sadie Hawkins Day. Officially February 29, but you can do it any time in Leap Year. Next Leap Year is 1980. Leap Years are the same as Presidential election years and Olympic Games years. Tradition holds that women can ask men to marry them in a Leap Year. Sadie Hawkins Day is the chance for the women to invite the men to a dance or party.

Make up your own holiday. Celebrate Founder's Day, the Birthday of the Organization, the day you get your tax exemption, the president's birthday, installation of officers, and of course, *all* your victories! You can also celebrate other holidays which are important to your own members, such as Seneca Falls Day (July 19) for a feminist picnic, Dr. Martin Luther King, Jr.'s birthday (Jan. 15) for a Black leaders award luncheon, or St. Joseph's Day (March 19) for an Italian dinner.

BIBLIOGRAPHY

GOOD CENTS—Every Kid's Guide to Making Money. The Amazing Life Games Co. and Friends. Houghton Mifflin Co., Boston, MA. 1974. 128 pp. $5.00. Lists eight projects connected to holidays. Especially good on the Haunted House, suggesting special twists to appeal to the strong stomachs of little kids. For example, their suggestion for making "monster breath" is to run your big sister's hair dryer over an open can of cat food. Blow this out the cut-out mouth of a monster face and any kid will believe it is monster breath. So will any adult with a hangover.

CHASE'S CALENDAR OF ANNUAL EVENTS. Apple Tree Press, Box 1012, Flint, MI 48501. $5. 80 pp. Published annually. You can dredge up an excuse for a party on *any* day of the year out of this book: presidents, authors and celebrities' birthdays, foreign country celebrations, commercial promotional weeks and months, and presidential proclamation holidays.

ALTERNATIVE CELEBRATIONS CATALOGUE. Alternatives, 701 N. Eugene St., Greensboro, NC 27401. 1975. 200 pp. $3.50. (Also available at most American Friends Service Committee office bookstores.) How to celebrate holidays without going broke or crazy.

THE MEMBERSHIP CANVASS

A membership canvass is an *organized* drive to get new members and money in a short period of time. You are selling new people on the benefits of belonging to your group.

The people. The preparation for a membership drive involves the three P's: the people, the plan, and the package. The people are the most important part of preparation. You need: 1) a chairperson to oversee the membership drive; 2) a committee to go out and sell the memberships; and 3) a clear understanding of who you are trying to sell—your market.

The *chairperson* can be either the president or the membership chairperson. Or you may elect someone just to chair the drive. The chairperson makes sure everyone has materials, is working on schedule, and gets whatever help is needed.

The *committee* of volunteers or recruits meets to make up the sales plan and the package they will use to sell. They decide who the market is.

The *market*. The market is the people who would like to join the organization. Consider who benefits from your program, where they are, and how you can reach them. Defining the market is the first step to making your plan.

The plan. The plan is a specific schedule for when and where the members will reach your market. If you have a city block club, your market is the neighborhood, so you go to people where they live. You may decide to have each of the ten people on your committee sign up everybody on the block. It may take three trips to recruit all possible neighbors, for instance one afternoon, one evening, and one weekend day. In that case allow two weeks for the membership drive.

If your group is fighting strip mining over half of Montana, it would be impossible to go ranch to ranch selling memberships. Instead, you have to go to your neighbors at places where they get together in groups. Your committee could divide up into pairs and sell memberships one Sunday after services at the five biggest churches. Then all ten focus on the biggest event in the upcoming month: the state fair, a rodeo, a calf sale.

A working women's organization sells where people work. You can distribute literature at subway stops and busy lunch-hour intersections. Or stage a big rally with good speakers for Secretaries Day, or April 15th, and recruit from the audience you attract.

A different challenge occurs when your market is people who share your feelings on an issue which does not have geographic limitations. This would include national issues like opposition to the B-1 Bomber and other defense spending fights, or even international ecological issues like opposition to the slaughter of baby seals. If you can't sell people where they live or where they work, you have to plan a way to collect the people sympathetic to your cause and sell them in a group setting. Some political clubs have each committee member hold a luncheon. Each is responsible for finding twelve guests who would want to join the club. The officers present a program on the club, their victories, and their goals. They can usually sign up 100 per cent of the guests at the luncheon.

Issue organizations like feminist or environmental groups can simply vote on a quota for the number of new members each committee member will recruit. If each of the ten committee members takes a quota of ten new members, the group gets 100 new members. Set a short time limit so everyone gets out and gets through. The committee members can sell memberships to their neighbors, to their relatives, at other club meetings, at their churches, sometimes at work, and can always write letters to sell sympathetic folks farther away.

There are really no limits on whom you can ask to support a good cause. People in Missouri who have never seen the ocean are members of "Save the Whales" because they oppose mechanized whale slaughter. If you have a broad, reasonable, human program—saving the environment, promoting gun control, improving the schools— everyone is your market. Just set your goals and quotas, then go out and get the members.

Make up a very specific timetable for the membership drive, the shorter the better. A good schedule might be: January 7—first meeting and practice sales pitch; January 14—second meeting, give out materials, divide up the area and practice sales pitch again; January 21—first turn-ins; January 28—final turn-ins. Tell people they must have the *money* to turn in, so they have to collect cash instead of promises.

The package. The package the committee uses to sign up new people would consist of:

1) A card for new members to fill in indicating name, address, phone numbers, and committee interests—like fundraising, publicity, property tax task force, senior citizen group, etc.

2) Receipt books. New members get a receipt for dues paid and the group keeps the carbon copy.

3) Your current brochure or fact sheet on the organization. This tells when the group was founded, current officers, goals of the group, how members can participate, regular meeting date, time, and place, and flattering comments by local celebrities.

4) A recent clipping of a favorable news story, exposé, or editorial.

5) Whatever regular members receive when they pay their dues: a membership card, a button, a decal.

6) A current copy of the newsletter or annual report. (See

"Dues" in "Ongoing fundraisers," chapter 8, for more information on what to give members in return for their dues.)

The package is the least important part of the sales program. The bare minimum you need is the card for new members to sign and receipts for their dues. If you have enthusiastic people and a well-organized plan, you need nothing more to sign up new members for your program. The most important thing they get is not on paper: their vote in the group. All the rest is simply information to help the sales people explain the group and to help the new members get actively involved right away.

You can use the membership drive whenever you need more money in a hurry because there is no overhead. You don't need to book a band, or print posters, or do any advance shopping. You already have your merchandise: an important, exciting organization. All you have to do is convince more people to join your group. It can be relatively simple to sell the memberships if people already know about the group, due to the work of the publicity committee. Of course, when you go in person to your neighbors most of those who join will do so because they know and trust *you*.

Membership drives work best for new groups that need to pass the word in person to their neighbors. The personalized membership drive is ideal for groups from 10 to 500; it expands their membership by using their best resource—the current enthusiastic members. After your first few years, you will have developed some system for asking the old members to renew and recruit new members. If you expand beyond one city you will probably want to professionalize your membership recruitment using either direct mail, door-to-door canvassing, advertising, or a combination of professional techniques.

PROFIT FORMULA: Your profit is the net profit from each membership times the number of new members you recruit. For example, if your membership fee is $5 and each person gets a membership card and a receipt that cost you 10¢, your net profit per member is $4.90. If you sell 100 memberships you make $490. If dues are $5 and each member gets the card and receipt that cost 10¢, plus a subscription to the newsletter that costs $2 per member annually, your net profit per new member is $2.90. If you sell 100 memberships you make $290.

MOVIES

Movie showings make easy small fundraisers since everyone likes to see good movies and they are easy to tie into your program. You can show one movie several times, run a film series with a theme, or show a movie in conjunction with a party.

Stick to 16mm; 8 mm or super 8 is too small to show anything except home movies. You cannot project a big enough image from 8 mm to entertain an audience of any size. Avoid 35mm films because they cost more to rent; you will have to rent a commercial theatre and hire a union projectionist to show the film. All this will run up your costs enormously. (See "Movie Premiers" in the "Big Fundraiser" section on how to do feature film fundraisers.)

The first thing to do is get some catalogs from companies that rent 16 mm films. These are listed in the yellow pages under Motion Picture Film Libraries. They offer feature films, travelogs, children's films and cartoons. If you want a film to provoke discussion or introduce your program to a crowd, write away for the catalogs listed at the end of this section under "Social Change." There are many excellent movies about current issues. You can choose a film simply for its fundraising potential or for its relevance to your current program.

The film catalogs will describe exactly how to order. Be sure to order at least six weeks in advance. You should get a confirmation slip in the mail about ten days after you place the order. If you don't, contact the distributor immediately. Films should arrive two or three days before your showing date; if they do not, contact the distributor again.

You can ask the filmmaker if he or she would like to attend the showing. Especially if it is a new film, the filmmaker may be curious about the audience's reaction and might like to talk about how they made the film—from idea to editing. Tell the filmmaker who you are, what you do, and why you are raising the money. Explain that the filmmaker's appearance will be a special attraction in your town, and that it will help you raise money. You should offer to pay the filmmaker's expenses. The director may be willing to do it for free out of sympathy with your group, or if yours is a new organization. If you expect to make a big profit ($1,000+), offer an honorarium too.

Preparation.

Arrange for a place to show the film. Try to find someplace free, like a church hall, or low-cost, like the YMCA. The most profitable places to show movies are college campuses. Ask a college student group to co-sponsor the film. As a student group they can get a free auditorium with a projector and screen. Colleges offer a captive audience with time, money and interest in films. You may be able to get a commercial theatre for a low rent if you show your film in the afternoon when the theatre would otherwise be empty.

If you will be showing during the daytime, be sure you can darken the room. Also check out how the sound will work in the room. Places with curtains and carpeting work best; big stark places like school cafeterias are terrible because they echo too much. Try to ask someone who has used the room before how it worked for them.

Preview the film. If you have not already seen the film, be sure to view it at least once before you show it. At the same time, have your speaker see it, so he or she can make remarks linked to the film's content.

Price the tickets slightly lower than the going rate for first-run films. If theatres in your area charge $3 for new movies, charge $2 for adults and $1 for children and senior citizens. You can also have $5 patron tickets for wealthier supporters. Try to pre-sell as many tickets as possible, especially the patron tickets.

PUBLICITY

Do as much advance publicity as possible. About five to six weeks in advance, send a notice to all the organizations that have members who might like your film. Ask them to include it in their newsletters.

Ask for a press packet from the filmmaker when you order the film. This includes photos from the movie called "stills," background on the film, the stars, the topic and the music; how it was made, what festivals it was in, and copies of reviews. All of this will help you get positive coverage.

Announce the showing in your newsletter, put notices in the bulletins of nearby churches, and offer tickets as premiums on popular radio shows. If you have lots of energetic help you can put up fliers and posters in the neighborhood too, but this is usually lots of work for very few customers.

Try to get a newspaper story on your film. If it is a brand new film you can run a special private showing for the movie critics in advance. Especially if it is a good social change film, you may be able to get a story connecting the film and your program. An interview with the director or star always makes a good story too, and works well for TV and radio shows. Include both campus and commercial newspapers.

SERIES

You can run a series of films on a theme. This can become a regular fundraiser since film buffs will keep coming back to see good films at low prices. Once you build a mailing list and publicity out-

lets you can get a predictable crowd with very little work.
    Some series that work well are:
        Science fiction movies or monster movies.
        Spectacles ("Ben Hur").
        Musicals.
        Crime, mystery and suspense films.
        Heroes: Women's heroines ("Antonia") or working class heroes.
        Schmaltz: Shirley Temple or Ruby Keeler movies.
        Spy films.
        Star series (Judy Garland, Humphrey Bogart, Kathryn Hepburn, W.C. Fields).
        Director series (Alfred Hitchcock).
        Foreign films (Cuban, French, Japanese).
        Love Stories: ("An Affair to Remember").
        Travelogs. These make good matinees for senior groups and are usually less expensive.
        Cartoons and children's films: these make good matinees for kids and the young at heart. Also animal series, classics ("Heidi") or westerns.
    Series work well because you can do one mailing for the whole series and get repeat customers without additional publicity costs. Be sure to check what the commercial theatres are running so you know what the competition will be.
    HOW TO SET UP: You need an experienced projectionist to show your film. Be sure you have run the beginning of the film on the projector you will use to make sure: 1) the film is wound correctly and in good condition and 2) the projector is in good working order. Check both the picture and the sound.
    Get a crew to set up chairs and the concessions stand. Besides your projectionist, you need a door committee to sell tickets and distribute literature, a committee of ushers, a team to sell the candy and popcorn, and a clean-up crew.

WHAT YOU NEED BESIDES THE FILM AND PROJECTOR:
A large white wall or the largest possible movie screen. Do not use
    a sheet or paper.
Table for the projector.
Take-up reels. If you are showing several films of different lengths
    it is good to have several reels.
Extra bulbs and instructions on how to change them.
Extension cord.
A three-pronged adapter if needed for the power cord.
Masking tape to tape down the cords.
Know the location of circuit breakers or fuse box and which circuit
    you will be using. Be sure you can get at it during the showing.
    Opening night. Set up everything well in advance. Have your
tickets, cash box and newsletters by the door. If you are showing the

movie at a free hall, plan to run a concessions stand. Real movie
theatres pay the rent with the proceeds from their concessions stand.
Sell candy, popcorn, coffee and lemonade.

It is fun and profitable to show a short cartoon before the feature. Cartoons make it seem like you're "at the movies", they make
allowance for the late-comers, and make more time for people to
buy concessions.

PROGRAM. You can run the movie strictly as commercial
entertainment. Then you show it like any other movie: charge admission, play the movie, and send everyone home.

On the other hand, you can link the movie to your program.
Print up simple fliers on the group, what it does, how the audience
can join, and how to contribute. Before the movie the president can
welcome the audience, thank everyone for coming, and ask them to
take home the flier. If the movie has an intermission you can sell
coffee or lemonade and circulate members through the crowd to sell
memberships or issue materials like buttons and T-shirts.

You can also add on a short program at the end of the movie.
Try to get the filmmaker or a person who is in the film to speak.
Most of the crowd will stay to hear more about how the film was
made and what has happened to the people in the film since it was
made. The president or chairperson of the issue campaign can also
give a short talk on the issues affecting the audience.

MOVIES WITH A PARTY. You can run a good short movie
as a focus for a fundraising party. Invite people to a large home or
high-rise party room. Charge them, say, $10 each and offer wine and
cheese before the movie. After the movie have a local celebrity do
an inspirational pitch along the lines of "If they can do it, so can we!
Here's the president of XYZ to tell you what is being done right
here in Metropolis to win a fight just like the one we just saw." Then
the president outlines the importance and urgency of the fight, the
overwhelming resources of the opposition, and the group's need for
money right now. The celebrity comes back and says, "I've seen a
lot of good causes in my day, but I think these folks have the most
exciting and most significant battle in America right now. I'm giving
them my check for $100 and I'm asking you to do the same." Then
the celebrity and the president collect the checks.

JUST FOR FUN. Of course you can always show movies just
for fun. The Lincoln Park Zoo officially opened its new Great Ape
House with a box supper and "The Great Ape Film Festival" featuring (what else?) the original *King Kong*. Some small town police

or fire departments show cartoons for the kids on Hallowe'en to keep them off the streets.

Afterward. It is your responsibility to promptly return the film according to the directions in the catalog. You are liable for the film if it does not reach the distributor, so be sure to insure it when you mail it back; $50 worth of insurance for a short film will cost you 60¢, and $220 worth of insurance for a feature film will cost you $1.20. Buy the insurance at the post office.

Where to get advice. The Public Library, Film Curator. The library may have films individuals can check out for free, but not for groups to show for fundraisers. The curator can advise you on good local filmmakers and where to get catalogs.

The Art Museum, Film Center. If your art museum has a film center, the head person there can suggest catalogs for you.

The Film Festival. If your city has a "film festival" it should be listed in the telephone directory under the name of the city film festival. They can also suggest catalogs for you.

The college, university or high school. Contact the film, video, media or drama department head. Ask who would be the person who knows the most about current film-making and who could give you advice. Also, contact the student activities director and the head of the school film series (if there is one) to see what catalogs they have.

Your national office. If your group is a chapter of a national organization, the national office sometimes has films produced specifically for chapter use. The national office can also tell you which films other chapters have used successfully. The Greater Cleveland Chapter of ACLU used *Sacco and Vanzetti* and the Arizona chapter used *I. F. Stone's Weekly* and *Joyce at 34*. These successful fundraisers were reported to the other ACLU chapters by the national office.

Most national church denominations have films local parishes can use free of charge. Most of these run from dull to mediocre, so only order one that has been recommended by a viewer.

Other organizations. Ask other organizations like your own which films they have used successfully for fund-raisers.

Filmmakers. Someone you know who makes movies or videotapes may give you a special deal on a new film in order to get exposure, and will probably know about other good new films available.

Movie critic for the local newspaper. The movie critics should know where you can get catalogs and they should also know the names of the best independent filmmakers in your area.

Television station. Your local television station should also be able to refer you to the best local independent filmmakers.

Public Relations Professionals. P.R. people can recommend local filmmakers. They would know who does the commercial promotional films for the banks, corporations and United Way campaign. Sometimes you can find a filmmaker who's having a guilt attack for selling a "What's good for your local power company is good for you" film for an outrageous price and wants to work off the guilt by making a film for you.

Free Catalogs
GENERAL INTEREST & FEATURE FILMS

BUDGET FILMS (290 pp)
4590 Santa Monica Blvd.
Los Angeles, CA 90029

FILMS INCORPORATED (372 pp)
440 Park Avenue South, New York, NY 10016
5589 New Peachtree Road, Atlanta, GA 30341
733 Greenbay Road, Wilmette, IL 60091
5625 Hollywood Blvd., Hollywood, CA 90028
716 Cooke St., Honolulu, HI 96813
Kohli Motion Picture Services, Box 2079, Anchorage, AK 99501
Deseret Book Co., 60 East South Temple, Salt Lake City, UT 84110
Knight's Film Library, 3911 Normal Ave., San Diego, CA 92103

MACMILLAN AUDIO BRANDON (440 pp)
34 MacQuesten Parkway South, Mount Vernon, NY 10550
8400 Brookfield Av., Brookfield, IL 60513
2512 Program Drive, Dallas, TX 75229
3868 Piedmont, Oakland, CA 94611
1619 N. Cherokee, Los Angeles, CA 90028

SOCIAL CHANGE FILMS*

APPALBROCHURE—1977 (30 pp)
Appal Shop, Inc.
P.O. Box 743
Whitesburg, KY 41858
Films about Appalachia and Appalachian culture.

CHURCHILL FILMS (40 pp)
662 N. Robertson Blvd.
Los Angeles, CA 90069

----

*Unfortunately, there is not at this time (1977) a comprehensive catalog or distribution system for social change films. This is a list of distributors recommended by filmmakers and fundraisers who have used their films. Since this list is neither complete nor current, ask each distributor you contact to recommend other catalogs, distributors, and filmmakers.

FILM IMAGES (60 pp)
1034 Lake St.
Oak Park, IL 60301
Rents *By the People,* the best film on how to put together a precinct organization for an independent candidate. It documents a successful campaign that beat the best political machine in the Free World. Also *The Emerging Woman,* history of American women.

HAYMARKET FILM AND VIDEOTAPE (one page brochure)
1901 W. Wellington
Chicago, IL 60657
(Has *Now We Live on Clifton* about working class kids moved out of their neighborhood by real estate investors and a university expansion.

NATIONAL FILM BOARD OF CANADA
Order films from:
Contemporary & McGraw-Hill Films
1221 Avenue of the Americas
New York, NY 10020

NEW DAY FILMS (22 pp)
P.O. Box 315
Franklin Lakes, NJ 07417
Specializing in "films about men and women." Produced *Union Maids,* about women organizing in the 1930's; *Growing Up Female,* and *Men's Lives,* on how one learns gender roles.

ODEON FILM CATALOGUE (20 pp)
1619 Broadway
New York, NY 10019
(Includes films on health care, women, children and prisons)

PYRAMID FILMS (242 pp)
2801 Colorado
P.O. Box 1048
Santa Monica, CA 90406

RED BALL FILMS
P.O. Box 298
Village Station
New York, NY 10014

TWYMAN FILMS (228 pp)
329 Salem Ave.
Dayton, OH 45401

UNITED FILMS (200 pp)
1425 S. Main St.
Tulsa, OK 74119

VIEWFINDERS, INC.
P.O. Box 1665
Evanston, IL 60204

VISION QUEST (100 pp)
7715 N. Sheridan Rd.
Chicago, IL 60626
or
Box 206
Lawrenceville, NJ 08648

FOR LISTS OF DISTRIBUTORS OF 16MM FILM

THE JUMP CUT GUIDE TO 16MM DISTRIBUTION Jump Cut,
3138 W. Shubert, Chicago, IL 60647. Issue No. 9, Oct.-Dec. 1975. pp.
17-21. Most comprehensive list available, includes evaluation of quality
and quantity of films plus a comparison of prices. Also good inside information, such as which distributors you have to check and double-
check for delivery.

NAM FILM GUIDE. Julia Reichert and Loren Weinberg. National
Office, New American Movement, 1643 N. Milwaukee, Chicago, IL
60647. 1973-74. 75¢. List of distributors of revolutionary films and
instructions on how to do a film showing and lead a discussion. The
nuts and bolts advice is excellent; you can take the socialist view-
point or leave it.

STAR: a people's film library (16 pp)
The Haymarket Foundation
2 Holyoke
Cambridge, MA 02138
Has a low rental fee film library. For New England organizations
only.

THIRD WORLD FILMS*

NEW YORKER FILMS (64 pp)
43 W. 61st St.
New York, NY
Good selection of Third World feature films.

THIRD WORLD NEWSREEL (38 pp)
RESOLUTION
630 Natoma Street
San Francisco, CA 94101

TRI-CONTINENTAL (44 pp)
333 6th Ave.
New York, NY 10014
Good collection of Third World political documentaries.

*Includes international issue, cultural, foreign language, minority
and some domestic issues films.

Catalogs for Sale

FILMS BY WOMEN/CHICAGO '74—$2.50 (40 pp)
Features and shorts directed by women around the world.

REVOLUTIONARY FILMS/CHICAGO '76—$2.50 (54 pp)
Political films from around the world.

TRICKFILM/CHICAGO '75—$2.00 (48 pp)
Important animated and special-effect films made around the world
between 1879 and 1975.

Order from: Film Center
School of the Art Institute
Michigan at Adams
Chicago, IL 60603

You must send your check with your order; they cannot bill
you. Each catalog lists twenty to thirty of the best films in each
category, describes each film, and tells where to order it.

WOMEN'S FILMS IN PRINT
Bonnie Dawson
Booklegger Press
555 29th St.
San Francisco, CA 94131
$4.00, 1975, 165 pp.

FEATURE FILMS ON 8MM AND 16MM (4th edition)
R. R. Bowker Co.
P.O. Box 1807
Ann Arbor, MI 48105
$16.50

FILM PROGRAMMERS GUIDE TO 16mm FILMS (2nd edition)
(210 pp)
Peel Research
P.O. Box 6037
Albany, CA 94706
$8.75
(Highly recommended. Lists films alphabetically by title and direc-
tor, and indicates where to rent each.)

Where to Get Free Entertainment Films:

These are for program filler rather than fundraising.
Call the chamber of commerce. Many big businesses, like the
phone company or food processors, put out free films for their public
relations campaigns.
The National Association of Manufacturers publishes "Program

Notes." This quarterly newsletter lists films and speakers non-profit groups can get for free. Most have tacit commercials for the company whose public relations department produced the film, but they make good light entertainment filler for meetings. Write The National Association of Manufacturers, 1776 F Street, N.W., Washington, D.C. 20006, to get on the mailing list.

Other free promotional movies are available from: Modern Talking Picture Service, 2020 Prudential Plaza, Chicago, IL 60601. Ask for free brochure on "Free Films For . . ." (choose one): colleges, church groups, men's clubs, business & industry, or adult groups. They also have free sports films. All are public relations films. For example a spark plug company produced the sports film about the Indianapolis 500 auto race featuring safety tips and a plug for their plugs.

The Public Library, Film Department. The library may allow non-profit organizations to check out films for free. Ordinarily you may not charge admission for the film. You may use it as entertainment for a regular meeting, however, and then announce your own film series and sell tickets to that.

Labor unions. Contact your local labor council and any large labor unions in your area. Address a letter to their "Education Department." Some unions with free film catalogs are:

AFL-CIO
815 16th St., N.W.
Washington, D.C. 20006

International Ladies Garment Workers (ILGWU)
1710 Broadway
New York, NY 10019

United Steelworkers of America
5 Gateway Center
Pittsburgh, PA 15222

Amalgamated Meat Cutters and Butcher Workmen of North America
2800 N. Sheridan Road
Chicago, IL 60657

International Longshoremen's and Warehousemen's Union
150 Golden Gate Ave.
San Francisco, CA 94102 (For Western U.S. only)

NOTE: See also p. 171 and p. 180 for information on producing slide shows and leading film discussions.

The Pot Luck Supper

The pot luck supper is a delightfully high-calorie, low-cost fundraiser. It is a great way to get families together and an excellent way to introduce small groups to each other.

Preparation. Choose a date and tell each person what you want them to bring, such as "a dish to serve ten people." Get a large free room with tables and chairs and running water so you can make coffee. A church or school hall is fine. If you can get a big kitchen too, that's even better.

The sponsoring group usually provides beverages like coffee and milk. Have the shopper get milk, coffee, cream, sugar, napkins and placemats. If the place does not have plates, cups and silverware, buy or borrow those too.

BEFORE THE DINNER. Have a committee come in early to make sure the room is clean, the tables and chairs are set up, and the coffee is made. Set the tables with placemats, napkins, silverware, salt and pepper shakers, cream and sugar, and bread and butter. You can add simple centerpieces from the members' gardens or have the kids make holiday placemats for Valentine's Day or Christmas.

The committee makes up a buffet table on which to put all the food, and makes sure there are enough large spoons and forks to serve everything. It usually works well if you can put long tables in the middle of the room so the diners can serve themselves in two rows from either side of the table.

At the dinner. Have two people be the hosts—responsible for getting all the food out, keeping early dishes warm, and making everyone feel welcome. They say nice things about *every* dish. In addition, they recruit a team of waiters and waitresses to pour coffee. clean up spills, and help serve anyone who needs help at the buffet.

Set up a ticket table by the door. Most groups charge about $2 for adults and $1 for senior citizens and children.

PROGRAM. You can have a simple program consisting of the president welcoming everyone and telling a little about what the group is doing now. If there is a piano in the room you can always have a sing-a-long with dessert. Keep the program short, since most people really come to eat and talk with their neighbors.

Afterward. If you are using the school's dishes, you need a team to wash up and put everything away. Put all the tables and chairs back the way you found them. Be sure people take their empty dishes home, or that one person takes all the empty dishes to a central location to be picked up. Be sure to thank the principal for the use of the room. Turn off all the lights and stoves and lock the room after the last person leaves.

MIXER. Pot lucks are a good way to get a couple of small groups to meet each other. Be sure you have a host or hostess who introduces the guests to each other; use name tags, and try to mix up the seating so everyone gets to meet someone new. One gimmick that works well at rearranging people is to get up twelve tables and mark them with zodiac signs and dates; e.g., Gemini, May 21-June 20 or Aquarius, Jan. 20-Feb. 18. People will pick up their food and sit at the table for their sign. Clip the horoscope from that day's paper and mount it on the sign to make a dandy conversation starter.

The zodiac mixer works best with all-adult groups. It does not work if there are many families so that adults must sit near small children. For groups with lots of kids, you can mix them up by school, neighborhood or parish, or simply in order of arrival. If there are a lot of children, it is good to have another large room nearby, in which the kids can play, since they usually finish first.

PROFIT FORMULA. Your profit is all the ticket sales minus your costs. The costs should be no more than paper products like placemats, plates and cups.

Variations

You can also run a picnic as a pot luck. It is easiest to have everyone bring cold dishes like fried chicken or meat loaf rather than trying to grill hot-dogs. You can add soft-ball games or frisbee contests.

Have a theme. For the Fourth of July you can have all American or regional dishes. For Christmas or Hanukkah you can have holiday specialties. Or you can have an ethnic dinner in which everyone brings an ethnic dish like sauerkraut, tamale pie, lasagne or borscht. This works well in big cities where there are lots of ethnic groups. Tell your people to bring grandma's best dish.

Use a pot luck to launch the sales drive for your group cookbook. If you have put together a cookbook of the members' best recipes, ask each person to bring the dish he or she submitted. Then people can have personal recommendations to make when they sell the book, like "Try the 'Rice that Stands Alone' on page 27, or 'Grandmother's Snickerdoodles' on page 104." Invite the food editors and feature writers of the local paper to the picnic to sample the fare. Give them cookbooks and press releases, and encourage them to do stories on the cookbook.

International Food Feast

The International Food Feast is a large-scale, dressed-up pot luck dinner. Whereas the pot luck has just random donation from the group's cooks, the International Food Feast has well-organized donations from each ethnic group represented in the membership. Besides highlighting the cuisine of each ethnic group, the feast can also present an entire program of entertainment, costumes and decorations to portray each group's customs.

This is a natural event for organizations with great ethnic variety in their membership—urban parishes, metropolitan community organizations, senior citizens coalitions. It also makes a great fundraiser for regional get-togethers of youth groups, women's clubs or civic organizations. It works perfectly for organizations which promote international understanding like the American Field Service, urban visitors' centers or university international programs.

The "Taste and Tell": For smaller groups, a delightful variation on the International Food Feast is the "Taste and Tell." This can be done at a luncheon or coffee hour, or as an addition to a monthly meeting.

Recruit about twenty people to make their special family dessert recipe and bring it to the Taste and Tell. They tell the history of the recipe and its creator, and may have stories to tell about the unusual equipment they use to make the dessert, like a krumkake iron or the old family bundt pan. This is a grown-up "show and tell" where everyone else walks around and samples your goodies.

The Taste and Tell works especially well at Christmas time. Some churches have each ethnic group decorate a small Christmas tree in the style of its homeland. Others display cherished Christmas decorations like handmade ornaments or creche sets. Each person tells the story of the decorations and serves the national dessert. It is an honor for the tellers and a joy for the tasters.

You can either charge a flat price for the Taste and Tell or put baskets near each table for donations, with a suggested price per sample. You will probably make more charging 50 cents per sample since most people lose all self control at the sight of homemade chocolate torte or raspberry trifle.

THE RAFFLE

A raffle is a game of chance. You sell chances to win prizes. All of your customers support your program and hope to win a prize.

Raffles have been popular in America since Colonial days. Boston ran a raffle in the 1660's to help Harvard. Today, thirteen states run raffles called lotteries. Illinois' lottery, the most profitable, grossed more than $144 million the first year.

Preparation

1. Make or buy chance tickets—printed with the name of your organization, date and place of the drawing, list of prizes, price and a number. Add "Winner need not be present" if true. Each ticket has a detachable stub with the same number, and spaces for name, address and phone.

Chances can simply be mimeographed, cut up and collected. Or they can be printed by a commercial printer. The printer may try to sell you a "cover" for a book of five or ten chances. A cover is just heavier paper sandwiching the chances. It is just an extra expense for something you will throw away. Order your chances without covers.

2. Choose the prizes. Everyone's favorite is cash. Other attractive prizes are appliances, trips, and gift certificates. A team of members should try to get prizes donated by local merchants. Remember: the less you have to spend on prizes, the higher your profit will be.

One advantage to cash prizes is that the jubilant winner will often donate a part of the prize back to the organization. If the winner asks how much would be right, say that most people give 20 per cent. So if the prize is $500, you may get $100 back; if it is $100 you may get $20 back. This is not mandatory, of course, simply a nice tradition to encourage.

For bookkeeping purposes you should pay out cash prizes with a check. Record the winner's name and social security number for your tax reports. It is the organization's responsibility to make out a "1099 form" for miscellaneous income. One copy goes to the winner, one to the IRS and one to the organization's files. Get 1099s from your IRS office.

It is the winners' responsibility to report cash prizes on their income tax forms. Some people think if they win money from a tax-exempt group they don't need to pay taxes on it. Alas, Uncle Sam says income is income.

ADVANTAGES OF A RAFFLE.

1. The price is low. Most groups price tickets at 25¢ each or five for $1. Anyone can afford a raffle ticket.

2. It gets everyone involved. Because of the low ticket price, *everyone* can sell them. A raffle allows you to include your lowest income members, children, students, and senior citizens in your fundraising program.

3. You are selling people something they want to buy anyway. Customers do not have to be crusading consumers or ardent environmentalists. Everyone loves a chance to win.

4. You can increase attendance at your meeting or party by scheduling the drawing there.

5. Sales are traceable. You find out who your leadership really is, who has networks, and who produces.

6. Once you establish your sales networks, it is easy to repeat a raffle. State lotteries run weekly drawings and some community organizations run monthly raffles.

7. A raffle can be combined with any other event—dinner, meeting, pet show, theater party, or dance.

8. It's fun.

9. You can use a raffle to turn a valuable but useless merchandise gift into usable cash. Mother Teresa, a nun working among the poor in India, used this technique. Pope Paul VI gave her a Lincoln limousine that someone else had given him. As a car it was useless to her work. As a raffle prize it brought in some $100,000 to help feed and clothe poor people.

Closer to home, many groups use a raffle as a spin-off from an ad book campaign. As the members solicit the business community for ads, they always find five to ten merchants who insist they have no money to give but will give you merchandise or gift certificates. Save the merchandise and certificates and use it to run a raffle, either separately or during the event at which you distribute the ad book.

DISADVANTAGE: NUMBER OF TRANSACTIONS. Raffles require a very large number of transactions for success. It takes lots and lots of 25-cent sales to make a decent profit. Evaluate how you want to invest your members' time. Is it better for them to sell a hundred $1 raffle books, twenty $5 dance tickets, or one $100 page in an ad book?

How to boost sales.

1. Be sure everyone has tickets all the time. If each member carries a few books in a purse or pocket, chances can be sold to everyone the members run into.

2. Set an ambitious goal. Have frequent money turn-ins so you know how you're doing. Build in some friendly competition between your committees or regions.

3. Use incentives. Reward the top sales people. Have each seller put his or her name on the back of each stub. Whoever sold the ticket to the first-prize winner also gets a prize.

4. Work systematically. Learn where and how you can sell. Set up a table outside a supermarket on Saturday or a church on Sun-

day (with permission from the manager or pastor). A team of two people can sell $75 worth of tickets in about three hours this way.

Try going door-to-door. Selling chances to your neighbors gives you an opportunity to identify potential new members.

Kids love to sell chances, especially the ten-to-twelve age group. Offer a modest commission or a party at the end of the afternoon and you'll be amazed at the results.

Ask business people to buy more chances to support your group. They can easily buy $10 to $20 worth.

5. Ask *everyone* to buy a chance. Remind them of your victories and how these results have helped them personally. A national survey showed that only four per cent of those interviewed had contributed to political campaigns. However *89%* said they would contribute *if asked*. Raising money proves you are serious about your goals. Everyone should support your important work—*ask them*.

6. Keep in touch with your sales team leaders daily and keep up the pep talk.

MECHANICS.

1. Number all tickets. Keep track of who has which tickets out and what money is due in.

2. Be sure you get all the stubs in *before* the drawing.

3. Democratically select an impartial person to do the drawing. If a small child does the drawing, even the most cynical gambler won't complain of a fix.

4. Decide whether you want the staff to be able to enter the raffle. It makes for very poor public relations if staff members win the prizes. Since some people are skeptical about the honesty of all forms of gambling anyway, it is much better to simply make a rule forbidding the staff to enter the raffle. Even if they say they never win anything, the only way to guarantee they don't win is to make sure they don't enter.

The Raffle As An Ongoing Fundraiser

50-50 Monthly Raffle. A small town civic group runs a "50-50" monthly raffle. It gives away half of the money collected and keeps half. Since it sells about $500 worth of tickets a month, it regularly nets about $250.

The tickets are distributed through the chamber of commerce and the tavern association. Some of the businesses re-sell the tickets. Others just consider it a regular contribution and "eat" the tickets. Members of the civic group also sell tickets. One bartender, whose wife is on the group's board, makes customers buy a ticket before they can buy a drink.

The drawing is held every month at the group's regular meeting, which boosts attendance and adds some fun to an ordinary business meeting.

The advantage of a monthly raffle is that once you establish the sales networks is is an effortless, dependable source of income. It also permits the business community to support the group in an ongoing way.

No. 1107

NAME_____

ADDRESS_____

_____

PHONE_____

SAMPLE:

MISSISSIPPI ACTION COUNCIL
3rd Annual Convention
Saturday, May 20, 1978
1:00 PM—International Room
Jackson Hotel—200 Main St.
Jackson, Mississippi 39222

1st Prize
$500 Cash
2nd Prize
Black & White TV Set
3rd Prize
A year's supply of pralines
(Winner need not be present)

25¢ Each   5 for $1.00

No. 1107

Chapter 6
Intermediate
Fundraising

An auction is simply an entertaining sale. You make money because the auction items are all donated. Extra excitement comes from celebrity auctioneers, unusual donations, and friendly competition.

Preparation: The major part of the work for an auction takes place before the auction itself: soliciting the donation of goods and services to auction off. There are three ways to do this. The wrong way is to go out and buy the art and other items you want to auction off, then auction them and try to make more than you spent. This will produce a fundloser, or at best, a very small profit and very large worries. The second way is to ask several artists to donate works for you to auction on commission. Then you get part and the artists get part of each sale. This limits the variety of your auction items—and your profits.

The right way to do an auction is to get everything donated. Rural groups have asked farmers for hay, farm equipment, sides of beef, and even cattle to auction. Ask artists to donate works for the publicity involved. Ask stores to give you merchandise. Best of all, ask people to donate their services and talents. Dinners, lessons and recreation donated by interesting people make the best auction items since they bring in high bids but cost you nothing.

SAMPLE AUCTION ITEMS

ART—paintings, photographs, sculptures, prints
CRAFTS—jewelry, pottery, macrame, weaving
CARTOON ORIGINALS—especially political cartoons. Write the artist in care of the newspaper.
AUTOGRAPHED BOOKS or RECORDS
CONTRIBUTIONS OF SERVICES BY PEOPLE:
RECREATION: Offer the chance to ride on a sailboat at a lake, ride on horses at a ranch, drive a race car, have a wine-tasting at a vineyard, or drive a snowmobile at a farm.
INSIDE TOUR: Tour backstage at the opera, aquarium, museum, guided by the director.

MEALS: Donors offer to prepare and serve in your home or theirs, their famous curry dinner for twelve, or fondue for four, or the ultimate romantic dinner for two.

LESSONS: Professional, teacher, or prize-winning amateur can donate lessons in belly dancing, scuba diving, speed reading, woodworking, self-defense, bowling, auto repair, Chinese cooking, knitting, etc.

PARTICIPATION: Arrange with the sponsoring agency for the highest bidder to get to: play in the symphony, sing in the chorus, be a batboy/girl for the professional baseball team for a week; be a Senate page, be an extra in a movie, carry a spear in the opera, do the weather on the TV news, or sit on the bench with the hockey/football/rugby/basketball team.

TALENT: For the high bid, you get an artist to design your stationery, interior decorator to design one room in your house, a plant doctor to perk up your plants, a professional to help your swing/serve/punt/swan dive or whatever, a mechanic to tune up your car or motorcycle, a barber/hair dresser to cut/style your hair, veteran parents (or grandparents) to put on a birthday party for your kids and guests, jolly person to play Santa Claus for your family or group, seamstress to replace all missing buttons, handyman to fix all the odds and ends that need repair in your house, carpenter to build anything wooden of your own design from a birdhouse to a rolltop desk, Santa's helper to address and mail all your Christmas cards or to wrap all your presents, veteran host/hostess to supply you with hors d'oeuvres for 50 for your next party, healthy teen-ager to mow lawn/rake leaves/shovel snow for a season; responsible babysitter to watch your kids for a whole week-end including a trip to the zoo; or person with car to be your driver for a day.

As you can see, the possibilities are almost endless. The beauty of an auction is that you can sell anything that one person will donate and someone else will want to buy. Some of the most unusual auction items make the most money and get the best publicity. For example, the Massachusetts ACLU auctioned off the chance to have your name in Kurt Vonnegut's next book—and got $550. The Chicago ACLU auctioned off the chance to have your name in lights—on the marquee of the famous Biograph movie theatre. The Biograph is the place where the FBI gunned down John Dillinger in 1934. After much spirited bidding, a politician bought the privilege for $127.50. The bidding was so much fun that the theatre owner, who was at the auction, gave them the marquee again, which they promptly sold for $125.

SOLICITING CONTRIBUTIONS: As you collect your contributions, catalog each item very carefully so you know who gave it, the value, the recommended starting price. With the advice of an experienced auction producer or auctioneer, arrange the contributions in order so you have a variety of price and interest.

Next solicit celebrities to serve as guest auctioneers, and schedule them at intervals through the evening. They can auction off their own contributions, or else just serve as auctioneers for a few items. Some possibilities are sports figures auctioning off lessons or autographed equipment, TV or radio stars auctioning off autographed scripts or clothing, or politicians auctioning off a service (like dinner in the governor's mansion—not ticket fixing). These can also be great publicity-getters.

Print your program at the last minute so you can include everything. You may even want to mimeograph the program to allow yourself the most time to include all items.

AUDIENCE: Obviously, for the auction to be a success you need an audience of people who will buy the merchandise. The more money the people have, and the more likely they are to spend it, the more money you will make. While your own members may dig deep to make contributions, and others may spend foolishly to fulfill their fantasies, you still have to consider how to get people with bigger budgets to the auction.

There can be a problem if there is a big difference between the average income of the membership and the average income of the auction audience. On the one hand the members may complain, "Everything was too expensive—I didn't get to buy anything." On the other hand, if you don't have the rich people you will not make enough money or have enough bidders to make it fun. One compromise is to auction a wide variety of items so everyone can at least bid on something. The other is to take all of the lower-priced items, like crafts, prints, or plants, and set up a sale where you just mark things with a price and sell them. This eliminates the least profitable items from the auction itself. You will still sell all the crafts and plants, and you leave more time to raise the bids on your more exciting donations. This way everybody can go home with something and the organization will end up with the highest possible total.

LISTS: Try to get lists of people who would be likely buyers for your art and services. This would include the lists of guests from any other auction held in town in the past year, lists of museum members (for an art auction), lists of rich supporters of the local politicians, plus names from every person on the committee. Just ask everybody to suggest everyone they can possibly think of and send them an invitation. (Of course, be sure to make a list at the auction for the next time.)

Send invitations and try to pre-sell as many tickets as possible. The ticket price should cover the room, printing, a professional auctioneer if you have one, and refreshments. Get a tempting door prize and list it on each ticket with "Winner must be present" to encourage people to attend.

Do lots of advance publicity, with photos, to inform the public of your exciting and unusual bargains. An auction is one fundraiser to which people will come as a result of publicity and will buy even if their feelings about your group are neutral. There are people who love the thrill of bidding and the chance to get a bargain. They watch for notices of an auction.

Your own members should sell as many tickets as possible in advance. You should promote the auction in the newsletter and do a mailing to your own contributor list. Urge everyone who donates auction items to take several tickets, too. If that seems too crass, give them free tickets.

At the Auction

AUCTIONEER: Hire a professional auctioneer unless you are very confident about an amateur whom you have seen work. Use your celebrities for variety and to attract the audience, but you have to depend on your auctioneer to keep the auction moving, keep people bidding, and get the totals up in a fun way. The auctioneer's most important skill is controlling the tempo so people don't get bored and start to chatter or wander away. The auctioneer also has to know how to work several bidders against each other so they spend a lot of money but still feel good.

Be sure to observe an auctioneer's style before you hire him or her, since some professionals are used to working high-price, high-powered shows and may overpower your crowd. You need someone who understands that the purpose of the auction is both to raise money and to impress the audience with the organization.

VOLUNTEERS: Line up volunteers to work the door, serve refreshments, carry and display the auction items, accept payments and give receipts, pass out numbers for the bidders, help the auctioneer identify bidders, and make sure everyone goes home with the right thing. Make a complete record of who bought what. Artists especially need to know who has bought their work in case they ever need to borrow it for a show. It's also nice to include the information with your thank you's so the donors know how much they have helped the group.

THE KEY TO SUCCESS IS THE TEMPO. You need to keep people interested, keep them buying, and simply keep them in the room. It helps if you start early (7:30 pm on a week night; early afternoon on weekends), and have people circulate with coffee and snacks. Have each auction item on display with a tempting description and the starting price so people can decide what they want. Intersperse celebrity auctioneers to add excitement, and vary the merchandise to increase bidding. Another gimmick is to have your "winner must be present" door prize drawing at the end of the evening. Since the people have already bought their tickets, and want your door prize, they will stay to see if they won. Limit the auction to about two hours. One problem is created by people who get bored easily or early and want to talk in the back of the room. They distract the rest of the crowd. Have several ushers who will shoo the talkers into another room, explaining that they will be notified when the item they want comes up.

PROFIT FORMULA: The profit on the auction is your sales total minus the cost of invitations, tickets and the auctioneer. If you auction art work on commission, it is your percentage of the sales minus the costs.

Variations

There are three variations on the auction which are less profitable but which are also less work:

THE AUCTIONEER'S AUCTION. There are auctioneers who will deliver a whole package auction to your audience. They bring the art, the carriers, the auctioneer, the prices, the bookkeeper: the whole show. All you have to do is deliver an audience that wants to buy the art. This works best for upper-income groups that have spenders who will buy the art. Your profit is the percentage you get from the total sales.

THE DUTCH AUCTION. This can be tied onto any dinner, meeting, or rally if you have a group of 50 or fewer. Each guest brings an item to auction off, either an unusual artifact, homemade baked goods, handcrafts, or a gift-wrapped mystery item. A peppy, funny auctioneer convinces the crowd to buy one another's treasures.

THE MEMORABILIA AUCTION. This is good for a quick fundraiser for a group which has been around more than two years. Get together in someone's home, or your regular meeting place, and auction off organizational mementos with special historical significance or sentimental value. You can auction off the first button, the original art for the first logo, early bumper stickers, the first convention program autographed by the first slate of officers, the first T-shirt, autographed copies of the first legislation you got passed, signed letters from the President, Governor, Senator or Mayor, secret corporation memos telling their employees to have nothing to do with you or the original draft of the organization song.

THE BAZAAR

The bazaar is a modern-day version of the medieval fair, offering novelties, bargains, food, drinks, and entertainment at the same time. In the middle ages, itinerant merchants would set up their wares in the market place at holiday time, offering shoppers new and varied merchandise. Today the shoppers come to you, but they are still looking for bargains, novelty, and entertainment.

The key to success is plenty of advance planning to produce as much variety as possible, because the way you make money at a bazaar is by seducing your customers into making a lot of small purchases. Although a customer may not buy the $25 silver candlesticks in the flea market, they will drop $1 on the pony ride, $2.50 at the bake booth, 50 cents at the raffle, $1 for bayberry candles, $1 for handmade Christmas ornaments, 50 cents for a handmade catnip toy and $3.50 for a cookbook. They have now spent $9.50 and still have to get their lemonade. The more you offer, the more they will spend.

Preparation:

Choose a day or a weekend, preferably in the spring or the fall. Fall works best because people are shopping for Christmas decorations and gifts. You can also reap a lot of good things for the flea market and old clothes sale from the members' fall cleaning. You can run the bazaar on Saturday from 10 a.m. to dusk, or Saturday and Sunday, or Friday night and Saturday.

Choose a large space. You can set up indoors or outdoors or both. It is easier to set up indoors, because you can get ready ahead of time. If you have the room, you can sell all your merchandise inside, while you run games and sell food outside. Try to get a prominent location on a busy street with plenty of parking. A church or school hall with adjoining parking lot is excellent.

MERCHANDISE: The attractions of the bazaar can be divided into three categories: things to buy (merchandise), things to eat and drink, and things to do—games and entertainments. The more you have of each, the more money you will make. To get a lot of each, you must plan ahead to get your committees working several months in advance. When you have chosen your location, make up a sample floor plan, dividing the area into booths or tables for each thing you will sell or game you will play. When you know how much space you have, and what kinds of booths you want, then you need to recruit a committee to get the merchandise, to price and mark it, and to serve as salespeople the day of the bazaar. For some booths, like the lemonade stand, you will need a crew to make and sell the lemonade just for that day. For the handcraft booth, you will need to sign people up several months in advance to give them the time to produce the goods.

HANDICRAFTS: Handicrafts include anything made by hand. These are usually great sellers because they are attractive, they are one-of-a-kind pieces you cannot buy in a store, and they make great gifts. You can ask people to donate completed items to the booth. If you can get quantities of material free, you can give the workers the materials for their project. They contribute the labor and the talent. If any members complain they are not talented, have some simple, fool-proof projects ready to suggest for the beginners, like fringed placemats or catnip mice. If you will all be working on the projects for several months, you can get together one night a week, with simple refreshments, to work on your handicrafts. Some people may decide to contribute something just to get in on the weekly "sewing circle."

Encourage people to make simple, colorful, salable, completable projects. It will take as long to make one embroidered tablecloth as it will to make fifty animal bean bags, but it is a lot easier to sell fifty $1 bean bags than it is to sell a $50 tablecloth, If you get something really special like a quilt, you might consider putting it in as a raffle prize or using it for a silent auction. (See p. 103)

Some sample merchandise for the handcraft booth could include: afghans, pillows, placemats, napkins, aprons, spectacles cases, bookmarks, potholders, hats, shawls, ponchos, mittens, scarves, baby things, tote bags, covered hangers, pet toys, baby blankets, candles, picture frames, dried flower arrangements, and paper weights. Also handmade renditions of the current dumb fad, like the pet rock.

CHRISTMAS BOOTH: A subdivision of the handicrafts booth is the booth for all the handmade things that are Christmasy. These include tree ornaments, house decorations, wreaths, card holders, bayberry candles, and Christmas cards if you have your own design to sell. (Avoid selling other people's Christmas cards because you do not make enough profit.)

HERB BOOTH: The old herb cottage can sell herbed vinegars, potpourri sachets (made from your dried rose petals), dried herbs from your garden, small potted herb plants, like chives, plus the ever-popular catnip toys. You can also sell here all your bottled or canned foods—jams, jellies, preserves, pickles, relishes, chili sauce, spaghetti sauce, brandied fruit.

USED GOODS: Divide your used goods into wearable and non-wearable items. Put the clothes into the "Boutique" and put everything else into the "Flea Market."

BOUTIQUE: Used clothes. Pre-sort all the clothes and throw out everything that is dirty. (Ask donors to contribute clean items only.) Hang everything on a hanger. Sort by men's and women's, boys' and girls' wear. If you have the space, put men's things in one room, women's things in another and kids' clothes in a third. Mark each item, pricing everything very low, because you need to sell it in one day. Have enough room for people to look at the clothes and, if you have the space, make a fitting room, too. Borrow some full-length mirrors. You also can sell accessories like purses, wallets, hats and jewelry. Don't bother with shoes and boots unless you can get almost-new kids' shoes or specialty items like imported sandals or clogs.

FLEA MARKET: The flea market is where you sell everything else that is second-hand—dishes, glasses, ashtrays, trays, planters, books, records, candlesticks, appliances that work, knickknacks, pictures, bottles, etc. The biggest job of the flea market committee is getting everything out attractively and putting a price on each item. Again, price everything low so it will sell.

Whereas the attraction of the handicrafts booth and the herb cottage is the variety and quality of handmade goods, the attraction of the boutique and the flea market is the variety and *quantity* of second-hand goods, and especially the bargains. If your prices are low enough, bargain hunters will load up, go home for more money, and come back again. If you have collected all the members' white elephants over the past few months you should have more than enough merchandise. Of course your members always can ask their neighbors for their cast-offs too.

THE BAKE BOOTH: The bake booth is a real gold mine that can be run as an independent fundraiser or added on to almost any daytime event. You need an energetic chairperson who will recruit literally everyone in the group to make something for the bake booth. Don't take no for an answer. Anyone can bake. If they never did before, it is high time they learned. At least ask them to buy two boxes of brownie mix for someone else to bake. The bake booth needs two kinds of goodies. First, you want small portable things like brownies and cookies which the customers can munch on while they are shopping. Second, you want things they will buy to take home: bread, cakes, and pies.

A variation on the bake booth works well next door to another event which will draw a lot of traffic. For example, one church in a big city is on an alley where the neighborhood association sponsors a two-day antique sale that attracts several thousand people. The church had all the members contribute boxes of brownie mix, then made and sold brownies all day for two days. The fragrance of baking brownies drew the shoppers like bees, and the brownies sold as fast as they could be made, If you wanted to get fancier you could sell ice cream too to go with the brownies. The advantage of brownies is that you don't have to price them individually and they will sell themselves.

OTHER FOOD: Decide what other food you would like to sell according to your theme, the weather, and your facilities. If you have an outside barbecue you can cook hot dogs or bratwurst. If you have a kitchen you can also sell corn-on-the-cob, chili, tacos, or whole dinners. If you don't have a kitchen you can sell sandwiches and candy. If you have a liquor license you can sell beer in the summer or mulled wine in the winter. (You can sometimes get special short-term licenses for special events; check with your local liquor license director, usually in the department of revenue at city hall.)

You can also sell coffee, hot chocolate, lemonade or soft drinks. ice cream too to go with the brownies. The advantage of brownies in the fall, too.

The major consideration here is how much money you will make on each item. Remember, your bake booth is 100 per cent profit so you want most of your food sales from there. If you also sell donuts you will only make about 5 cents on each donut and detract from your bake booth sales. Keep the food as simple as possible and have plenty of waste containers around.

ADULT ATTRACTIONS

Fortune teller, palm reader, tea leaf reader or horoscope caster. Authenticity is less important than entertainment value. Remember, good news is good news.

Button making—buy or borrow a machine for making buttons. Custom make each with a slogan or photo of the customer's choice.

Calligraphy—A talented art student or professional artist can prepare favorite proverbs, prayers, or sayings suitable for hanging.

CHILDREN'S ATTRACTIONS

Face painting—an artist with a steady hand paints small flowers, stars, ladybugs, etc. on the face of the customer with water-based tempera paint. Charge 25 cents for children, $1 for complicated designs on adults like a dragon or train.

OLDIES BUT GOODIES

Bean Bag Toss
Balloon Pop
Hit the Nail into the Log in Five Hits
Guess the Number of Beans in the Bottle
Penny Toss
Basketball Freethrow Contest

FOR BABIES

For the smallest customers set up a small pile of clean hay with trinkets hidden near the surface. Babies crawl through the pile until they grasp a trinket—they "win" whatever they grab.

LOSS LEADERS

Offer a special attraction for the kids, because where the kids go the parents will follow. Although you will not make a profit on the attraction, it is an investment to build your crowd. Grocery stores offer special sales called "loss leaders" to get shoppers into the store. You can do the same thing. You can ask for contributions to help underwrite the expense of the attraction.

Some attractions that work well are: pony rides (especially in the city), a carousel or calliope, a magician, a puppet show, a band, a ride on the fire engine, or a visit from the most popular children's TV show host or hostess.

GATE

Ask for a modest donation (e.g. 50 cents) at the gate from everyone who comes in. Offer trinkets at the gate for everyone, like bright neckerchiefs for a Western Round-up, medallions for the Medieval Fair, or balloons. If you print the balloons with "Boise Fall Fair" on them, each kid who leaves becomes a walking advertisement for the fair. The income from the gate pays for publicity, dram shop insurance, and decorations.

Add-on Moneymakers

THE ALL-DAY RAFFLE. You can add on a raffle to the bazaar. Collect prizes from merchants and include the best contributions to the flea market, like new appliances or silver. Sell tickets all day long and have a drawing every half an hour. List the names of all the winners as the day goes on and post on a large blackboard or sign the time and prize for the next drawing. You can have several people circulate through the crowd with raffle tickets.

You can raffle off dinners or lunches at local restaurants. Even better, combine several prizes into one grand prize. Offer the "Grand Prize Week-End in Metropolis," including lunch on Saturday with the mayor, alderman or congressman, a dinner and show for Saturday, a "free pew" at the church on Sunday morning, Sunday brunch, a guided tour of the zoo or museum by the director, plus Sunday dinner and movie tickets. Top it all off with an offer of free babysitting for the lucky winning couple.

SILENT AUCTION:

You can run a silent auction any time you get something that is very appealing and unusual. You may get more money by auctioning it off than by simply marking a price on it. Good candidates would be an excellent handmade quilt or valuable antique.

Simply place the item on display with a note about its history and value. Put a poster next to it with a marker and a beginning (minimum) bid on the top. Then each bidder puts a higher bid under the last:

	Handmade Quilt
Minimum bid:	$100
Mark Twain:	120
Martha Washington:	130
Will Rogers:	140
Etc.	

Post the final time for bids, say 4 p.m. Make a final announcement at 3:45 that it is your last chance to bid on the quilt. At 4 p.m. whoever has the highest bid gets the quilt.

Variations

If you have several organizations who want to jointly participate in the bazaar, there are two ways to do it. One organization serves as the sponsor, sells tickets and does all the publicity. Each participating organization pays a fee for a booth and gives a percentage of their profits to the sponsoring organization.

The second way is to simply divide up the booths on a first-come, first served basis. Each booth is responsible for its own set up, operation, and clean up. Thus the 4-H club can sell garden produce and flowers; the consumers group can run the games; the block club can sell beer and lemonade; the church can sell hot dogs and corn-on-the-cob; the PTA can sell handicrafts, and the fire department can give rides on the fire truck. Each participating organization gets to keep its own profits and the gross is larger because there is more to attract the customers.

SAMPLE REPORT — URBAN CHURCH
1976 FALL YEAR

BOOTH	REVENUE AND CONTRIBUTIONS	EXPENSES	PROFIT (LOSS)	PERCENT PROFIT
Boutique (resale clothes)	$202	$——	$202	100
Kids' Games	128	50	78	61
Baked Goods	515	—	515	100
Beer	116	108	8	7
Handicrafts	1,136	155	981	86
Candles	99	—	99	100
Herbs	163	—	163	100
Barbecue	236	70	166	70
Dinner and Cocktails	1,549	942	607	39
Flea Market (resale items)	913	—	913	100
Ice Cream	91	38	53	58
Silent Movies	1	—	1	100
Raffle	507	—	507	100
Gate (publicity expenses)	344	63	281	81
Melodrama	56	51	5	9
Pony Rides	56	145	(89)	(Loss)
Total	$6,112	$1,622	$4,490	73%

CELEBRITY LECTURES

The celebrity lecture series offers your community a chance to hear famous people speak on the issues of the day. You make money, provide an educational and entertaining service to the community, and get the chance to meet fascinating people from all walks of life. Series usually offer six to eight speakers on a weekday evening during the school year (September to May.) Summer audiences are usually much smaller and less profitable, unless you offer a series tailored to the season, such as a sports forum.

You can choose a theme such as Law, Crime, Prisons and Justice, the Modern Working Woman, You and Your Taxes, the Future of Metropolis, or The Decision Makers. Using a theme makes it easier to repeat every year and to build your audiences. For example, one college offers an annual community forum on "Law: Great Cases I Have Known." The first speaker each year analyzes a great historic legal case—the trial of Thomas More, Joan of Arc, Socrates. This unusual kick-off guarantees the attendance for the rest of the series. You can offer a variety of celebrities, using the speakers themselves as the draw rather than the topics. Authors, entertainers, politicians, media stars, professors, national consumer advocates, and sports stars all attract large audiences. You can also offer a debate format with experts from opposite sides arguing the pros and cons of nuclear power plants, women's liberation, energy conservation, or gun control. Or offer the first-person expert, perhaps a former burglar to tell homeowners how to make their houses safe.

For the big national celebrities, you will have to pay them either a lot of money, or none at all. If they sympathize with your cause they may agree to speak for free. You will still have to pay for their transportation and expenses. Try writing the celebrity in care of his or her employer: the TV station, movie studio, or sports team. Ask your local newspaper critic or columnist for advice on contacting celebrities through their agents, at work, or even at home.

Most likely you will have to use a lecture bureau to reach the celebrities. Due to the volume of requests that the stars get, the only efficient way they can coordinate their time and travel is by letting a lecture bureau arrange their speaking engagements. If you are able to reach someone personally and get them to donate a speech, that is a bonus for your budget. But for an entire series that will be repeatable year-in and year-out, get to know your lecture bureaus.

Lecture bureaus are listed in the telephone book yellow pages under "Lecture Bureaus." As you will see, some offer a variety, others specialize in one kind of speech such as motivational or humorous speeches, and others specialize in one kind of speaker, such as the Black Women's Speakers Bureau. If you live in a small town, look up the lecture bureaus in the closest large city (phone books are available at your local phone company office). The phone company also will send you on request the books for Manhattan, Washington, D.C., and Los Angeles which would list the best national lecture bureaus.

Write each lecture bureau and ask for a catalog. Go through all of them and decide whom you would like to book for this year and next. Call the appropriate bureau and find out what arrangements they can make. Be prepared with second and third choices since the most popular people may already be booked. After you have run your lecture series for a few years, it will get a lot easier to get the people you want since you can order them a year or two in advance.

You can also fill out your series by alternating the high-priced national stars with local sports heroes or politicians. Be sure you get a written contract in either case. This guarantees you that the speakers will show up on the date arranged and guarantees the speaker that you will pay. The standard lecture bureau contract includes commitments to provide a substitute of equal stature if your celebrity cannot appear.

Setting Up the Series

Once you have lined up celebrities for, say, six Thursday nights from November to April, you'll need to get a large auditorium with comfortable seats and good acoustics. Many groups use a high school or college auditorium, but you can also use a church, a business building's auditorium, or even a movie theatre. When you start, aim for a hall to hold 500 to 1,000 people. As you get more successful promoting your series you can either sell two speeches the same night or move to a bigger hall. Get a written contract for use of the hall and payment.

CHOOSING A MODERATOR. You can have your president serve as moderator of the series, which will give him or her more exposure in the community. Or you can choose someone else to moderate—a popular judge to moderate the law series, or the best sports columnist to moderate the sports series. Some groups ask the local gossip columnist to moderate to get extra free publicity. It is best to stick with one person as moderator for the whole series so you have a reliable professional you can depend on.

PUBLICITY. Do a big publicity campaign, especially your first year. Try to get a feature story on the whole series to help ticket sales, as well as stories on each speech. You can also make arrangements for TV and radio interviews, depending on the wishes of the celebrity.

SELLING THE SERIES. The best way to sell the series is in person. Many groups go door to door the first year to sell out their tickets. It is best to pre-sell tickets for every seat in the house to guarantee your income. Since not all the series ticket holders will attend every speech, you can also sell tickets at the door for the extra seats. The advantage of selling the series is that people will buy the whole series even if they only want to hear three or four of the speakers. Again, after the series has been in business for a few years, the tickets get easier to sell. Also, after the first year you can mail an advance subscription offer to your list of last year's ticket holders.

Before Each Lecture

Write the celebrity you have booked (or the agent or lecture bureau) and ask for:

1. Publicity materials. There should be a *press packet* including a biographical sketch, a photo, and a summary of the speech. It may include the complete text of the speech if it is a regular topic. Many celebrities, especially news commentators, tailor their material to the latest events so they will send only the topic, title and length. Ask them if they want you to set up *TV and radio interviews*. Some celebrities love to do a lot of interviews, some don't do any, some let the lecture bureau handle it, and some have their own publicists. Never make any commitments without approval. *Logo.* Some entertainment celebrities have a logo, a visual trademark. Ask for permission to use it on your publicity. Ask for "stats" of the logo; these are black and white photostatic copies which can be easily used on your own fliers and releases.

2. Hospitality. Get the date, time and flight number of the celebrity's arrival. Find out whether he or she wants to be picked up, to have a rental car reserved, or to be left to his or her own devices.

3. Format: Find out what audio-visual equipment, if any, the speaker needs, and what other conveniences would be helpful, such as a table on which to display the speaker's latest book.

Send the celebrity your fact sheet or brochure so they know who you are and what your group does. Include a letter welcoming the celebrity, with a name and phone number to call for any other information. Say who the moderator will be, the expected attendance, the history of the series (e.g., first year, ten years old, most successful in central Arizona, etc.), and the format.

If you have any other requests to make of the celebrity, be sure to ask in advance. For example, if you want O. J. Simpson to have cocktails with the leaders and top ticket sellers after the lecture, be sure he knows it so he can avoid scheduling something else in that time. You are paying only for the lecture. All the rest of Mr. Simpson's time is his own. *Ask* him if he wants to tour the city, come to a meeting or action, or have dinner. Never assume he'll have nothing else to do.

LODGING: If the celebrity will be staying overnight, you may offer your hospitality. Since there are enormous demands on the energies of most celebrities, your speaker may need to retreat to a quiet, undisturbed hotel. If your invitation is accepted, ask your guest whether he or she has any allergies or special dietary needs.

If the celebrity prefers to stay in a private home, the series committee should consider both the celebrity's comfort and the organization's politics in deciding who will be host. If the president is not the moderator, the logical place is the president's home. If the president *is* the moderator, the celebrity could stay with the coordinator of the series, the fundraising chairperson, the top ticket seller, or a big contributor. The celebrity should never stay with a staff person unless they are lifelong chums. Being the host is an honor; consider how to use this honor organizationally.

Brief the celebrity on the local issues, the history of the group's activities, and the size and makeup of the audience. If your group is controversial, be sure the celebrity knows what you have done recently so that he or she has an answer to "What is an important person like you doing here in Metropolis for a group like that?" Check the hall beforehand to see that the sound system meets the speaker's needs, and that other items like a podium, ashtrays and chairs are available.

If you have time, it is nice to give your speaker a little tour of the town, and a good meal with a minimum of alcohol. Introduce the leaders to the guest either at the meal or at a small reception immediately after the speech. Plan to give the speaker some time and space alone before the speech to collect his or her thoughts and to freshen up.

Treat the celebrity courteously but humanly. Remember that it's refreshing for the celebrity to get away from New York or Washington and meet people who are really doing something about what everyone else only complains about. Ask for advice on other speakers for the series, and also on your campaign strategies. You will probably be pleasantly surprised at the celebrity's concern and cooperation; he or she may be able to suggest other groups for you to contact on your issues, or offer to encourage a celebrity-friend to speak for you.

Format

A good format for a lecture is a short introduction by the moderator welcoming the audience. The moderator explains the purpose of the group, tells who else will be speaking in the lecture series, and then introduces the speaker. The most effective introduction is very brief and includes an anecdote about the celebrity. Then the celebrity gives the talk, usually about thirty to forty five minutes, never more than one hour. Then open up for questions.

The questions are usually the most popular part of the program. It is quickest to have people write their questions on 3" x 5" cards which are then given to the speaker. The speaker can eliminate the duplicates and answer the most interesting questions. Otherwise, set rules—"limit your question to the topic" and "keep it under two minutes." If it is a very large room put floor microphones in the aisles so people can line up to ask questions. Have two or three people planted in the audience to start the questions on the right track. Find out in advance whether there is a question the speaker wants to get. If so, have it planted. It is the responsibility of the moderator to cut off anyone who talks too long, asks the same question twice, or just wants to give a speech without ever asking a question.

Allow some time at the end for the celebrity to autograph copies of his or her new book or record, or the evening's program. Again, have about ten people chosen in advance to form the line for autographs.

Try to get a volunteer photographer to take photos at the lecture for your newsletter. A candid shot with some action is best, though your leaders may prefer the formal shots of the celebrity with the moderator and officers. Don't distract the celebrity with flashbulbs during the speech.

Afterward: Take care of your celebrity until you've put him or her on a train or plane. Be sure to get to the airport or station early with all the luggage. Ask for an address to mail anything the celebrity may have forgotten.

Send copies of newspaper clippings about the speech with your thank-you note the next day. Also send along copies of the newsletters with the advance notice and the follow-up story with photo for the celebrity's scrapbook.

Above all, be proud of who you are, what you do, and your home town. A hotel executive who has worked in Chicago, Denver, New Orleans, and Los Angeles said the most successful welcome she ever did was for celebrities coming to a resort in Smithville, Indiana, population 300. Usually celebrities get a bottle of champagne in a silver ice bucket and a basket of fruit. For a change, she put out cartons of milk in the ice buckets and homemade sugar cookies with a handwritten note, "Welcome to Smithville. You're back home in Indiana." The celebrities said it was the best welcome they'd had all year.

For the best advice on how to treat celebrities from their point of view, read Barbara Walters' *How to Talk with Practically Anybody About Practically Anything*. (Dell Paperback.) Besides giving you lots of practical advice on guest speakers, she will have you *believing* you can carry on a conversation with her and Paul Newman and Harry Belafonte as if they were the ticket committee members.

THE COCKTAIL PARTY

The cocktail party as described here is a method for soliciting upper-income people. If your membership includes affluent people the cocktail party should already be a familiar fundraiser. This is written for organizations with low- or middle-income members who want to take their message to upper-income citizens for support.

Ideally, the way to do cocktail parties is to find a sympathetic rich sponsor who will hold a party for you once or twice a year. Your speaker explains that your group is doing the work, and that all you want from the rich people is their support, specifically their money. This is similar to the church model for supporting missionaries. Once a year the church's missionary to Outer Bosnia comes back and tells the congregation what the mission has accomplished, how many souls have been converted, and what the mission plans for the next year. Then the group chips in to support the missionary. It works because you are making the program *personal*. Instead of asking for support for "the missions" you are asking for support for your missionary, Gladys Ormphry. In the same way a community organization can send a leader to ask for support for their work. The cocktail party guests then are giving to Joe Smith, president of the Mayfair Community Association, instead of giving to "better neighborhoods."

People go to cocktail parties for several reasons. They may want to see the house, they may want to meet the host or hostess, they may want to meet the other guests, or they may want to support your cause. Most likely the guests' motivations are more social than idealistic, but that's all right. Your job is not to transform their consciousness; your job is to raise money. If they leave the party a little smarter too, that is simply an extra benefit.

Preparation:

How do you find a rich person to throw a party for you if none of your members is rich or knows anyone who is? Before you do anything, you have to decide that your work is important to the entire community. Everyone will benefit, including the rich people. If you have an effective, hard-working publicity committee the rich folk have probably already heard about your work and are curious about who you are anyway. Now you need to do a systematic search to find one rich person to invite others to learn more about you.

It is essential that you overcome any stereotypes about rich people before you start. If you go about your search with a chip on your shoulder, or if you treat the rich sponsor as a frivolous auxiliary to the enemy forces, you will never achieve any ongoing, respectful working relationship with the people you want to reach. Just as you want to be taken seriously for the work you are doing, so the rich people want to be taken seriously for the contribution they can make. If you want allies on your team for the long run, treat your rich sponsors as equals.

How to Find a Host/Hostess

The first place to look for help is your own contributor list. You have kept careful, complete records of all your donors; now go over them looking for the right names or addresses, or simply the biggest donations. You may find you already have a candidate on your list.

Second, talk with any sympathizers you have in the media. Although they cannot ethically throw a party for you, since they need to maintain a facade of "objectivity" for their job, journalists get invited everywhere and know lots of people. Ask them who they would recommend as a host or hostess. They may even set up an introduction for you.

Third, try any sympathetic clergy, especially clergy with rich congregations. They usually have the best reading on people's budgets, altruism, and networks. In addition, they are sure-fire door-openers since almost no one will turn down a request from a pastor.

Fourth, read the society columns with a careful eye. Clip them regularly so you can go back and see which names pop up with regularity. Most likely the names you see the most are people with "new money" who use their money to meet the people with "old money" and to make an impression on the local social world. These people are the best bet to sponsor an event for you, because they like an excuse to invite other folks they want to know. They can get away with inviting Horace Gotrocks IV to a party for a worthy civic organization, even though H. G. IV would never come to their purely social function.

Fifth, read the business columns. The self-made millionaire is still a reality in America. Financial columnists figure there are probably about fifty new millionaires made every year in a big city. You need to do the same thing the fancy "Director of Development" does for a hospital, disease, or university. Play "Find the Millionaire." Read the gossip column in the business section of the paper, and the gossip columns in *Fortune* or *Forbes*. When you find the name, look it up in "Who's Who" at the library and see if there is any connection between your leaders and the new millionaire: school, business, or church. If not, you can always just call him cold, introduce yourself and ask for a meeting.

Sixth, ask politicians for recommendations. Most politicians protect their big funders like a tigress protects her cubs. Look for a politician who has retired recently, one who is in mid-term in a non-election year, one who is exceptionally well-adjusted, or one who owes you something. Ask the politician to introduce you to a good prospect.

Seventh, cultivate your old school ties. Everybody went to school with somebody who has subsequently struck it rich (usually the person they kicked out for going up the down staircase). Don't be shy. Even if the person doesn't remember you sat behind her in geometry fifteen years ago, she may be curious enough to agree to meet you again.

HOW TO ASK: Obviously all of these people are virtual strangers. You are going to ask them to throw a party for you in their home at their own expense. Why would they do it? They will do it because they like giving parties, they want a chance to invite bigger shots to their home, or they want to back your work. Mostly, they will give a party for you if they believe in you and like you personally. So it is important who from the group does the asking.

Your most important officer should be the one to ask for the party. Someone else, the pastor or politician, can arrange an introduction, but it is the president who has to go *in person* to convince the host to be a host. Mail information and clippings on the group before the meeting so they know what you have done, why you need the money, and what you intend to do next. If you have another leader who is recognizable from TV, send him or her too. Consider it from the host's point of view. The host is going to have to tell friends, "I want you to meet so and so." If the host admires you and your work, you may get your party.

Be frank. Explain how much money you need and why. Say that none of your members know the kind of people the host does and that is why you want the host to have the party. Explain that the host only has to get the people there, that you will ask for the money.

Answer all the host's questions. Say how many people you want to have and which dates you think are best. Leave all the decisions on food and drinks to the host. People who entertain a lot are skilled at estimating the quality and quantity of refreshments needed. They will do it right.

Be clear that you want the host to cover all the expenses. This can run from $100 to $1,000 depending on the size of the crowd and the elegance of the party, so you must both be clear it is the host's donation. Although this is a lot of money, some people think nothing of throwing a party like that but would never just give you a check for an equal amount. Offer all labor for addressing invitations and clean-up.

INVITATIONS

You can print invitations or send a hand-written note on the host's personal stationery. They must look good. Send the invitations about two weeks before the party and follow up with phone calls. It is best if the host and some friends do the follow up phone calls.

Ask for a specific donation on the invitation (usually $10 to $25). This guarantees a minimum amount from each guest. It also tells the people who cannot attend the right amount for a donation. The callers should urge the no-shows to send in a donation anyway. The invitation should indicate that the guests will be asked for more money at the party. They know it anyway, but it is best to keep everything clear.

Sometimes the host will recommend a very high price per person, say $100, because he or she knows from experience that people will pay that much to get into that particular home. In that case you need to have a strict but gracious door team to admit only paid customers. Otherwise cocktail parties run on the honor system. If a guest says he paid, you take his word for it. Even if he did not, you still have a chance to get a check from him at the party. Besides, no one can get away with freeloading for long, because freeloaders will be purged from the invitation list.

LISTS: If your host is a veteran party giver, he or she may have a complete list of people to invite. You can add on the big donors ($50+) from your own list. In addition, you can mail to any other big donors in the same zip code from lists you can get from politicians or other groups.

REHEARSAL: Try to line up a celebrity to introduce your speaker. A media figure, a sympathetic politician, or nationl leader are all good. Practice your pitch before the party. Do it for the host and ask his or her advice.

AT THE PARTY: Have the top four to six officers attend the party. They should relax, stay sober, and decide to have a good time. Their job is to tell people about the organization in a low-key way. This is not the time for lectures. It is best to simply *listen* to the guests. Successful people usually consider themselves experts at everything and will want to tell you what you should be doing. As Talleyrand said, "If you wish to appear agreeable in society, you must consent to be taught many things which you know already." Thank everyone for their good advice. Try to learn and remember their names.

THE PITCH: After everyone arrives, have the host introduce the celebrity. The celebrity explains the issue, what the group is doing, and why it is so important, and then introduces the speaker. The president thanks the host and leads a round of applause for such a far-sighted, community-minded person.

The pitch must be short, simple, and above all, personal. More than anything else, the guests want to know who you are. The celebrity has already told them what you are doing, and they have your brochure that gives the facts and figures. The speaker's job is to make it personal and real:

"My name is Joe Smith. I was born in the Mayfair neighborhood, and I hope to die there. My first job was selling scorecards right there at the Babe Ruth ball park, when you could still get there for 7 cents on the trolley. I have four kids who all went to the Robert Frost Grade School, and Carl Sandburg High School.

"The other folks in the Mayfair Neighborhood Association are just like me. We are working people raising families in a community we love. We are fighting to save that community. We run a Bingo every Friday at the Masonic Hall and we run a bazaar every spring. Ninety per cent of the families in Mayfair pay dues to support our group.

"But now we find we're up against the toughest fight we've ever had, the Beltway Corridor Plan. That's why we're here tonight, to ask your help. We've gone to the hearings, we've gone to City Hall, and we've gone to the Capitol. It's clear this is going to be a long, hard fight. We intend to stay in and win. We can do the work if you will help us with a donation. If you can give $25, $50, or $100 tonight, it can mean we can save our neighborhood. And I'll get to see my grandchildren grow up right there, in Mayfair, just like my kids did."

Answer any questions simply and briefly. The celebrity wraps it up and tells how much he is giving. Have one or two other people primed to say how exciting this is and how much they are giving, too. Then the organization team and the celebrity collect the checks, or pledges. The host does not get involved with the money collection.

RULES FOR THE PITCH:

1. Keep it simple.
2. Keep it short.
3. Make it personal.
4. Be proud of yourself, your organization, and your goals. *Never apologize* for who you are, or what you do, or how you do it.
5. Be positive. Paint a picture of determination to win, soon.
6. Don't get bogged down in details. For facts and figures refer the audience to the written materials.

WRAP UP: Stay until the last guest leaves. Be sure to thank everyone who gives you a check and to make sure that you have their names right. Thank the host again for the hospitality. Offer to do any clean-up even if there are servants. If there are no servants, *insist* on cleaning up. Don't linger after the clean-up unless invited, and then don't stay too long.

Send a thank-you and a complete report the next day. Be sure to stay in touch with the host through the year with copies of good clippings, the newsletter, and invitations to social events. A friendly call from the president is good, too, and a request from the fund-raiser for advice is superb.

The Do-It-Yourself Cocktail Party

A variation on the cocktail party makes a super emergency fundraiser. This is for your own members, to raise money on the spur of the moment or to celebrate a victory and raise money at the same time.

One member with a large home is the host, who sets up a bar with glasses, mixers and ice. A few people volunteer to bring snacks and dips. Each person brings a bottle and puts it on the bar. Then each time they make themselves a drink they charge themselves a dollar. Teetotalers can charge themselves 50 cents per Coke.

This can raise $50 to $100 an evening. Many people figure they are going to go out on a Saturday night anyway. This way they party together and donate the money they would have spent at Joe's Bar to the organization. And they all get a chance to get to know each other better.

THE COOKBOOK

Unlike other fundraisers, the cookbook is not a project that can be done by just any group. Although any group can do a bake sale, a pot luck supper, or a dinner, not every group can do a profitable cookbook. What you need, obviously, are good cooks who have good recipes which they will share. If you have, or know, a number of good cooks, read on. If not, consider something else.

Making money on a cookbook is a three-part proposition. First, you must identify the good cooks, collect the recipes, eliminate the duplicates or unoriginal recipes, and choose a theme. Next, you must organize the book so it will be useful and attractive, test and check the recipes, type and proofread all the copy, and supervise printing and production of the book. The third step, which is just as important as the first two, is the marketing plan. No matter how great your book is, it will not sell itself. Businesslike and aggressive marketing is the recipe for cookbook success.

Preparation

Before you get the recipes, you have to find the cooks. There are several ways to do this. You can have a giant pot luck supper, asking everyone to bring a favorite dish and a copy of the recipe. Then you have a chance to sample all the dishes. You can ask for contributions from people on your mailing list, and ask them to ask their neighbors and friends. Or each person on the committee can take a quota to find twenty good recipes in the next week from people in the parish, neighborhood, or ward.

SET CLEAR RULES: Give everyone clear rules in writing so you don't have to do anything twice. For example, say you want all the recipes to serve six. List ingredients first, then instructions, include any interesting history, and a note about the cook. Ask people for original recipes, or at least recipes they have "improved." Decline anything that has been clipped from the paper, or that you recognize from the *Reader's Digest*. Make a rule about duplicates. If you want to take everything, resign yourself to five fudge recipes and three tuna casseroles. Otherwise, it is more tactful to take the first fudge recipe that comes in and tell the others you already have a fudge recipe, but how about their almond torte or chicken paprikash? To avoid hurt feelings, set a limit on recipes per cook, so everyone is equally represented. Test all the recipes. It will give your families a chance to try lots of new dishes.

CHOOSE A THEME: In order to have something that will sell,

choose a theme that will make your book stand out. It can be a memorial, say for the centennial of your town or church, like "A century of good eating in Metropolis." It can be all one course, such as the book of "Appetizers" put out by the Crippled Children's Hospital and School in Sioux Falls, South Dakota or the Infant Welfare of Chicago's "Once Upon a Toothpick" hors d'oeuvres book. It can have an ethnic theme like the American Indian Center's "Indian Cook Book" or the North Shore Hadassah's "Bagels, Blintzes and Borscht." It can be based on the character of the group, like the 44th Ward Independent Political Organization's "Stirring Things Up" or Women Employed's "The Working Woman's Cookbook: Recipes for a Small Salary."

After choosing your theme, consider whether you want a local literary figure to do an introduction. The Washington, D.C. Junior League got Art Buchwald to write a humorous intro to their "Think Christmas" book. The Jackson, Mississippi Symphony League got a wonderful introduction from Eudora Welty for "The Jackson Symphony Cookbook"; it captured the complete flavor of the South as well as the recipes in the book.

Production

Once you have collected the recipes and chosen a theme, organize the recipes in a logical way so the book will be both useful and attractive. You can organize the recipes by course: appetizer, soup, entree, dessert; by ingredients: meat dishes, fish dishes, vegetables; or by menus: brunch dishes, party dishes. The Chicago Junior League's "Soupcon" has the recipes organized by season in four color-coded sections for spring, summer, fall and winter (to include holiday dishes and maximize use of seasonal fruits and vegetables).

Type each recipe clearly and have several people proofread each page. (One classic charity cookbook boo-boo is a banana cake recipe that calls for everything—except the bananas!) Proofreading out loud (with one person reading the original and another reading the proof) seems to catch the most mistakes. Decide on the order of the recipes, number each recipe, make up a table of contents and an index. You can include simple illustrations, too, if you have good volunteer artists. *Be sure to include several order blanks* in the back of the book.

Get the best possible design for the cover—it is worth paying a professional, since many people think you *can* tell a book by its cover. Also, many people buy cookbooks as gifts, so they want it to look impressive as well as be a good book.

PRINTING: Try to get the printing donated, or ask several "angels" to underwrite the printing. Get several estimates on printing, paper, and design features like binding. There are two ways to think about the printing. If you are doing a one-edition memorial book for the town centennial, get the best printing bargain you can. If you intend the book to be an ongoing money maker, get the best printing you can afford. It is worth spending more on the first edition, selling out, and doing more editions, than scrimping on the first edition only to have the books sitting in your office forever. It is possible to sell multiple editions of good cookbooks. "Soupçon" is in its fourth printing, "Think Christmas" is in its second edition and fourth printing, and "The Jackson Symphony Cookbook" is in its sixth printing.

Marketing: Retail

There are two levels of marketing: retail and wholesale. All your members sell at retail. For retail selling you print enough books to saturate your own market—members of the parish and friends, or residents of the town and visitors. Plan to do one edition and price the book at one-third more than its cost to you. If it costs you $4 per book, charge $6 per book.

Once you get the books, plan an introductory luncheon to launch the sales and introduce the book to the press. Do a midday meal so the working press will attend; they will not come to anything too early, or too late. Give them a kit containing a selection of recipes, a copy of the cookbook, and a press release describing the book, the sponsor, the history of the book, and how to order it. Invite the food writers and editors as well as the feature writers and the reporters who ordinarily cover your work. Invite everyone who contributed to the book, praise their work, and send everyone home with at least ten copies to sell.

The marketing committee goes into full swing once the book is launched. They try for every possible column mention, "new ideas" column plug, and "good gifts" column plug. In October they send the book and press release again to all the column editors for the Christmas gift columns. They get on every talk show they can to promote it, and take it to every art fair and sale they can get into.

Most important, they get it sold commercially in the local department stores, the book stores, and the specialty cooking stores. This means they make an appointment to see the buyer of books, in person, at his or her convenience. They take in the cookbooks and make arrangements to deliver more. Most stores buy books at a forty per cent discount, but some will buy local organizations' cookbooks at a thirty per cent discount, leaving you seventy per cent.

The way to sell a lot of books is to get them in a lot of stores. The marketing committee should cover every possible store, in your home town as well as every other store they can reach. Any time any committee member travels to another town, for business, shopping, or just vacation, he or she should take a copy of the book and a supply of order blanks to introduce the book to the buyers at the right stores. Once you have established your cookbook in several stores and have re-orders, it is easier to get it into new stores on the strength of your record.

A buyer at a major big city department store explained what she looks for. She wants a professional look, an index, clarity and variety in the recipes, a simple layout, an interesting theme, and a good appearance throughout—clean type and nice illustrations. The store prefers local organizations' cookbooks since they sell best. Although there are 40,000 new books published every year, there is always a demand for new cookbooks. Many people buy cookbooks as gifts or as books to read, as well as for their practical value.

The marketing committee is also responsible for all the book-keeping and mailing. They fill orders for the cookbooks, including gift cards, and do the shipping and billing. This can become a full-time job for the committee if the book is a success, but it produces a dependable source of income over the long run.

Since serving on a successful cookbook committee involves this drudgery, try to dream up some entertaining and glamorous events for the committee, too. One group threw together a gala spring house-walk. The "ticket" to see a special old home was a cookbook sold at the door. Then the guests were served May wine and tidbits made from the recipes, like the samples you get at the grocery store. Everyone was so impressed with the goodies that most people bought four or five more books when they left the house.

Another group had an old-fashioned box supper auction. Each cook made his or her special recipe from the book, and prepared an appropriate setting for the dish. The pheasant mousse was served on heirloom china, and grandma's fried chicken came on paper plates. An auctioneer read off the tempting menus and the non-cooks bid on the privilege of sharing each dish with the cook. It was a super promotion, good for both cookbook sales and the cooks' egos.

Marketing: Wholesale

If you have a high quality cookbook, which can be impartially determined from the opinions of the food editors and store buyers, and if you sell out your first printing in less than six months, consider going to wholesale marketing. For wholesale marketing you have to figure out how you can sell your books by the thousands, rather than ones, tens, or hundreds.

There are two major outlets for wholesale cookbook sales. First are department stores and book stores, which buy all their books at sixty per cent of the cover price. In other words, you sell in quantity to stores at a forty per cent discount. In order to make money, your cover price must be high enough that you can still make a profit when you sell the book at sixty per cent of the cover price. This is done by going to larger printings, which reduces your cost per book, and selling thousands of books to stores. If your book is good enough to sell through regular store outlets, you can make more money selling 20,000 copies wholesale than you made selling the first 5,000 retail—and there is less work for the committee.

The second major wholesale outlet is mail order catalogs. Get a list of catalogs from a list dealer. Eliminate those which are obviously not for you. Some sell only imported or cheap goods, and others sell only luxury goods over $10. Choose the middle-range catalogs that sell good, medium-priced American products. Write all of them, giving a description of your book and its sales history. Follow up with a phone call to determine if they are interested. You will have to negotiate a wholesale price with the catalog publishers. If you can get listed in both an East Coast and a West Coast catalog, the book will sell thousands. Although it takes a lot of work to get listed originally, once you get into a good catalog you can maintain a mutually profitable relationship for years.

You can also sell wholesale to other chapters of your national organization, either through the national newsletter or by displaying it at the national convention. You should also consider buying a booth at the best trade show to sell your book to the buyers for all the national stores.

Banks are another outlet for bulk sales. Since every bank pays exactly the same rate of interest, they compete for accounts by offering "premiums" to attract new customers. Try to convince the bank's vice-president for marketing to buy the cookbook as the next premium. Explain that it has a double value, as a marketing tool and a public relations tool. The book is a tempting premium, and the bank's money will be going to a worthy civic organization rather than just another trinket peddler. Especially if you have the name of the town in the book's title, it is a natural for the town's bank to promote the town and the bank at the same time.

In addition to the larger profit you make by selling thousands of books wholesale, you will also expand your retail sales from the mail orders you receive from the order blanks in each book.

THE DANCE

A dance can be a fun-filled costume party with a band, or a formal affair with a big dance band, or a come-as-you-are bash with the latest disco hits played on a record player. If you have people who like to dance, good music, and fun extras, you can make a lot of money for your cause.

The secret to success is a peppy committee of people who like to plan parties. If they are people who like to go out and have fun, they will plan an event which will leave the guests asking, "When is the next dance?"

The arrangements for a dance can be divided into two parts. First, everything that needs to be done before the dance, and second, everything that needs to happen at the dance to make it a success.

Before the Dance

Before the dance, the committee has to choose a date and a theme, book a band and reserve a room, print the tickets, sell ads for the program and print the program, plan the agenda for the evening, and choose the refreshments.

THE BAND: The most important element of success for the dance is the band. If you get a popular band everyone will have a good time and will want to come to your next dance. If the band is a bore it will take a lot of ingenuity to keep the party rolling, and even more to sell tickets to the next dance.

How do you find a good band? First consider what kind of band you want for your crowd. Do they want rock and roll, polkas or the fox trot? Or a combination? The best bands can play a variety of fast and slow numbers, as well as a few group participation songs like "Hava Nagila," "The Bunny Hop," "The Hokey Pokey," or "Zorba the Greek." First, ask everyone on the committee to recommend good bands they have heard at weddings, parties or other dances, and whether they know anyone who either plays in a band or books bands.

Look in the Yellow Pages under "musicians" and call several bands for prices and availability. If there are local clubs which feature live music, the committee could also have a "research night on the town" (at their own expense, of course) when they go around and listen to the bands. This is one of the more pleasant aspects of serving on the planning committee so you might want to do some research even if you already have a band. (As you and your committee members go out during the year, remember always to get a business card from the leader of any good band you hear for future reference.) You can also call your opposite numbers in other organizations and ask their advice on a band.

You will probably have to reserve a band at least several weeks in advance of the night you want. The more popular the band, the more advance notice they will need. In fact, if there is one band that is outstandingly popular (and still affordable) you should reserve a night as soon as you decide to do a dance. Even if you decide in January to do a dance in September, it is not too early to reserve the best band for the date you want.

It is better to pay more for a band and scrimp on everything else than the other way around. The difference between a $200 band and a $400 band can be the difference between a repeatable event and a flop. Of course you should always try to get the best for the least money, but if you have to spend a little more for a popular band, do it.

Free Band: If you have a not-for-profit organization, and you are getting everything else free (the hall, refreshments, etc.) you qualify to get a free band from the musicians union. Each local of the musicians union has a fund to pay bands to play for non-profit groups. Call the musicians union's local secretary and ask if you qualify. Then find out how to get the band you need. Unfortunately, you seldom get the first-rate bands this way, but it is a great way to get a free band for the after-convention party or other occasions that are more festive than commercial.

CHOOSING A THEME: Although you can always have the "First Annual Friends of the Forests Dance," it is more fun if you choose a theme for the dance. Carry out the theme in the invitations, program, decorations, menu, skits, favors and costumes.

SAMPLE THEMES

Holidays: Halloween costume party, New Year's Eve, Twelfth Night Elizabethan Revelry, Valentine's Day, Mardi Gras (literally "Fat Tuesday," the day before Ash Wednesday, last chance to feast and revel before Lent), May Day.

Movies: The Way We Were, Camelot, Cabaret, Showboat, Hello Dolly, Guys and Dolls.

Places: Evening in Paris, New Orleans—French Quarter, A Funny Thing Happened on the Way to the Forum, or Comedy at the Colosseum (Rome), South Pacific, Fiesta in Mexico, Hawaiian Luau, Carnival in Rio, Emerald Isle, Night on the Nile.

Eras: Roaring Twenties, Gay '90's, Fabulous Fifties, Hard Times ('30's); 2001, Renaissance, Medieval, Ancient Greece, French Revolution.

Costume themes: Butchers, Bakers and Candlestick Makers Ball (worker's costumes), American Revolution, Best or Worst Politicians, "Enemies Dance" for action groups, Barn Dance, Movie Stars, Villains and Tyrants, Gangsters & Gun Molls.

Fantasy: Wizard of Oz, Lost in Space, Never-Never Land, The Good Old Days, Lost Atlantis, Garden of Eden.

Seasonal: Spring Fling, Harvest Moon Ball, Saturnalia (Winter solstice December 21), First Day of Spring, Summer, Autumn, Winter, Midsummer Night's Dream.

Books: Canterbury Tales, Romeo and Juliet, Vanity Fair, 1001 Arabian Nights (Scheherazade), Cinderella.

PLACE

Once you get a firm date for the band, look for a place to hold the dance. Any large hall with a hard floor will do. It is better if it has a stage and a kitchen, and better still if it has a built-in bar. Other features which are nice, but not necessary, are a coat room, nearby free parking, handy public transportation, and few or no stairs. Try to find somewhere free (you may have to do your own clean-up) or as inexpensive as possible. Again, ask your committee members where they have been and what they recommend.

You can use the occasion of the dance to show off your own building, too. Some museums do this to get donors into the building, and many a church kindergarten has become a Roaring Twenties speakeasy for a night. If you do not have a big enough room of your own, consider having a cocktail hour in your offices before the dance so the guests can see firsthand why their money is needed. Then go on to the nearest hall for the dance. Do not reject your own free but humble hall because of its appearance. As long as it is clean, your clever committee can transform any hall into the Taj Mahal with a maximum of creativity and a minimum of lighting.

Besides the church basement, the high school gym, or the rented hall, any large space with electricity will do. Some original ideas that have worked well in the past include:

Dices and Pisces (dance with gambling) held at the local aquarium. An action organization could sponsor "Making Waves" at the aquarium.

The Red, White and Zoo Ball, held at the zoo on the Fourth of July.

Spring Revels on the village square.
Venetian Night Gala on a barge.
Super Circus in a tent.
Harvest Moon Ball in a barn.
"Hard Times" dance in a warehouse.
St. Valentine's Day Massacre gangster-style costume party in a garage.
"Take Me Out to the Ball Game" at a ball park.
"Fabulous Fifties" sockhop at a roller rink.
"Pretty as a Picture" at an art museum.
Wild West square dance at a shopping center mall.
And the ever-popular summertime block party with dancing in the street.

PRINTING: Once you have chosen the date, band, theme and place, you can print the tickets, posters and invitations. A few energetic salespeople can start lining up door prizes and selling ads for the program. The program can be a single page mimeographed in your own office, or an elaborate ad book. (See ad book, chapter 7). On the program list the schedule of events, the names of the band and other entertainers, the names of the committee members, a paragraph about the organization and how to join, and a note of thanks for everyone who gave donations.

At the Dance

Once all the advance arrangements are made, the committee moves into phase two, which is a thorough plan of what will happen at the dance. It is the committee's responsibility to make sure everyone is welcomed, the ticket desk runs smoothly, and there is a place with helpers where guests may leave their coats. The committee members set up everything, give precise instructions to the band, sell drink tickets and raffle tickets, and generally mingle to make sure everyone is comfortable. Find someone outgoing to serve as MC to welcome everyone, introduce the band and any other acts, and give a running report on what happens next. This could include the drawing for the door prizes, the raffle drawing, or introduction of the president. It is the president who "frames" the party by telling the guests what the group is doing and why they need the money, recognizing the committee and top ticket sellers, and thanking any merchants present who contributed to the event. All of this should be planned in advance, so it all goes smoothly, and the president has time to prepare a good *short* talk.

The committee members become the social directors at the dance. They make sure everyone is having fun, start the dancing, and plan games or dances to mix everyone up. They are also the security force if any race, sex, alcohol, dope, marriage or outsider problems develop. It is the committee's job to remove the problem as quickly, tactfully and quietly as possible. Perhaps you will not have any problems at all, but just in case, decide *beforehand* who will handle it.

REFRESHMENTS: Merry dancers will work up a thirst so decide what kind of liquid refreshments you will serve. If you choose to have alcoholic beverages find out if the place has its own dram shop insurance or if you need to get your own. Unless you are expecting several thousand guests, or are holding the dance in a hotel that requires union bartenders, you can recruit your own committee of volunteer bartenders to work the bar. Keep the bar as simple as possible; leave the fancy blender drinks like brandy alexanders to the pros.

Sell drink tickets at a table near the entrance so that bartenders only have to serve the drinks. You can buy rolls of tickets at any novelty store or carnival/Bingo supplier. Either sell different colors for soft drinks, beer/wine, and hard drinks, or get rolls of 25-cent tickets and sell soft drinks for 25 cents (one ticket), beer and wine for fifty cents (two tickets), and hard drinks for $1 (four tickets). The other advantage to selling drink tickets is that the guests will buy more tickets than they will use and your profit on the unused tickets will be 100 per cent.

You can also offer something to drink for free, like a non-alcoholic punch or coffee in a self-service urn.

You can put out free salty snacks like pretzels or popcorn, which you buy in bulk and double salt to increase the bar revenue. The committee can recruit a team to bring hors d'oeuvres and finger food. Specify cocktail type salty or spicy things which are portable and can stand at room temperature for several hours. Discourage sweet dessert-type contributions—they stifle the drink sales. Or you can sell sandwiches, pizza or tacos from a table near the kitchen.

Add-On Moneymakers

In addition to the regular dance, there are several other moneymakers which you can add on. As already mentioned, you can sell ads in the program, run a raffle, sell drinks or sandwiches. For a Roaring Twenties party, you can have "taxi dancers" selling tickets for "ten cents a dance." This also makes a good mixer. You can sell photographs of groups at a table (as night clubs do), of posed couples (like the high school prom), or of corny Tarzan and Jane or American Gothic facades with holes cut out for the faces (like the grammar school fun fair). Ask your local camera shop for advice.

Run a dance contest. Charge 50 cents to enter, and give ribbons for first, second and third place by audience applause. Depending on the crowd, have a waltz, charleston, cha-cha, jitterbug, twist, polka, hustle, or bump contest. Or have an "oldies but goodies" dance contest to see who can *still* do the: black bottom, dip, tango, mashed potatoes, locomotion, monkey, swim, Soupy shuffle, Bristol stomp, or Lindy hop.

THE HOUSE TOUR

If you have ever walked by an unusual old house and thought, "I wonder what it's like inside?" you are a potential customer for a house tour. The house tour is literally a tour through one or more houses. It gives all the do-it-yourself decorators a chance to get new ideas, and gives everyone the chance to satisfy curiosity.

The range of possibilities is endless. The Jaycettes in a small town in Wisconsin sponsored a simple tour of two old homes plus tea at the library to raise money for a flagpole. The women's board of a New Jersey hospital put on a full-tilt, month-long extravaganza at a redecorated mansion with fourteen boutiques running in the carriage house. They made $260,000. You can put together a combination of interesting homes that will appeal to your community and raise money with very little work.

The first thing you need for the house tour is the houses. You can use your members' homes or ask people outside the organization to let you show their homes. Figure out how many homes you can move people through in a day. You may want to start with two the first year, then go to four, and then to six. You can have them all open all day, or show half in the morning and half in the afternoon.

Successful Tours

HOUSES: Aim for a variety. Show a colonial, traditional and modern, or a big family home, a young married couple's home, an older retired couple's home, and a bachelor's apartment.

THEMES: Show four examples of one architect, historical examples of the oldest or newest houses in town, or houses in one historical area. You might show houses owned by famous people from the town.

SHOW OFF ONE ROOM: You can have a kitchen tour or a "cook's tour" showing only kitchens and selling your cookbook. Others have run tours of just nurseries, just children's rooms or just dining rooms.

WHERE PEOPLE WORK: Run a tour of artists' studios in the

artists' quarter of the city or executive suites of the top corporations

GARDENS: Sponsor a garden walk in the spring or summer to show off the prettiest gardens in your neighborhood. This provides an extra boost for people to spruce up their yards. You can also sell seeds, bulbs and plants at the end.

Once you have several houses for the tour, choose one weekday when you should have good weather. Never attempt a house tour in the winter. Sell a limited number of invitations—usually 500 to 2,000, depending on how many people you can move through the house. Print clear rules on each invitation. Standard rules include: Adults only. No smoking. Be prepared to remove your shoes. Follow the traffic plan. Mind the hostesses who are wearing the green nametags.

The invitations are also the tickets, and the programs. They describe what is special about each house and the history of each house and the town. Include a simple map.

Other Preparation

1. Get adequate insurance to cover large numbers of people going through the houses and climbing stairs. Some organizations have run house tours for twenty-five years without an accident, but you still have to get complete insurance to cover anything that might occur.

2. Get flowers donated for each house from local florists. List the florists' names in the program and put a sign in each house.

3. Notify the police of the day of the tour and the location of the houses. Ask for help directing traffic where you need it.

4. Give the hosts any cleaning help they want before the tour.

5. Arrange for someone to entertain the host families *away* from home on the day of the tour.

Try to get all the printing, insurance and flowers donated. Especially if you are doing a historical tour, house tours are great community booster events. They should be supported by your local printer and insurance broker.

DAY OF THE TOUR: Get a team of volunteers lined up to work each house. Before anyone comes, they set out a marker to mark the house as a tour house, put up a saw horse to block the driveway, set up a table to check the programs (which are also the tickets), put out a container for cigarettes, and double check that everything is clean and orderly. Each house needs a greeter to check each ticket/program so each person goes through each house only once. Several volunteers serve as guides. The guides tell guests the history of the house and information about the decor. They are also the security force, keeping an eye on everything in the house. Finally, they clean up the house and yard after the last guest leaves.

The day after the house tour the president delivers personalized gifts to the hosts and thanks them again for the use of their homes.

REFRESHMENTS: If people are on their feet all day seeing the houses, they are going to want to take a break for something to eat. Offer a package of a meal with the tour. You can get a deal from a local restaurant and add on two dollars per meal price. You can offer a box lunch in a big yard; serve the lunches and beverage from a decorated garage. Or serve "soup, salad and sweets" in the church hall.

PRICES: Charge a dollar a house, that is $1 for a one-house tour and $4 for a four-house tour. Price the luncheon at double the cost to you: if it costs you $2, charge $4. Sell the luncheon as a package with the tour so that only house tour patrons can attend the luncheon. Limit the luncheon to people who have pre-paid tickets so you know exactly how many lunches to make. Do not sell luncheon tickets at the door.

If you are showing only one or two houses it is easier to have tea and cookies in a free room. Charge 50¢ for the tea and cookies.

REPEATABILITY: The house tour is a very repeatable event. If people learn you have interesting homes, that you run an efficient tour with little waiting, and limit the number of tickets, they will buy their tickets early every year. After you have run your tour two or three years you will find the tickets sell themselves. Do not be afraid of running out of houses. You can always show a house a second time ten years later if it has been redecorated by new owners. And you can add on an unusual church or studio for variety.

Variations

THE CHRISTMAS SALE HOUSE TOUR: Use the houses to display your handmade Christmas decorations. Decorate three or four houses with your handmade merchandise. Run the tour in October and you will find you can sell everything off the walls. Try to have a variety of settings: early American, modern, baby's first Christmas, teenager's Christmas, or ultra-elegant Christmas. Some churches run the Christmas sale house tour every two years. Then they have two years to prepare the merchandise and need to find hosts only every other year.

THE BUS TOUR. Instead of showing people through houses in your own community, you sell them tickets for a tour of another community. This is a dependable fundraiser for small groups of people with spare time, curiosity, and no cars. You can arrange tours of churches, museums, old restored neighborhoods, country places, and gardens. Include lunch and it becomes an all-day adventure. Charge double your expenses. Any travel agent or school teacher can tell you how to get buses.

THE SHOWCASE HOUSE. The showcase house requires a big investment and an upper-income membership that can get donations of high-priced talent and merchandise. Find an old mansion and recruit professional interior decorators to re-do one room each at their own expense. The decorators do it as advertising for new business. If your group is not the kind that can promise a large number of upper-income tourists, the showcase house is not for you because you will not be able to recruit the top decorators.

If you *can* deliver rich tourists, then you can approach the decorators because you can offer what they want: customers. Contact the local chapter of the American Society of Interior Designers (ASID). They can tell you if there is any local competition, and can make arrangements to discuss doing a showcase house for your group.

Your group needs to find an available empty mansion and make all the legal arrangements to use the house. It usually takes at least a year of advance work to get the house, choose the decorators, raise the seed money, redecorate the house, do the publicity, sell the tickets, and contract with merchants to sell in the boutiques. If you want more information on showcase houses, contact the local ASID and look up these references:

"How to raise money for a good cause and have a good time doing it" (*House and Garden*, November, 1976, pp. 144-147, 190-192) tells the story of the Women's Association of Morristown, N.J., Memorial Hospital Showcase House of 1975. They spent eighteen months transforming the Geraldine Rockefeller Dodge House—and raised $260,000. They emphasize that your success depends on "who you know."

How to $ucceed in Fund-Raising Today. Helen K. Knowles. The Bond Wheelwright Co., Porter's Landing, Freeport, Maine. See Chapter XIII, "The Prestigious Decorator's Show House," pp. 123-140.

THE LUNCHEON

The advantage of a luncheon over a dinner is that it is shorter and less expensive. The challenge is to keep the entire meal and program in a tight time frame, so you must choose a place with good service and run a very well-orchestrated agenda.

You can also use the luncheon to kick off a campaign to get corporate or foundation funds, to sell an ad book, or to give awards. Or you can use it to present your program to a group, such as local merchants, then follow up with them individually.

It is easiest to schedule the luncheon at a restaurant or hotel that is convenient for most of the guests. Choose a simple menu. Most working people prefer a light lunch so they can stay alert in the afternoon anyway. If you want you can also arrange for a cash bar for wine or cocktails for the early birds.

People do *not* come to a luncheon for the food, so don't try to impress them with expensive dishes. They *do* come because of 1) who invites them, 2) who else will be there, and 3) the quality of the speaker and the program.

Format

The typical format for a luncheon is:

1) Greeting by the officers when guests arrive. Fruit juice, wine or cocktails for the folks who come early. If you want, you can arrange for the hotel to set up a cash bar.

2) Show the guests to their tables. Seating is *not* random. Be sure that you arrange the guests so that they all get to meet someone from your group.

3) You may have a minister or rabbi give a benediction or say grace.

4) A simple meal is served. This needs to be done quickly and efficiently.

5) The chairperson of the luncheon welcomes all the guests and introduces celebrities in the audience.

6) Present your program. This can be a few very short speeches on different aspects of your work, one "state of the organization" speech by the president, or a series of awards. Keep it all as short as possible. Avoid audio-visual aids because they will put people to sleep.

7) If you are going to ask people for money, have the member at each table armed with pledge cards to distribute to table mates. You can collect checks at the luncheon or take pledges.

8) Have plenty of written material, fact sheets, brochures or annual reports for guests to take when they leave.

You can also run a series of luncheons to get new members or patrons. For example, some big city groups will sponsor a luncheon the second Tuesday of every month. The guests pay for their own meals, so there is no cost to the organization. Then the leaders of the group ask the guests to pledge a monthly amount, usually $10 to $25. This is aimed toward executives and professionals who do not have the time to participate but sympathize with the goals of the group. The advantage to the organization is that they can sell the professionals in a group rather than one at a time. The series builds itself by asking the guests for both money and new names for the next luncheon.

PROFIT FORMULA

It will probably cost you from $5 to $10 for the luncheon. Be sure you set your price based on the total cost: meal plus tax plus tips. Sometimes a restaurant will give you a special price if the owner likes your work or if the owner will get the revenue from the bar. It will be higher at a hotel because you are also charged for set up. Depending on your market, you can charge from $10 to $25. Your profit is the total ticket sales minus the total costs.

Sample: A recent luncheon at a chic but sympathetic restaurant got a special price for a luncheon of $5.95. The restaurant got the revenue from the bar. The cost per person was $5.95 plus five per cent sales tax plus fifteen per cent tip for a total per person of $7.14. Printing and postage were donated. The group charged $19.76 for the tickets ("in this our Bicentennial year"). The program attracted 170 guests.

$$170 \text{ guests x } \$19.76 = \quad \$3,359.20 \text{ gross}$$
$$170 \text{ guests x } \$ \ 7.14 = - \ \underline{1,213.80} \text{ costs}$$
$$\$2,145.40 \text{ net profit}$$

Invitations

The secret of success is personalized invitations. Get your committee together at someone's house, and offer refreshments. This is monotonous work so it helps if there is an attraction like an interesting house, a tempting menu for the workers' lunch, or a host that the workers want to meet. Go through your lists to eliminate the duplicates. Then have the group address the envelopes by hand. The envelope addressing may take more than one meeting. If you are in a hurry you can begin addressing the envelopes before the invitations are ready. Be *sure* they are the right size.

You will need to send about ten times as many invitations as the number of guests you want. If you want 150 guests, you'll have to send 1,500 invitations. As you become more experienced and refine your guest lists, you can reduce the proportion.

Then deal out the envelopes so all the committee members get their own lists plus the names of anyone else they know from the other lists. Now add a note on each invitation, like "Hope to see you there," or "This will be Cecil Celebrity's only visit to Lexington this year." The best note is a personal invitation such as "Can you sit at my table?" or "I've got the company car on Tuesdays; can I give you a ride?"

Follow-up with phone calls if sales are slow. You must have an accurate reading of sales so you know how many lunches to order. You also need to know the number to set up the room so it will look full with a small crowd or fit in the extras for an overflow crowd.

Every invitation must include:

The date, time and place of the luncheon.
The price.
The names of the chairpersons and committee members.
A phone number for more information.
A description of the program. If you have scheduled a famous speaker it is nice to include a photograph.
A blank or extra card for people to return either to reserve seats or make a contribution.
An instruction explaining how to make out checks.

THE THEATRE PARTY

The theatre party is the simplest of the medium sized fundraisers. Since the theatre does all the production and publicity work, all you have to do is sell the tickets.

Preparation

FINDING A THEATRE: First call all the theatre companies and ask to speak to the business manager. Ask if there is any possibility that the company could do a benefit for your group. Make a record of each person's name, the company's policy, and how many seats the theatre has.

There is a range of benefit possibilities. Your best deal is for the theatre to "give you the house." That is, the theatre donates the performance, and you get to sell all the seats and keep all the money.

This is very rare and will probably happen only if the theatre owner or the producer, director or star of the show is a loyal friend of the group.

The usual policy is for a theatre to give you the house on a week-day evening for a discount. For example, if all 300 seats in the theatre usually sell for $5 each, you can get the house for perhaps $3 a seat. Thus your cost is $900 (300 x $3). If you sell all the seats at $6 each, you will gross $1,800 and net $900.

$$300 \text{ tickets x } \$6.00 = \$1,800 \text{ gross}$$
$$300 \text{ tickets x } \$3.00 = -\ 900 \text{ costs}$$
$$\$\ \ 900 \text{ net profit}$$

Get a written contract explaining exactly what you are paying the theatre. There are actually two ways to get a discount deal from a theatre. In the first case, you buy all 300 seats from the theatre. You owe them $900 no matter how many seats you are able to re-sell. This is the plan the theatre prefers since it is guaranteed its money no matter how well or poorly you do. Plus they can mark that night "sold out" on their publicity, which makes the play look good to the general public.

The second system is the best for beginners. In this case the theatre gives you the first chance to sell every seat for $3. If you sell them all, that is fine for both of you. If you sell only some of the seats, the theatre gets to sell the rest at its regular price at the box office the night of the show. For example, if you sell 150 seats for $6 each, the theatre gets $3 per set, or $450 and you get $3 per seat or $450. The theatre sells the other 150 seats at the regular $5 price. Obviously the advantage of this system is that you owe the theatre only for the seats you sell. If you were working on the "buy the house" system and only sold 150 seats, the theatre would make its $900 and you would make nothing. If you are not confident you can sell the whole house, ask for a discount on all you can sell, with the theatre selling the balance.

A third system for beginning groups is simply to buy a block of tickets. For example you only buy 150 tickets to re-sell. You usually get a smaller discount if you take less than the whole house.

Comedies and musicals are the easiest to sell. Avoid depressing plays or very avant garde pieces with no plot at all. They might be excellent theatre, but they will be hard to sell this year, and murder to sell the second year.

SELLING THE TICKETS

Since all you have to do is sell the tickets, concentrate on that. Have one team concentrate on selling patron tickets, priced higher than your regular tickets. Then systematically contact your big donors, politicians and business executives. Set a goal to have ten percent of the house as patrons. In our example, if you have a 300-seat theatre, thirty of the seats should be patron tickets. Let's say you price them at $25 each.

PROFIT: Patron seats

30 tickets x	$25	= $	750 gross
30 tickets x	$3	=	− 90 cost
		$	660 net

This leaves 270 seats to sell at the regular price:

270 tickets x	$6	=	$1,620 gross
270 tickets x	$3	=	− 810 cost
		$	810 net

Patron ticket profit = $ 660
Regular ticket profit = + 810

$1,470

Thus, you make almost as much money from ten per cent of the seats as you do from the other ninety per cent.

Ironically, most of the patrons won't show up. Although they paid the highest price, they were spending expense account money, not their own. Also, patron ticket buyers often buy tickets for several events occurring the same night, and obviously cannot be in more than one place. Usually, the only patron ticket holders who show up are the politicians who want to work the crowd.

Thus it is possible in real life to "oversell" the house. This means you gamble that less than 100 per cent of the ticket holders will actually show up in person. So you can sell more than 100 per cent of the seats. It is usually safe to oversell by about ten per cent, especially for a late show. Thus if you sell all thirty patron tickets, you can really sell all 300 seats at your regular price too. You then have 330 tickets sold for 300 seats, but will end up with only 300 people for 300 seats.

PROFIT FORMULA IF YOU OVERSELL BY TEN
PERCENT:

Patron seats   30 tickets x $25 = $ 750 gross
                30 tickets x $3 = − 90 cost
                                   _____
                                   $ 660 net

Regular seats 300 tickets x $6 = $1,800 gross
              300 tickets x $3 = −900 cost
                                   _____
                                   $ 900 net

Patron seats profit   = $ 660 net
Regular seats profit = + 900 net
                        _____
Total profit $1,560 net

If you don't want to gamble your first time out, keep careful
records of your first few theatre parties. Write down the total tickets
sold and the total attendance. This will tell you the safe margin for
overselling. If the committee votes to gamble and oversell, do it with
the understanding that *you* are the ones who will stand if you are
wrong and everybody comes.

At the Performance

Enjoy! You only need one or two people to take tickets and sell
memberships. You can have a speaker during intermission to "frame"
the event. The speaker welcomes everyone, introduces the organization, explains its work and thanks everyone for coming. The speaker
should also recognize and congratulate the top ticket sellers.

ADD ON MONEYMAKERS:

If this is too simple, add on other moneymakers. If it is a small
theatre (100 to 300 seats) and you are confident you can sell more
tickets, ask them to do two performances on the same night. It takes
very little additional work to sell the second show. You may be able
to get the company to do an early show, say at 6 p.m. and 8 p.m.
rather than their regular 8 p.m. and 10 p.m. This gives you a chance
to sell to your seniors, people with early-morning jobs, and people
who have to travel a long way. If you do two shows, you get double
the profit, in this example, $3,120.

Add on a door prize to produce a sign-up list.

Run a raffle.

Print a program with ads if the theatre does not have a program of its own. If the theatre already has its own program, print a one page insert with info on the group, how to join, the next benefit, and patrons' names.

Ask a percentage of the bar if the theatre also serves drinks. Tell the crowd you get part of the money so they drink up.

If you do not get part of the bar revenue, have a "Do It Yourself Cocktail Party" before or after the performance. (See Cocktail Party: Variation).

WHERE ELSE TO GO FOR ADVICE: Contact your local arts council, the community arts center, the arts service organization or the local Actor's Equity Union. They all work to promote theatre attendance and will have good advice for you about the local theatre scene. For example the Chicago Alliance for the Performing Arts (CAPA) publishes a directory of all the local theatres and theatre companies as well as a publicity manual on show business pubicity.

Variations

This same format will work for any "show business" performance just as well as a regular stage play. You can do the same thing to sell tickets to an opera, a concert, a recital, a ballet, a circus, or the legendary dog and pony show.

Some theatres offer other sorts of ready-made fundraising packages as part of their ongoing public relations efforts to introduce new customers to the theatre. For example, the Guthrie Theatre in Minneapolis offers organizations a "Costume Show." Costumes from past Guthrie productions are modeled by volunteers, who also explain the design and construction of theatrical costumes. Be sure to ask all the theatres to explain all the fundraising possibilities they offer.

While you are at it, use this opportunity to get to know the theatre professionals. They can give you invaluable advice in the future since they do professionally as actors what you do voluntarily as a fundraiser: offer people entertainment for money. Everything you do involves theatre, from the simplest presentation to an audience of one to an extravaganza rock concert for an audience of 30,000. Both require theatrical skills: memory, pacing, involving the audience, focus, variety, clarity, and casting. Theatre professionals are the best people to ask to teach you how to give memorable performances.

Chapter 7
The Big Time

Here are ten sample big events you can evaluate for your specific group. A big event assumes you will have a big membership, at least $1,000 seed money, at least six months of advance planning, and a huge publicity campaign. It is best to run these as annual events with a committee that starts planning next year's event the day after this year's event.

Some of these can begin as smaller events and get bigger every year. For example, the first year you do an ad book you are really discovering the market and training the salespeople. The profits should double the second year, and increase every year after that as the membership grows and the salespeople get more confident.

Each of these is described very briefly because there are other books and pamphlets written about each one. They are the fundraisers used most by big organizations, politicians, art groups, disease associations, hospital boards and universities. There should be several other people in your area to ask for advice when you try one the first time.

In addition, for more information on big scale fundraisers, get:

Handbook of Special Events For Nonprofit Organizations, Tested Ideas For Fund Raising and Public Relations. Edwin R. Leibert and Bernice E. Sheldon. Taft Products, 1000 Vermont Ave., N.W., Washington, D.C. 20005. $13.45. 224 pp. Advice on award dinners, charity balls, fashion shows, art exhibits, bazaars, fairs, house tours, theatre benefits and a smattering of other ideas gleaned from big organizations' newsletters. Lots of samples and excellent checklists. (The examples are almost all well established, non-controversial, big-city groups with paid staff and upper-income boards. Adjust the prices and style to match your own group.)

137

THE AD BOOK

Ad books are a high-profit fundraising device that have been effectively translated from their church and political origins to serve many community organizations. The most profitable contains nothing but ads. You simply sell ads to local businesses, politicians and individuals, then print a booklet. This book can be distributed at a meeting, party, or fundraising event. The biggest advantage of the ad book is it gives you a way to ask people outside the organization for support.

You can start small by recruiting ads from the churches, merchants and politicians in your immediate neighborhood. When you have more experience, go after the bigger corporations, institutions and politicians.

People buy an ad because you *sell* them on the idea of supporting the organization. They know that a $50 ad in your ad book is not going to deliver the customers that the same ad in a local paper will bring. So you have to take the time to plan your sales pitch in the committee. Why is it in the interest of your sales targets to give to your organization? Prepare a sheet on what the organization has done for the community, and what it plans to do next year. In addition, match the sellers and customers with care and caution.

Since you will never be able to offer the advertisers the circulation of the local newspapers, and since they are really giving to support the organization rather than advertise, you can print as few books as possible. You need one for each worker, one for each advertiser, and a stock to take with you when you sell next year. By limiting the number of books you print, and limiting the non-advertising copy, you can make about ninety per cent profit on the book.

Read *Helping NOW Grow—Fundraising,* Chicago Chapter, National Organization for Women, Room 1501, 53 W. Jackson, Chicago, IL 60604. 1975. $2.00. 20 pp. Good suggestions for any group plus precise details of how Chicago NOW ran its 1973, 1974 and 1975 ad book campaigns. Tells you how to set goals, plan a timetable, find prospective customers and record sales for next year's committee, prepare sales materials, organize the volunteers, produce the book, and follow-up. Plus sample ad book order form, letter of introduction and volunteer sales instructions.

Besides the all-advertising ad book, there are many other ways you can sell ads to raise money. Many groups sell ads to pay for the expense of printing the convention program. This will allow you to do a classy convention program for a large audience and make a small profit too.

Some small town volunteer fire departments sell ads to cover the cost of an attractive community calendar. Each page has a week on one side and ads on the other side. In addition, the book has information on the fire department and the town. Every fall, the volunteer firemen go door to door and *give* each household a calendar while other firemen give the kids a ride around the block on the fire truck. Then they ask each person whether they would like to buy two tickets to the Firemen's Ball. Virtually all say yes. The calendar gives necessary fire information to help the homeowners, a collection of ads from all the local merchants to help the business community, and a pleasant sales gimmick to help the fire department.

You can sell ads on anything you can print. High schools sell ads in the back of the year books, college groups sell ads on desk blotters, and churches sell ads on the back of Sunday programs. Fancy charity ball committees print their big donors' photographs between silver covers and call it a "Souvenir Journal." You can always print the names of patrons on any mimeographed program for any other fundraising event too.

ANTIQUE OR ART SHOW

Antique or art shows offer the community the choice of dozens of dealers or artists in one place. They appeal to both dealers and shoppers. Some people who would never go in an antique shop or art gallery will shop at a show because they can browse with no commitment to buy and they can do comparison shopping.

Shows have been run in big convention display halls, old mansions that provide an antique backdrop, schools, farms, garages, sports clubs, restaurants, and outdoors on the streets of a scenic neighborhood. You can invite antique dealers from the lists in the booklets at other shows, from the dealers listed in the phone book under "antique dealers", or from the membership of the city, state or national associations. You can invite artists from the lists of other shows, and suggestions from galleries, museums, art collectors, and other artists.

Most groups charge each dealer or artist a set fee for a space. Fees range from $15 to $250 depending on the convenience of the location and the size of the crowd. For an antique show each dealer is also asked to donate one item to the group's own booth. The group operates one booth, which sells antiques donated by the members as well as the dealers' donations. Legally, an antique is something 100 years old or more; commercially, an antique is anything that is old and appealing. You get all the sale revenue from your booth.

For an art show, ask each artist to donate one good work for an auction. If you have enough artists, you can run the auction all day long. The group keeps the revenue from the auction. It is in the self-interest of the artist to donate an appealing (profitable) work, because many browsers will watch the auction and note which works they see that they like the best. If they like the Karl Wirsum painting, they will seek out his booth.

To attract dealers and artists, explain the neighborhood and the anticipated number of shoppers. Add an appealing note, like "only show in downtown Topeka" or "first show of the season in Raleigh". The sellers also appreciate being able to buy food and beverages on the premises, handy washrooms, good security, and courteous movers. (You hire the movers or recruit volunteers; the dealers pay tips for special efforts like carrying the solid oak table or plaster column.)

Besides the sponsor booth for an antique show or an auction for an art show, you also make money by selling tickets in advance and at the door, printing a program with advertisements, and selling refreshments. This is another good place to run a bake sale.

THE CARNIVAL

Everybody loves a carnival. It combines professional rides and attractions with member-operated game booths and refreshment stands. Like Bingos, carnivals are successful because they appeal to the whole community. People come to ride the Ferris wheel and eat the cotton candy rather than support the organization, so they are an ideal way to reach people beyond your members.

Your location is your best advertising and the key to success, so choose it with care. You want a large open space in a relatively dense, lower-middle to middle class neighborhood. It should be within walking distance for kids and visible from busy streets. You also need a nearby building with washrooms, secure rooms to count the money, and possibly a large room to run a Bingo.

Call City Hall to find out what city permits you need. Call the police to find out what arrangements you need to make with them for traffic control. Ask the fundraisers at local churches, schools, or unions that run carnivals whom they recommend as competent, honest operators. Then call the carnival operators to get prices and available dates. They are listed in the Yellow Pages under "carnival suppliers." Unless you have planned far ahead, the first year you may have to take a date at the beginning or end of the summer when the weather is more erratic. As you repeat your carnival year after year, you can get better dates as you move up on the carnival operator's list. Try to run a minimum of five days, since your best publicity is word-of-mouth from satisfied customers. A longer run, seven to ten days, will make more money, and holiday week-ends like the Fourth of July are the very best dates to get.

The carnival operators are professionals and will give you the best advice on operation and promotion of the carnival. If you follow their advice, it is almost impossible to lose money on a carnival. The amount of your profit depends on the arrangements you make with the operator and the volume of customers.

Arrangements With the Operator: The package varies with each operator but a sample agreement would include provisions covering these subjects:

● The operator runs the rides and buys insurance to cover any accidents. Your members sell and take tickets. You will get twenty to twenty-five per cent on the rides.

● Games of chance or lucky jars. This is a raffle, the numbered chances come in glass jars. The customer pays 10 cents to 25 cents to draw a chance and win a prize. You purchase the jars set at the odds you want, usually a net of forty-five per cent. The pitch is "Every prize in this booth is in these jars!"

● Games of chance or lucky jars. This is a raffle; the numball, pitching nickels into glassware, or breaking balloons with a dart. You make the most money if you run these yourself. Then your profits are all the ticket prices minus the cost of prizes. Otherwise, if you are shorthanded, you can sell the space (usually about $100 to $150) to a professional game operator supplied by the carnival operator.

● Food concessions you can operate yourself, along with the never-failing bake booth. You can also add on a Bingo you run yourself if your state license allows.

Your other overall costs are the cost of wiring for rides and lights, renting the space, security forces, and advertising. Usually the operator will include 200 to 500 color posters in the deal for stores and schools around the site. You can put up a huge wood sign on the site several months in advance and string a banner above the street two weeks before the opening. Try to get a member who is a teacher or member of the PTA to make arrangements to get fliers passed out to the schoolchildren on opening day.

Your best advertising is word of mouth. Build up the hoop-la with newspaper stories, church bulletin inserts, scheduled appearances by celebrities, and prizes for the workers who do the best promotion. Some carnivals even print conversation-provoking buttons for all the workers and kids to wear before and during the carnival.

THE CONCERT

Because of the new laws on campaign contributions, the rock concert has become an increasingly important part of big political campaigns. Jimmy Carter raised almost $350,000 from rock concerts and government matching funds; Jerry Brown raised almost $150,000 through California talent and the matching funds; Tom Hayden raised $75,000, ten percent of his budget. Politics and pop music made the match because there is no legal limit on contributions of *time*. As long as the stars donate their performance the revenue is all legal and qualifies for matching funds. The pols get big chunks of legal money; the pop music business hopes to get favorable legislation.

The big political concerts show everyone else the right way to do a big money, big audience, big star concert. Woo the artists and their agents, appeal to their intelligence and their own interests, and deliver lots of good publicity. Then stay in touch and treat them nice for the next campaign.

The most important thing to know is that concerts can give you big, big profits or they can give you big, big losses. If you are planning to do a large scale concert with an investment over $10,000 and a major star, whether it is Stevie Wonder or Leonard Bernstein, hire a professional promoter. You can't do it yourself. There are too many risks involved for you. Also, if you do a bad show you will burn out your market for the star, and make you poison for future stars, so your first concert will be your last.

Of course you can always ask the promoter to donate his or her services. Otherwise consider the promoter's percentage as insurance against failure. Work very closely with the promoter to learn all you can about the business. After you have presented two or three concerts, you may consider doing it yourself.

The only exception is for college groups which can promote a concert in their own auditorium. Since they have the advantages of a captive market, free publicity, free location and labor, they can produce their own show with confidence. If you have to pay for union labor, a location, equipment, advertising, promotion, and ticket service, hire a professional promoter.

HOW TO FIND TALENT: Obviously, you can't do a concert without a star. If you don't know any superstars, you have to meet someone who does. This includes other organizations that have done concerts, such as Nader groups and presidential candidates' campaign organizations. You can also ask your local music and movie critics or the gossip columnists of local papers and TV stations. Ask the managers of local night clubs and theatres. Ask the writers on national magazines who interview stars, the public relations professionals who use talent, and the people who book talent for local universities.

You have to learn to be aggressive. Ask for introductions if you can get them; if you can't, introduce yourself. Attend concerts and arrange to get yourself or at least your materials to the stars. Then pursue them to do a concert for you. Emphasize that their audience is your constituency and visa-versa. Explain why you need them and all the benefits that will accrue to your community if they will do the concert for you.

Understand there is no free lunch. Even if the star comes free, it will still be very expensive to pay for all the other personnel involved in a concert. Be sure to interview some other fundraisers who have run concerts to learn the do's and don't's before you start.

If the star agrees to do your concert, use the opportunity to make friends with the star. Like any other business, it is a tight fraternity, so professional entertainers know lots of other professional entertainers. Once you get a good working relationship, your star may do repeat performances for you and introduce you to other talent.

To find out more about concerts, read:

Raising Funds For the Environment: The Benefit Concert. Leslie Millenson, "Environmental Quality Magazine". February, 1973. pp. 45, 46, 70-73. This is the best explanation of how to contact talent, including major booking agencies, plus step by step advice on presenting a concert. The magazine is out of business, so you will have to get a back issue at the library or from your local environmental group.

To track down information on a specific artist, follow this route:

1)   Go to a record store and find out what company produces his or her records. The company name is on the label of the record.

2)   Call the music director at the local radio station that plays this record. Ask for the name of the local record promoter for the particular company. Every record company employs people in every area to push its records.

3)   Call the promoter of the record company and ask for information on the artist. The promoter will have biographies and other information that will help you figure out the best way to approach the artist.

THE DINNER

A dinner is an overgrown luncheon. You do the same preparation but have more food, a bigger program, and charge higher prices. Because a dinner seems to be more of an "occasion", you can also use it as the basis for a corporate campaign, an ad book, or direct mail solicitation.

Like the luncheon, the draw for a dinner is *not* the food but the person who sends the invitations. Guests come because they want to please the person who asked them. Another gimmick common to dinners is the "honored guest." Many groups choose a beloved recently-retired politician, an earnest activist, a dedicated reporter, or a virtuous celebrity to "honor" at the dinner with an award. This gives you access to the honoree's lists. It also can serve as the bait for a top notch chairperson if that person wants to be associated with the honored guest. Some groups are crass enough to make their biggest donor the "Man (or Woman) of the Year," because they know he or she has the clout to force other people with money to make an appearance. This does raise money, but it can ruin your credibility as a sincere organization primarily concerned about your program.

Almost every politician has run big dinners, and so have many union leaders. Ask them or their fundraisers for advice.

Bibliography

"Award Dinners" in the *Handbook of Special Events For Nonprofit Organizations,* pp. 110-124. Lots of samples and great checklists. (See p. 137 for HANDBOOK listing).

Ten Steps To A Million Dollar Fundraiser, Mrs. Miles Berger. *Grantsmanship Center News,* 1015 W. Olympic Blvd., Los Angeles, CA 90015. Eight-page reprint. 75¢. 1975. How to link a big dinner-dance to a corporate campaign.

THE LAS VEGAS NIGHT

A casino night involves gambling, entertainment and refreshments, all presented with Las Vegas-style razzle-dazzle. These are especially popular in states that do not have legalized gambling because they offer people a chance to gamble for fun. Some will get merchandise prizes too. They appeal to organizations because they raise a lot of money and provide so many different ways to volunteer that everyone can star at some part.

One format for a casino night is to sell advance tickets which admit the players, give them a set amount of play money ($20,000), and serve as door prize tickets. The customers then get to gamble with their play money. Get the standard games and instructions from a carnival supplier. The games—roulette, craps, black jack, etc., are staffed by your most vivacious members, who can explain the games simply and encourage people to play.

Each customer gets an instruction sheet that explains the games and a list of the prizes with "prices" listed in play money. Get the prizes from your carnival supplier and solicit others, like dinners at local restaurants and gift certificates to local stores. Successful gamblers can trade in their play money for prizes if they want to leave early. If they lose all their play money they can get more at the "currency exchange" where you sell play money for real money. Unlike illegal gambling, you are neither taking nor paying out real money, and you don't need to worry about the dealers skimming.

The secret of success is getting the gamblers to stay and gamble all night. So keep the best prizes like the stereo, TV, trip to Hawaii, or ten-speed bike for an auction at the end. Then the best gamblers will bid for the top prizes with their winnings. Also, hold the door prize drawing at midnight.

In addition to the gambling, you can sell food and drinks. Have lots of waiters and waitresses to serve the gamblers drinks. Sell food in other rooms decorated as cafés. A school makes a great setting for a Las Vegas night because you can gamble in the gym, and run different shows and restaurants in other rooms. Sometimes groups combine the food and entertainment, like having the German band in the room with the beer and bratwurst and the Dixieland band in the room with the oyster bar. Or you can use the auditorium and put on a full-tilt musical production with singing and dancing. Sell the refreshments separately and include the entertainment in the ticket price.

Line up some celebrities to take a shift running one of the games for you, too. It is fun for the celebrities and the crowd. In addition it will build up your repeat customers, if they think they can get lucky with the senator or the second baseman dealing.

THE MARATHON

The walk-a-thons and other fundraising marathons raise money from a lot of people pledging to pay the participants money per output. For example, in a walk-a-thon, walkers will collect pledges for contributions from 10 cents to $1 for every mile they walk. The volunteers can walk, ride bikes, swim, dance, or play volleyball. Obviously the marathons offer tremendous publicity opportunities in addition to high income.

To be successful you have to recruit a large number of young people through school networks to solicit the pledges and do the walking. Then a professional staff takes over to do the billing and collecting of the pledges. Walk-a-thons work best for issues that appeal to young people, like environmental issues, or for issues promoted by the leaders young people respect, such as the hunger walks organized by popular church leaders.

To find out how to run a marathon, ask local fundraisers who use the technique and get this book:

Fundraising in the Public Interest. Section I: "Walk-A-Thons, Bike-A-Thons and Assorted Marathons for Money." David L. Grubb and David R. Zwick. Fundraising in the Public Interest, P.O. Box 19404, Washington, D.C. 20036. 1976. 186 pp. $4.50. Make checks to: Public Citizen, Inc.

You can also adapt the "pledge per output" concept to a small scale fundraiser. Politicians have collected pledges for contributions per pin in one line of bowling or contributions per lap for one hour of swimming. Hairdressers have run the "cut-a-thon" where they donate all the proceeds for one day of haircuts at $2 per head. Senior citizens have held "rock-a-thons" where they collect pledges for hours rocked in a rocking chair. The possibilities are endless.

THE MOVIE PREMIER

Movie premiers bring to mind the images of glittering stars, shiny limousines and crowds of fans. For a benefit premier, you can use the magic of Hollywood plus the methods of your hometown.

As with a concert, the first step is getting to know the people who distribute movies. Ask the groups you know who have done movie premiers, like the Nader groups and/or the big local charities. You can also ask your local movie critics for suggestions.

Unlike a concert, which is a one-time special event, a movie premier challenges you to persuade people to pay $10 to $50 to see a movie they will be able to see the next day for $3. You do this by running a high-powered publicity campaign plus adding extra attractions.

For example, when the Illinois Public Action Council ran the premier for "All the President's Men" they added a panel of investigative reporters moderated by Studs Terkel, plus a cocktail reception afterward. Some groups arrange for the star of the movie to appear. A group in Washington, D.C. held a party in the Smithsonian museum with all the airplanes when they did the Robert Redford's "Waldo Pepper" premier about ace pilots.

Besides the attractions, a movie premier needs an efficient and aggressive sales team. Their job is to reach every name on every list and make them believe this is *the* event of the year. They emphasize the importance of giving for the cause as well as for the entertainment.

To keep up with movies in progress, read *Variety*, the trade newspaper. This can give you an opportunity to be first in line to ask for a premier. *Variety*, 154 W. 46th St., New York, NY 10036. At the library, or subscribe for $30 a year. Fifty-two issues about 100 pages each.

THE TELETHON

Telethons and radio marathons seem very glamorous and enjoyable. They are also very expensive and tons of work. Don't do them.

Bibliography.
For an excellent explanation of the pitfalls and possibilities of telethons, including a sample cost breakdown, read:

Mediability: A Guide For Nonprofits. Len Biegel and Aileen Lubin. Taft Products, Inc., 1000 Vermont Ave., N.W., Washington, D.C. 20005. 1975. 110 pp. $6.50. See especially "Everyone wants to do a telethon," pp. 73-79.

THE TENNIS TOURNAMENT

The tennis tournament is an example of a fashionable fundraising event used to involve and integrate different audiences in your program. You can reach the people who play the sport, people who like to watch the sport, people who like to watch celebrities, people who like to be involved with the big, exciting fundraisers, and your own membership, too. All of these people will gain from the experience of working with one another.

You can use any popular spectator sport. Many politicians and unions use golf tournaments, hospitals use tennis tournaments and polo matches, and ecology groups have even used fly-casting tournaments. Since there is some risk involved the first year in accurately measuring the real enthusiasm in your town for a particular sport, it would be wise to bolster the income from the sports event with an ad book, corporate donations and food and beverage sales. After you have run the event a few years, you will master the publicity campaign and marketing strategy to insure the sports event itself will pay off handsomely.

For a good account of how a medium-sized organization ran a successful sport fundraising the first time out, get:

Doing a One Shot, Big Time Fund Raiser. Christine Pattee, 3405 Woodland, Apt. #28B, West Des Moines, IA 50265. 1976. 5 pp. Free. Send self-addressed business size envelope. Excellent report on 1976 "Rally for the ERA with Billie Jean King" tennis match sponsored by Iowa Women's Political Caucus.

Chapter 8
Fundraising Forever

DUES

It costs money to belong to an organization. Members have to pay for transportation, meals, phone calls, postal stamps, and baby-sitting. They have these expenses only because they are active members of the group.

It also costs money to run an organization. Even the smallest group needs paper, stamps and envelopes. As it gets larger it will need telephones, equipment, an office, furniture, supplies, and, eventually, paid staff. The base for the income to pay the organization's bills is the dues of the members.

Although it is always a good idea to try to raise more money from sources outside the membership, you must still depend on dues for your basic subsistence. This is the best guarantee that you will never go out of business as long as you are doing what the members want to do.

Setting the Dues

First, discuss what the group wants to do in the coming year. Then make an estimate of what it will cost. Let's say you will need $2,000 the first year.

If you decide to do a bake sale, a raffle and a dance to raise $100, $100, and $300 respectively, for a total of $500, you will need to get the other $1,500 from dues.

Divide this by your probable number of members by the end of the year to get the average dues. If you get ten members a month you will have 120 members at the end of the year. Each member would need to pay $12.50.

But let's say that that is too much for people in your neighborhood. So then you decide to try to get ten members a month for the first six months, then twenty members a month for the second six months. Now you would have 180 members at the end of the year, and each one would pay $8.33 to raise $1,500. This is still too high.

So figure in addition to these 180 members, you will also get ten new members at the bake sale, and ten new members at the dance. You now have 200 members. Then each of the five officers takes a personal commitment to find ten additional new members over the coming year, for another fifty. You now have a goal of 250 members at the end of the first year. $1,500 divided by 250 is $6. This is a figure which will pay for the organization and be accepted by the community.

You can do it the other way around—set the dues and then see how many members you get. The problems with this are:

1) there is no strategy or commitment for getting the members,

2) the dues are usually set too low in eagerness to include everybody, or sometimes set too high in eagerness to seem like a high-class organization.

Alternatives

There is no reason why every member has to pay the same amount. It makes neat arithmetic, but especially if your organization is made up of members with many different income levels, you may want to set different dues for different groups.

SWEAT EQUITY. For members who contribute a lot of their time and talent, but lack extra cash, make a sweat equity deal. This would cover students, seniors, unemployed and underemployed volunteers. For example, you might say that if any person contributes one hour a week or a total of fifty-two hours a year, the group will waive that person's cash dues.

SLIDING SCALE. This gets more money from those who can afford it. Women Employed's dues are set like this:

Dues	Income
$ 5	Less than $8,000
$10	$8,000 to $10,000
$15	Over $10,000
$25	Sustaining member

The sign up is on the honor system, so no one checks your income.

DISCOUNTS. Discounts offer real financial incentives in return for dues. The Arkansas Community Organizations for Reform Now (ACORN) developed food buying co-ops which sell food at substantial discounts to ACORN members. The Senior Federation in Minnesota offers its members the lowest prices in town at its own drug store. Many art museums give members discounts at the museum stores and special preview privileges for shows.

PERCENTAGE OF INCOME. Some churches ask their members to "tithe" or pay ten percent of their income for the work of the church.* Church members just assume that part of their income belongs to the church; it is not theirs to spend. As their income goes up, so does their donation to the church. The church also reminds us that, for some people, tithing is selfish. The people who make the most money ought to give away more than ten percent. Similarly, some organizations have voted not to spend time doing extra fundraising, but instead to focus 100 percent of their energies on their program. So instead of doing fundraising events, the members work at their regular jobs and donate a percentage of the income to the group.

LOWER RATES. For students, senior citizens, or any other category you want to create.

DIFFERENT RATES. For individuals and families.

AFFILIATE DUES. Some umbrella organizations have each affiliate group pay a lump sum based on either the number of members or their ability to pay. Voting power may or may not be proportionate to the size of the dues. Some groups also give the affiliates the means to raise the dues, such as selling ads in the convention program or newsletter.

PAYMENT PLANS. In order to get larger amounts from the members, you can have the members pay so much a month. Women Organized for Employment (WOE) in San Francisco started the "WOE One Hundred." Members pledge $100 to WOE and make twelve monthly payments of $8.25 each. If a member misses a payment, she is mailed a reminder. Since WOE's members are all working women, few can pay with one $100 check, but some can give $8.25 a month.

EQUIVALENTS. Make the dues equal to some other expenditure. In the WOE One Hundred, members are reminded that $100 equals the cost of one lunch a week. If she brings her own lunch and gives the money to WOE, both the woman and the organization will be healthier. Political organizations tell prospective members that good government is one of the basic necessities of life, just like food, shelter and clothing. They ask people to give what they would spend on one pair of shoes. Then the people who buy $10 shoes give $10 and the people who buy $30 shoes give $30.

You Get Only the Net

The most important thing to remember about dues is that you

---

*One Methodist minister claims he saw a bumper sticker saying, "If you love Jesus, tithe. Any fool can honk."

get only the *net*. You can spend only what is left *after* you subtract the cost of member services. In our example, the dues are $6 per member. What are some options we can give the members, and where does that leave our net?

1. Dues   = $6.00
   Vote   =   − 0
   ————————————
   Net   = $6.00

2. We decide to give each member a membership card (2 cents), a button (8 cents), and a four-issue mimeographed newsletter mailed first class (60 cents). Our costs per member are 70 cents.
   Dues   = $6.00
   Costs =   −.70
   ————————————
   Net   = $5.30

3. We decide to give each member a window decal (10 cents), a bumper sticker (25 cents), a twelve-issue printed newsletter mailed bulk rate ($1.65), and a consumer guide to local businesses ($1). Our costs per member are $3.
   Dues   = $6.00
   Costs =   −3.00
   ————————————
   Net   = $3.00

For every item you decide to give the members in addition to the vote, you need to estimate whether it will increase the number of new members enough to pay for what it costs you. It is always better to sell membership material like buttons, decals and research, rather than give them away.

BINGO

Bingo is currently legal in thirty-six states, and card rooms are legal in six states. These states have recognized that their citizens are going to gamble anyway, so they might as well make it legal and tax the revenues.* Gambling is both fun and profitable, very profitable. If you choose to run a Bingo you can get a high return for the effort involved.

——

*This is verified by the three-year study "summarized" in a 413-page book entitled "Gambling in America" (1976). The federal government spent $3 million of our tax money to find out what any citizen could have told them for free. The first sentence says "Gambling is inevitable."

First, the finance committee and the executive board should discuss among themselves and with the entire membership whether to sponsor a gambling operation. The negative is that some people have strong moral objections to gambling as a sin and as a regressive tax. The positives are that it is profitable, most people want to gamble, it produces a convivial social atmosphere, and the occasion can also be used organizationally to reach new people. If the board decides to do it, get a copy of your state laws and read them thoroughly. Every state has different rules and you must follow them scrupulously. Even if you know St. Bastion's is stretching the rules, it is a bad idea for you to deviate from the law in any way. Especially if your organization is controversial, or sometimes has conflicts with the state government, remember that one way the state can retaliate is by inspecting your fundraising program with a microscope. Keep your record squeaky clean.

If the board chooses to run Bingo and if the organization meets the state requirements, apply for a license. Get advice from the people who currently run successful Bingos. Play at several different halls before yours opens to learn how they entertain the crowd, get people to come back week after week, and offer special gimmicks. You may be able to use the hall and equipment of an existing group that already runs a Bingo on a different night. Otherwise, look for the best place in terms of conveniences, appeal to a crowd, and access to your workers. You can usually buy your equipment on the installment plan. It may be a good idea to own your own equipment anyway to use for other events.

The key to success with a Bingo is the appeal of the caller. The best callers have a following who come to play because they know he runs a fair game and he cares about them. When the star caller of Chicago Bingo, Bernie Willow, jokingly told his crowd that anyone who brought him a valentine would get a free card, he was overwhelmed by the creativity and care of his audience. One woman made him a valentine made like the Bingo Board, one gave him a decorated can of beer, and one dressed up her little girl as a valentine. The rapport between player and caller draws the crowd. Since every state law sets a ceiling on the total prize money, your caller is your drawing card.

The caller is also the best person to give you advice on types of games and gimmicks. For example you can run a "friendship" Bingo where the people on either side of the person who Bingos get prizes or cash. This builds up team spirit. You can have the crowd sign the back of this week's card and put it in a box when they leave. Next week draw out three cards and give them extra cards, prizes, or cash if they show up. This will help build repeat attendance. You can also run a concessions stand and sell supplies.

Rotating teams of workers sell the cards and verify the Bingos after they are called. They also serve as the hospitality committee to assist the players so they don't need to leave their cards to get change, more chips, or an ashtray. Working the Bingo can be a very rewarding job as the teams get to know the customers and vice-versa.

In addition to the income, some groups use their Bingos to introduce political candidates, circulate petitions, recruit new members, pass out issue papers, and pick up information on local problems. But the big pay-off is financial. People come to play because they love Bingo and hope they will win big. They do not need to support your program to support the Bingo. Although you can anticipate a loss while you build up a regular crowd, after the first six to twelve months a successful week-end evening Bingo can bring in $40,000 to $80,-000 a year—enough to support a medium to large-sized organization.

GOING INTO BUSINESS

Katharine Hepburn once said, ". . . My first real, thrilling job was filling balloons with gas, then tying strings around them and making people buy them. They all said, 'VOTES FOR WOMEN'." Selling good products can provide a dependable source of income for the group as well as provide a satisfying form of involvement for your volunteers.

Some of the advantages of selling things are:

You can work at your own pace. You can start small with an inventory of your own buttons and bumper stickers and work up to a wholesale business of cookbooks, calendars, how-to manuals, posters and pamphlets.

You can start with one or two people, then increase the committee as the sales increase.

You can find the right job for every volunteer. One person can sell the products to the president of the largest department store, another can sell at meetings, and another can bill orders and keep the books in the office. There is a place for every personality in selling things.

You have a means to reach beyond the membership for support. When you begin you can sell at every meeting and public activity to raise money from new people. When you get to be very big you will be filling mail orders for the whole country in response to ads in national media.

Your members are learning valuable and marketable job skills.

Anyone who can sell anything, keep track of an inventory, manage the orders and billing, or do the promotion of a retail business, will have skills to sell in the business world.

You can always start by selling membership materials to your own members. These might be buttons, bumper stickers, issue papers or T-shirts. Unfortunately, for these your market is limited to your own members and collectors. Buttons and bumper stickers build morale and team spirit, but return such a low profit per piece that they are not really considered money-makers. In fact, most groups either lose track of their inventory or over-order so they become a promotional expense.

What you want to sell is something that will appeal to the public at large. It can still be issue-oriented, but focus on the issue rather than the organization—for example, balloons that say "Votes for Women" instead of "The Chillicothe Suffragettes". When Business and Professional People for the Public Interest was opposing Mayor Daley's proposal to put an airport in Lake Michigan, it produced buttons and bumper stickers saying "Don't do it in the lake." They sold out and are now collector's items. When the Seattle-King County NOW chapter wanted a poster about job discrimination, it came up with a picture of Israel's Prime Minister, Golda Meir, captioned "But can she type?" It launched the group's retail business. Save Our Cumberland Mountains (SOCM) in Tennessee has marketed a postcard showing the "before" and "after" of strip mining.

What Should We Sell?

You can make more money with a product that is the only one of its kind—an original cookbook, a calendar, consumer guides. Consumer Advocates in San Francisco prepared books comparing prices of used car dealers and banks in California. C.A. cornered the market and raised more than $30,000 a year from the guides. The Southwest Network in California publishes "El Calendario Chicano," the first calendar featuring original Chicano art work and recognizing the Chicano holidays, heros and heroines. Now in its sixth year, Southwest Network has doubled its sales every year and raises most of its budget from this unique work.

Start with a good product, sell to your own members, then expand to progressively larger markets. Here is a description of how the Seattle-King County NOW chapter did it:

"We started selling our products at our own meetings. With the money we made there, we paid two members' expenses to sell at the National NOW convention. With some of those profits, we began to contact other NOW chapters and we ran an ad in *Ms.* Magazine. And with that money, we rented an office, installed a telephone, bought a mimeograph and typewriter, provided child care at our meetings, and generally support out budget! Step, walk, run."*

For more on marketing your own merchandise get:
From Those Wonderful Folks Who Brought You Golda . . . The Moneybook. Seattle-King County NOW, 2252 N.E. 65th St., Seattle, Wash. 98105. $2.75. 1974. 18 pp. The best book on retailing. How to choose products, get ideas, raise seed money, prepare graphics for posters, buttons and brochures, market locally and nationally plus advice on legal problems, records, taxes, and structure.

General Information on Copyright. Copyright Office, Washington, D.C. 20559. 11 pp., free. How to copyright anything you want to retail.

WHAT TO AVOID: Don't sell somebody else's products. Many firms like to use organizations' members to sell their cleaning products, candy bars, fruitcake, trinkets, greeting cards, or Christmas cards. They pitch you on the "fundraising opportunities" when really they want to hire you as their short term, low paid, no benefits salesforce. You never get as good a deal from an outsider as you can give yourself. Why sell somebody else's fruitcake and make thirty percent, when you can run your own bake booth and make one hundred percent?

Opening Your Own Business

More and more organizations are exploring the idea of operating for-profit businesses. This would give them the chance to raise money, provide a service to the community, and establish a permanent, visible commitment to the people in the neighborhood.

If you want to consider opening your own business, first do a survey of your own members to catalog their skills, experience and interests. Find out how much time each would be willing to contribute to start the business, and then to keep it going.

Second, write the Small Business Administration, Washington, D.C. 20416, or call the SBA field office listed in the phone book under "U.S. Government", for a catalog of free and low-cost publications. They have good over-all advice, like the "Checklist for going into Business" as well as pamphlets tailored for specific businesses such as restaurants, florists, or gas stations. Ask the SBA to refer you to your area SCORE (Senior Corps of Retired Executives) volunteer who can match you with an experienced business person to give you advice.

In addition, try to line up some local business people to serve

---

*From Those Wonderful Folks Who Brought You Golda . . . The Moneybook, p. 11.

on an advisory committee to help you through the first few years. They can offer invaluable advice on marketing and record keeping to help you grow faster.

The biggest problem with starting your own business is getting the seed money to get started. Ask your business advisory committee and your banker to review your plan and to give you advice on all sources of seed money.

The other potential problem in running a business is the conflict it can cause in the organization. You have to establish firm rules to avoid any real or apparent conflict of interest for the board members. You also have to consider whether running the business will conflict with your program. For example, if you choose a business licensed by the state, like a pharmacy or health clinic, will this restrict your ability to vigorously campaign for reforms in these or other areas in the state legislature?

Besides the SBA publications, other helpful books are:

Food Stamp Sales As A Community Business. John MacPhee. Center for Community Economic Development, Suite 316, 639 Massachusetts Ave., Cambridge, MA 02139, March 1976 Newsletter reprint, 4 pp., 25¢.

How To $ucceed In Fundrai$ing Today. Helen Knowles. The Bond Wheelwright Co., Porter's Landing, Freeport, ME 04032. 1976. 250 pp. $7.65. Especially good on thrift shops, with sample consignment contract.

Non-Profit Food Stores. A Resource Manual. 1977. 64 pp. $3. Case studies and how to start one. *Democracy In the Workplace.* Ithaca FED. 1977. 100 pp. $4. How-to manual for worker-controlled businesses, covers organization, finances, laws, and marketing. Both from: Strongforce, 2121 Decatur Pl., N.W., Washington, DC 20008.

CORPORATE GIVING

Corporations represent a pool of potential giving which has been underutilized in the past. They have regularly subsidized the arts, disease associations and big hospitals partly due to the historic "charity by consensus" where all gave to a few charities which were "safe", and partly due to the fraternal round-robin caused by every executive serving on a charity board so that Fred gave to Nancy's hospital and Nancy gave to Fred's opera. But this is beginning to change as the corporations hire more professional staff and social change organizations learn to ask with the same skill as the big charities.

Although the corporations may legally give up to five percent of their pre-tax earnings, the average is around one percent. In 1975, corporations gave away a total of $1.2 billion. The trick to getting a piece of this pie is 1) finding the right corporations and 2) finding the right person in the corporation.

Finding the right corporation. According to the Filer Commission's data, of all companies filing tax returns in a recent year only twenty percent reported any contributions. However, of 457 companies responding to a Conference Board survey, ninety-nine percent made contributions during the previous year; ninety-three percent had a formal corporate contributions program, seventy-three percent "loaned" executives and fifty-three percent had a company foundation. Thus, although a minority of corporations give, those that do are proud of it, and give to several projects. They are the best place to start.

Unfortunately, there is very little information published about the giving history of corporations, so your preliminary research will be based mostly on word of mouth and circumstantial evidence. Ask other organizations' fundraisers for recommendations. Get the big charities' ad books to see which corporations took the biggest ads. Read the financial section of the newspaper. Ask at the Regional Library of the Foundation Center (see Appendix) for corporate foundations' tax returns. Or just take the twenty largest corporations in your area and start calling.

Finding the Right Person. Traditional advice for soliciting corporate donations suggests that you get the executives on your board to write a letter of introduction for you to the president of the corporation. Then pitch the top executive. This presents two problems: A. What do you do if you don't have any executives on your board, and don't know any? and B. What do you do if you can't get to the president?

A. If you don't know any executives, try to get an endorsement from the most important local person you do know. This could be the pastor of the biggest church in your area, or the top politician. It also helps if you can show local support for your program, such as "the local chamber of commerce has reviewed our plan, and has pledged complete support plus $100 a month toward its success."

B. If you don't get to see the president, don't be discouraged. One characteristic of successful executives is that they learn to delegate work to capable people. If you are referred to a vice-president for public relations or urban affairs, you still have just as good a chance to get a donation.

In fact, if you are not one of the giants of the community—the hospital, the symphony, or the heart fund—you are better off starting out asking for the head of public relations. The experience of smaller groups shows this is the best way to work. Call the company and ask for the head of public relations.* Tell the P.R. person who you are and what your organization does. Sometimes you will be told right away your organization does not qualify. For example, most corporate giving programs exclude individual churches but will fund church-sponsored programs for emergency food distribution, child care, or senior citizen activities. Ask how to apply for their corporate giving programs and the name of the person to whom you should send your information. Some companies, like public utilities, have lengthy application forms and printed reports about their program. Others have nothing in print and just want a letter from you.

When you get the right name and information, send a letter explaining who you are and why you want money. Like foundations, most corporations prefer to give one-time donations for a specific project rather than on-going general support funds, although there are exceptions. Ask for a specific amount of money which is in the range of the company's giving record. Most will not give anything less than $25; average donations may range from $100 to $5,000 depending on the size and success of the company. Find out the company's average gift by asking other groups, reading the company's reports, or asking the person in public relations. At the end of the letter, say that you will call for an appointment.

Call back in a week to confirm that your letter has been received. It is your responsibility to call. Don't assume that if they like it they will call you, or that if they don't call, they don't like it. You are selling your program to them, so you have to be the one to call.

Try to set up a personal meeting. It will probably have to be during the regular business day. You can also take your president or the person chairing the proposed project.

Then go and sell your program. The best corporate programs have staff people who may come out to a meeting or to a project, but for the majority, the only thing they will see of your organization is you.

Be sure to send a note right after the meeting thanking the corporate officer for meeting with you. If you get the contribution, be sure to keep in touch and ask the officer for advice on approaching other corporations. If you are not funded, keep in touch anyway because they may simply be taking a "wait and see" attitude. They may fund you next year if you show some progress this year. Also,

---

*According to *Profiles of Involvement: The Handbook of Corporate Social Responsibility,* the departments handling giving programs break down as follows:

Public relations	—	18%	Community affairs	—	10%
Chief executive	—	16%	Urban affairs	—	9%
Public affairs	—	11%	Contributions	—	6%
Personnel	—	10%			

policies change, so they may turn you down this time, and put you at the top of the list next time.

Bibliography

Ten Steps to a Million Dollar Fundraiser, Mrs. Miles Berger. "The Grantsmanship Center New", 1015 W. Olympic Blvd., Los Angeles, CA 90015, 8 page reprint. 1975. 75¢. Step by step account of how Sally Berger and her partner conducted a $1.4 million corporate campaign linked to a ball for a major research hospital. Adapt the techniques for your own organization and goals.

Read the financial section of your daily newspaper as well as *The Wall Street Journal* to learn about the business world in general and identify the self-interest of specific corporations. Also read *Business Week, Forbes* and *Fortune* at the library to keep up with businesses in your area. You want to learn all you can about the company, its products, its executives, its internal structure, and external marketing scheme.

Standard and Poor's Register of Corporations, Directors and Executives. Available at the library. Useful to look up the specific names and departments which handle a corporation's social responsibility programs. Always call to confirm it is current information.

After you get the name of the executive to see, look them up in *Who's Who in America* at the library to get clues on their personal interests.

The Handbook of Corporate Social Responsibility: Profiles of Involvement. Human Resources Network, 2010 Chancellor St., Philadelphia, PA 19103. 1976. 629 pages. $42.00. The basic source for information on corporate giving in the U.S.A. Unfortunately its thoroughness makes it too expensive for most groups. It is available at some regional Libraries of the Foundation Center (see Appendix) and at some public libraries. Urge your library to get it.

Those corporations which have corporate foundations (53%) must file tax returns on their giving programs just like other foundations. These *corporate foundation tax returns* are on file at the Regional Libraries of the Foundation Center (see Appendix) for the companies in the states served by that library.

DEFERRED GIVING

Deferred giving refers to all the ways someone who is still living can make a large donation that will accrue to the benefit of the organization in the future. This includes bequests, life insurance, annuities, charitable remainder trusts and transfer of property.

Many big plant-heavy institutions like universities and hospitals employ someone whose sole job is to recruit deferred gifts. In all cases, the basic assumption is that the organization will be in existence for a long time. If you cannot guarantee the donor your organization will be in business in 2077, it is probably unrealistic to explore the deferred gifts area.

If you are confident that your group will be alive and kicking in a hundred years, it would be wise to ask the ways and means committee to research deferred gifts. Donors use deferred gifts to get a break on their income taxes and estate taxes, so the people to ask for advice are tax experts, lawyers, the trust officer at your bank, and life insurance experts. They can show you sample forms such as letters of intent, clauses for wills, and special types of life insurance that will benefit your group.

For more advice on the role of the board in recruiting deferred gifts, read:

Fund Raising—A Crucial Role for Board Members. Federation of Protestant Welfare Agencies, 281 Park Avenue South, New York, NY 10010. $2. 1974. 44 pp. Includes best introduction to deferred giving: bequests, remainder trusts, annuity trusts, memorials, letters of intent and charitable gift annuities.

DIRECT MAIL

There is no such thing as a one-shot direct mail campaign. Direct mail is a scientific system for mailing a very large number of letters to a very large number of people and then soliciting the people who respond again and again. It is a means of prospecting for the people in the country who want to give to your group. When you find them you've struck gold.

Although the returns will vary according to the importance of the issue, the quality of the package and the currency of the lists, there is a formula which generally has proven to apply to direct mailing efforts. This is:

For the first mailing to all lists, expect a one percent return. This means one person in a hundred will give.

Of the people who give, sixty percent of them will give again when asked a second time.

Of the people who give twice, seventy-five percent will give when asked a third time.

As you can see, it is very expensive to get started because it costs a lot of money to do the volume of mailing necessary to find the people who give. But it pays off handsomely in the long run. If you chose to begin a direct mail program, you should plan your budget with the understanding that you will lose money the first year if you are a 501(c)4 group or just break even if you are a 501(c)3 group.

If you can afford or can borrow the money to launch a direct mail program, probably a minumum of $20,000, and if you are doing work which will appeal to a national audience, hire a professional to advise you. Successful direct mailing requires many, many decisions on the package: the letter, the envelope, the response device, and other enclosures as well as the many, many decisions on the actual mechanics of mailing: dates, lists, type of postage, repetition, and testing alternatives. Ask the big disease associations and top politicians in your area whom they recommend.

To give you an idea of the number of choices involved in a successful mailing program, as well as give you a grasp of the vocabulary, read the following books before you interview professionals to do your program. There is a lot of specialized jargon involved here, too, so don't be intimidated when your mailing pro says "zip code multivariate regression analysis" when he means counting the returns. Remember, the pro works for *you,* so just keep asking him to explain until you are certain you know what he is talking about. After a few mailings, you can show off and say things like "revolving budget concept for new contributor acquisition programs" as though you've done it all your life.

Bibliography

BEGINNER'S BOOKS

Fundraising in the Public Interest. Section three: "A Citizen's Guide to Direct Mail Fundraising." David L. Grubb and David R. Zwick. Fundraising in the Public Interest, P.O. Box 19404, Washington, D.C. 20036. 186 pp., 1976, $4.50. Make checks to: Public Citizen, Inc. Excellent explanation for groups beginning a direct mail operation, with lots of examples of letters, envelopes, response devices, etc.

Spend Less, Raise More. A Cost-Conscious Look at Direct Mail Fund Raising. Elizabeth Broder Peterson. Direct Mail Fundraisers Association, 810 Seventh Ave., New York, N.Y. 10019. 1974. 22 pp. $1. Do's and don'ts to increase your direct mail profit. Good introduction to the quantity and variety of decisions which affect a mail campaign.

A Consumer's Guide to Postal Service and Products. U.S. Post Office Publication Number 201. March, 1974. An assistance to mailing any second or third class bulk mail. Read it cover to cover before you ask any questions of a postal employee. Get from any post office. *How to Prepare Second and Third Class Mailings.* U.S. Postal Service Manual. See especially Chapter One. Pick up at any post office.

FOR THE PROFESSIONALS

Direct Mail and Mail Order Handbook. Richard S. Hodgson. The Dartnell Corporation, 4660 N. Ravenswood, Chicago, IL 60640. 1974. 1575 pp. $43. This is literally the encyclopedia of direct mail. 49 chapters on every aspect of successful retail or fundraising direct mail with specific samples and arithmetic.

Small local efforts

Assume you have a list of 1,000 names of people in Alabama. If you did a traditional direct mail approach to your 1,000 names and got the average one percent return, you would get ten donations. This is hardly worth the effort, especially if you have reason to believe these people will support you. The best clue to their inclination to give you money is whom and what they have given to before. If the people on the list gave to an organization similar to yours in the past six months, they should give to you. There are too many people to visit in person and they are too spread out to call on the telephone or get to a meeting. How can you reach them through the mail?

The best thing to do is send a personal letter. Take your 1,000 names and simply divide them up. If you have ten people on the committee, each person gets 100 letters to write. If each committee person gets one helper, making the new committee twenty people, each person has to write fifty letters. If you can write six letters an hour, it will take a little over eight hours per person, or three evenings of volunteer work.

Have two or three people each write a draft of the letter. They should pretend they are telling a good friend about the group, why they personally are involved, and why the group needs money. Add a specific amount and a reason for that amount, for example, "$15 will pay for one evening's personalized college counseling for our students." When they are finished, combine the best elements of each letter into a sample one- or two-page letter. Give this as a sample to the letter committee. Each letter-writer can add in a short paragraph on his or her personal reasons for involvement.

Write all the letters on organizational stationery. If the writers have *very* clear handwriting, the letters can be written by hand; otherwise they should be typed. Each letter should include the inside address of the person who will get the letter and the salutation should use surnames: Dear Mr. Smith, Dear Mr. Jones, Dear Mrs. Brown.

Sign it with the writer's full name, "Sincerely yours, Tom Scott". Include a line to the effect that, "I volunteered to write you, on behalf of the entire membership of Junior Educators of Tomorrow, because I wanted the chance to tell you about our exciting new program to offer college counseling to the students, who have no counselor at all at their high school."

Include a copy of your fact sheet or brochure. There are two kinds of envelopes to include for donors to mail their contribution to you. The first is a regular organization stationery envelope with the address written on it. It usually works best if the return address is the home of an officer. Include a note like: "Please mail your contribution in the enclosed envelope. We ask you to add your own stamp because we want all of your donation to go to help our students, rather than go to subsidize the post office."

The second method is to apply for a business return envelope permit. This takes about ten minutes at the main post office in person, or write and ask the post office for form 3614. It costs $30 per year for the permit number which is printed on a business reply envelope. The post office or your printer can show you the correct form for the envelope. Then you pay the letter carrier 25 cents for each envelope returned to you. This is obviously expensive, and means you have to start another ledger to keep track of the cash spent on return postage. Include a notice on the return envelope—"your stamp on this envelope saves JET 25 cents"—but expect to pay for the postage anyway. If you expect to do a lot of mailing throughout the year, it is worth the expense to print a number of return envelopes and pay the postage. The mailing pros have proven it will increase the number of contributions.

Put your letter, fact sheet or brochure, and return envelope in the organizational stationery envelope; address, stamp and mail them. Then keep track of the returns so you know who sent you money. Make a donor's card on each contributor and prepare a final report showing the total number of returns, average donation, and a breakdown of returns by zip code. You can use this to guide you the next time you write a large group to ask for money.

A small mailing is a good opportunity to ask sympathetic local business people for an in-kind contribution of postage. If you have met with a corporate executive who told you how much he or she regretted they had no funds to give you " at this time" but said "if there is anything else we can do for you, just call," now is the time to call. Explain that you are mailing 1,000 letters to ask for money from people in Alabama and you could use postage. The executive may offer to give you the postage or let you run the letters through the company's meter. (Stamps are better.) This is a favorite method by which corporate executives contribute to controversial organizations without their support showing up on their books or in their board meetings. If they give you stamps for both the inside and outside envelopes, it is a $260 donation (13¢ x 2 x 1,000). If they meter the outside envelopes, it is a $130 donation (13¢ x 1,000). This is a great saving for you, but a small donation for the corporation, which can bury it in the postage account with no trouble at all.

DOOR TO DOOR CANVASSING

Door-to-door canvassing is a labor-intensive, high-profit, recession-proof method of raising money. To work well, it must be done professionally all year round. There are currently scores of canvassing programs in operation in cities throughout the country. If you have a program with mass appeal and high publicity in a medium- to large-sized city with a large pool of available labor, you can consider a canvassing program.

Check with the charitable trust division of your state attorney general's office to get the laws on canvassing in your state. Then try to work with a successful canvassing team for at least a week, to get a first-hand understanding of the labor involved. If the board chooses to begin a canvassing program based on your research, try to hire an experienced canvassing field manager, or arrange for the director of your canvassing program to intern with another program at least a month before beginning your program.

Although it takes a lot of very hard work to run a successful canvassing operation, there are many pay-offs in addition to the income. It gives you a chance to reach fifty to seventy-five homes every evening to get an immediate and on-going reading of the public's reaction to your work. You can find out first-hand what the public thinks are the pressing problems of Metropolis.

In addition, it offers a superb training ground for prospective leadership or organizing talent. The skills you need to be a good canvasser are also the skills you need to be a good leader or a good organizer—the willingness to work long hours, the ability to explain the issues quickly and clearly, the skill to solicit a reaction to the problem, the courage to ask for money, and the capacity to listen.

There are two problems that can occur with a professional canvassing program. The first is the problem of adding four to forty employees to your staff. You need to develop your structure so that the canvassers are neither isolated from the rest of the staff and the leaders nor dominate the rest of the organization. The second problem can also develop if you hire a direct mail professional or any other professional fundraiser. That is that the professional fundraiser will want the organization to focus its energies and research on issues that make it easy to raise money. These may not be the same issues which are really the concerns of the members. Those issues which pay off best in canvassing or direct mail may not be the issues which will build the organization and bring in new members. This is why it is essential that the elected leaders of an organization continue to raise money in addition to their canvassing or mail program, and that they make sure the fundraiser works for the leaders and not the opposite.

Bibliography

Fundraising in the Public Interest. Section 3: "Knock, Knock . . . Who's There. A Citizen's Guide to Door-to-Door Canvassing." David L. Grubb and David R. Zwick. Fundraising in the Public Interest, P.O. Box 19404, Washington, D.C. 20036. 186 pp. 1976, $4.50. Make checks to: Public Citizen, Inc. An introduction to professional door-to-door canvassing. What you need, how it works, and samples of forms, ads and "pitches." Unfortunately, the samples are limited to one professional canvassing program, while there are many different working models in the country today. Be sure to interview several canvassing directors to get other ideas on how to adapt canvassing to work best for your own group.

Canvassing by Members

If you want to do an occasional door-to-door solicitation in the community to raise money quickly using your own members, read the pages on canvassing in: *Helping NOW Grow—Fundraising.* Chicago Chapter, National Organization for Women, Room 1501, 53 W. Jackson, Chicago, IL 60604. 1975. 20 pp. $2. Explains in detail how Chicago NOW raised $200 for local ERA effort with fifteen people in two hours on a Sunday afternoon.

NEWSLETTERS

Most membership organizations have some sort of newsletter which they use to communicate with the members, publish original research, and promote the organization. You can make money with newsletters two ways. One way is to sell subscriptions, and the other is to sell advertising.

Selling subscriptions is usually the least profitable. In order to encourage new people to join, most groups include the subscription to the newsletter in the price of the dues. In fact, *all* that members get for belonging to some groups is the newsletter. In order to make their information available to the largest audience, most groups try to keep their subscription prices as low as possible. For those groups in which "member" and "subscriber" are synonymous, this means the subscription price is kept low so that the dues are kept low. Thus they make very little profit, if any, from selling subscriptions.

The way to make money with a newsletter is to sell advertising space. This is how almost all magazines make money. When you start you can have members volunteer to sell the ads. Build in some competition between clubs or committees to promote sales. You can even divide the ad displays by area, which is another incentive to make the Chelsea chapter want to sell more than the Dorchester chapter.

For an ongoing money-maker, after you have worked out the most profitable newsletter format and advertising price arrangements, hire someone to sell the ads. This makes a good part-time job for a member, and gives the responsibility of selling a monthly amount to a professional rather than volunteer fundraisers.

For more information on selling ads, use the advice in:

Helping NOW Grow—Fundraising. Chicago NOW, 53 West Jackson, Rm. 1501, Chicago, IL 60604. 1975. 20 pp. $2.00. Simply adapt it for monthly renewals instead of annual renewals.

For more advice on the writing, editing, and printing of newsletters, see:

How to Do Leaflets, Newsletters and Newspapers. Nancy Brigham. The New England Free Press, 60 Union Square, Somerville, MA 02143. 1976. 44 pp., $1.25.

SERVICES

Services can make money when you run them like a business. You do it by selling your work instead of by selling things. Services can also pay off with positive publicity on your energy and creativity. Since all you need is lots of pep, service fundraisers are naturals for children and young adults. Remember Amy Carter's lemonade stand?

Service fundraisers might include charging by the hour or by the job to:

Walk dogs or wash dogs
Babysit

Put on birthday parties
Pick up newspapers for the recycling center
Outside work: wash windows, rake leaves, mow lawns, shovel snow
Errand service
Wash or park or fix cars or bikes
Address envelopes or Christmas cards
Distribute samples
Serve as a "typical consumer" for advertising agencies to test their ads, jingles and commercials
Take movies or photographs of kids or families
You can also ask at your State Employment Agency for temporary jobs.

Some groups run regular, year-round services as professional businesses. They let the members keep a percentage of the money they raise. Since it costs money to participate in any group, for car fare, meals, phone calls, postage and babysitting, this a good way to recruit part-time paying work for your volunteers and raise money for the organization at the same time.

For the best advice on running service fundraisers, get:

Ways and Means Handbook—A Chairman's Guide to Money Making Projects. The Sperry and Hutchinson Co., Consumer Relations, 2900 W. Seminary Dr., Fort Worth, TX 76133. 1964. 25¢. 34 pp. This is *the best* how-to on services; see pp. 18-19.

For the best advice and most examples for kids, get:

Good Cents—Every Kid's Guide to Making Money. The Amazing Life Games Co. and Friends. Boston, MA. Houghton Mifflin Co. 1974. 128 pp. $5.00. 44 projects for kids, which are adaptable to anyone with little seed money, less time, but lots of energy.

Talent Bank

Instead of running one service, like catering or deliveries, set up a "talent bank." Ask the members to record on a card what work they can do, what they would like to do, and when they are available to work. Then publicize the "Metropolis Talent Bank". Make your reputation for having (or finding) the right person to do any odd jobs. Then if a club needs a speaker, or a family needs a Santa Claus, or a company needs its valentines addressed, they will learn to call you. You will need a variety of talents, from the strong and boring, like shoveling snow, to the exotic and entertaining, like telling fortunes. This will allow you to find work for a larger number of volunteers.

Have a special division called the "Quitters' Relief Corps," consisting of all the members who are good with their hands. They relieve the folks who find they really can't build a color TV from a kit, or hook a rug with all the state flowers, or panel their den. The "Quitters' Relief Corps" allows them to save face and save their investment. One group even saved a marriage after the man of the house had all the pieces for not one but *two* sailboats hopelessly mixed up in his basement. His wife needed the basement for a wedding reception, and either the boat pieces or the man had to go. The town Talent Bank built the boats (one went to the YMCA), and saved the happy home.

THE SPEAKERS BUREAU

When you need more money, one question to ask is: "What are we giving away now, that we could be charging money for?" In other words, "What are we good at?" and "What do other people want?" Some examples might include charging a fee for giving advice on welfare regulations, tenants' rights, property tax changes, credit rules, or job possibilities. You can also charge money for people to hear your leaders speak about your issues.

A speakers bureau takes advantage of the fact that you have an exciting organization with something to say and someone to say it. Begin with a publicity campaign to make your group *the* source of expertise on your issue and make your leader the authority. The second is more important than the first for selling speakers. There are hundreds of consumer organizations, but Ralph Nader gets all the invitations. The key to success is TV. When your leaders are recognized from TV they become "somebody"—an expert. Of course they must also *be,* or become, experts on the issue before their first speeches.

When you are just getting started, place your leaders on as many TV and radio talk shows as possible. Your local publicity guide should list the shows which take guests. If you do not have a publicity guide, make your own list of talk shows from the newspaper's TV directory. Call them all. Tell the producer who you are, who your leaders are, and what topics they can discuss. It is best if you can link it to a current event—"Mrs. Gonzales, who will be testifying on nursing home abuses at the Senate hearings tomorrow . . ."

In addition to the TV and radio talk shows, fill all the free speaking engagements you get to give the leaders experience in giving their speech and fielding questions.

After your speakers have some experience and the organization has built its reputation through research, exposés in the press, and testimony before government bodies, you can launch the speakers bureau. Get copies of the brochures from the professional bureaus listed in the phone book under "Lecture Bureau." Use these as models to make up your own brochure using photographs of the leaders, provocative titles for their speeches, short descriptions of the speakers, and a history of the group. You can also offer slide presentations and training workshops as well as speeches.

Selling the Speakers

Give your service a name and buy a listing under "Lecture Bureaus" in the phone book. Print up about 200 brochures and mail them to the program chairpeople of all the civic organizations, professional associations, churches, and schools in your area. They are all listed in the phone book. You can also mail to the director of student activities and student government president at all the colleges and universities in the state.

Follow-up with telephone calls, to confirm that they have received your brochure and to sell your speakers. The best people to work with over the long run are the student activities people and the student government leaders. They get a large amount of money each year from "student activities" charges. Since they have to spend all of it every year in order to justify taxing the students, they are ideal sources of speaker's fees for your group.

Fees

Make a sliding scale based on the number of people in the audience, the group's ability to pay, and the type of presentation they want. A dollar a head works well for group charges, unless the group is a professional association or business group, in which case charge a minimum of $50. You will have to learn what the market will bear in your area, but most groups charge from $25 for appearing on a panel to $200 for running a daylong workshop.

The advantages to you of having other groups pay for the leaders are:
1. You raise money.
2. You really do limit the demands on the leaders.
3. You have a criterion for determining who is serious about wanting to learn more about your issues and hearing your speaker. If they will pay, they want it; if they won't pay, then they don't want it, regardless of what else they tell you.
4. Your speaker will speak to larger audiences. If the chamber of commerce pays $200 to hear your president, the chamber's program chairperson has to justify the expenditure by turning out

a big group to hear the speech. If the speaker comes for free, it doesn't matter to anyone—except perhaps the speaker—how big the audience is.

5.   Since we all suffer from consumer brainwashing, we "know" that the more something costs, the better it is. This works both ways. The audience will pay more attention knowing they paid for an expert, and the speaker gets a real ego-boost knowing someone will pay $200 to hear him or her.

HANDLING COMPLAINTS

Common complaints about your fees and the answers that work are:

1)   "I thought you people wanted to help the public."

A.   We sure do. It costs us $50,000 a year to run our program. We raise all of our money ourselves, and our program will help you too. So we will have to ask you for an honorarium.

2)   "Con Ed is sending Peter Power and we don't have to pay for him. Why should we pay to hear your side?"

A.   You already paid for Peter Power. His *job* is to give speeches for Con Ed and his salary comes out of your rates. Our leaders are all volunteers. They donate their fees to the work of the group so all the citizens of Metropolis have someone to speak for them against Con Ed.

3)   "But this is a real opportunity for you to talk to us! You want money too?"

A.   We get more requests for speakers than we can handle. All our leaders are volunteers. They do all their work for the group in addition to their regular jobs. So the only way we can limit the demands on their time is to ask people to pay.

4)   "Why should we pay for Mrs. Washington? She's just a housewife."

A.   That's right, she is a housewife, which is why she will be able to communicate with your audience better than some academic egg-head who will put them to sleep. She is also president of the Metropolis Concerned Citizens by virtue of her election by 1,500 people at our convention in October. Can 1,500 people be wrong?

EXCEPTIONS

There are times when it really *is* an "opportunity" to address a crowd, such as the keynote at an important convention. In this case, the publicity and the goodwill of the other group are more important than the money. This is a political decision rather than a fundraising decision.

PAYMENT: Checks should be made payable to the organization. If for any bookkeeping or political reason the check must be made payable to the leader instead of the group, the leader endorses the check to the group and is reimbursed for the difference it will make on his or her income taxes. Leaders are also reimbursed for any money they have to spend to make the speech, such as carfare, baby-sitting, or meals.

Bibliography:

Speaking Out. #299. League of Women Voters of the United States, 1730 M Street, N.W., Washington, D.C. 20036. 1977. One page. 15¢. How to set up a speakers bureau.

Leading Film Discussions. League of Women Voters of the City of New York, 817 Broadway, New York, N.Y. 10003. 1972. 42 pp. $2.00. Excellent guide on planning a program and leading a discussion as well as tips on operating sound and projection equipment.

Chapter 9
Publicity

Good fundraising is inseparable from good publicity. Your fundraising events attract public attention to the group, and publicity will attract customers to the fundraising events.

The publicity committee is the only exception to the rule "more is better." Every other fundraising committee works to attract as many volunteers as possible. The publicity committee, on the other hand, works best with only one or two people who will do a consistent, competent job.

Recruiting a Publicity Chairperson. You need to find a person who will make a commitment to do the job for a year. It works well if you have one person who heads the committee for a year, and another who is assistant for the same year and becomes head the next year. The ideal person is articulate, well informed, likes to talk about the group, writes clearly, and meets deadlines. They must understand that their job is to promote the entire organization, and especially the elected leaders, but not themselves. From a practical point of view, news people need to work with someone who is accessible, intelligent, and honest. Your publicity people must be able to make and receive phone calls during the day. Typing and secretarial skills are an advantage. Although the publicity chairperson's job is fun and sometimes even glamorous, it is also hard work. It involves a good deal of monotonous work like typing envelopes and mailing releases. Be sure your candidate realizes this and accepts both parts of the job.

TRAINING A PUBLICITY CHAIRPERSON: New publicity people should order and read the books listed at the end of this chapter to learn the mechanics of working with the press. The best help your committee can get is advice from an experienced volunteer publicity chairperson or a friendly professional publicist. They should try to get "adopted" by a veteran to get impartial, objective criticism of their press releases and publicity ideas. The most important information to get from a veteran is a current list of relevant members of the working press in your town, and some indication of their individual interests. Some high school adult education or college evening classes offer courses on publicity for community organizations. Encourage your publicity people to take one of these.

What Is Publicity?

Publicity, for our purposes, is all the information about your organization that you can get before the public. You should think of it in two categories. The first is general image publicity—all the work you do to create a positive impression of the organization. The second is fundraising publicity—information used to introduce the organization to potential donors, plus all the promotion you do to boost profits for a specific event.

GENERAL PUBLICITY: You need a strategy and an annual calendar for your general image publicity just as you need them for your fundraising. Although there will be spontaneous interviews and stories initiated by the press, most of the press coverage you will get will come because it was planned by your P.R. person.

First of all, make a list of what you have to "sell" to the press —your expertise on the issues, your admirable leaders, your actions, your testimony, your meetings, and your fundraising events. Lay out an annual calendar of events: the convention, election of officers, major hearings and testimony, major fundraising events, and major meetings. After you know what is scheduled, make a plan for getting the maximum publicity from each event. Be sure to treat the press fairly. If you give the morning paper an exclusive on your nursing home study, give the evening paper the next exclusive on car repair prices. If you give one television station the first interview with the newly elected president, give its rival station the first interview after you win the property tax reform.

In terms of your fundraising efforts, the purpose of general image publicity is to create a positive image of the organization in the minds of the public at large. People should identify the name of the group with the idea of a growing, effective and efficient organization. You want people to be able to say, "I saw your meeting with the mayor on TV. You know, my taxes are way too high too. I'm sure glad you're trying to do something about it," or "I read the story about your president in the *Gazette*. Gosh, I'm a working woman too, and I sure like it when someone tells how it really is for us. It's about time they reported that women work because they have to, instead of that outdated drivel about 'pin money'." You want to make people identify with your leaders and goals. Good publicity makes people realize that your organization is a good investment, because you are doing what they want done and saying what they want said.

The first goal of the general publicity program is this creation of a positive image in the minds of the public at large. The second goal is the creation of a positive image in the minds of the members. It is important that the members think of themselves as winners. You cannot take their attitude for granted. It is human nature for people to wonder "Is this doing any good? Does anyone know what we're doing? Does anyone care?"

The members need to know that what they are doing *matters*. Getting attention from the public via coverage in the newspapers and TV lets members know they are recognized and they are appreciated. As a side effect, press coverage, especially TV coverage, will deepen the members' commitment to the success of the organization. They gain a sense of responsibility from being—among their friends and neighbors—a spokesperson for that organization that's on the evening news all the time. They want the group to succeed because they are identified with it and their reputations are on the line.

Fundraising publicity

In addition to your general image publicity, you need to prepare a package to introduce your group to new people.

CLIPPINGS: To introduce your group to people with money, supplement your own material with copies of the good press coverage you have received. Systematically clip stories about the group and mount them on paper. Record the name of the newspaper or magazine, the date, page, and edition. All your clippings should be preserved in chronological order so you can prepare a package of clippings on the organization as a whole, or a package of clippings on specific issues. For an introductory fundraising package, include a variety of your best clippings. For example, an effective package would have a neighborhood weekly paper's in-depth article on the leader, a daily newspaper front page story on your research project, a feature story on the accomplishments of the organization, a national magazine story on your most important issue featuring your group as a good example, and an editorial from a daily newspaper paper products. The brochure introduces you to the public. If you praising the organization's stand on the issue.

FACT SHEETS OR BROCHURES: In addition to your collection of clippings, you should prepare a fact sheet or brochure to introduce your group. The information is the same in both cases. Include the history of the organization, the purpose, the current leaders, the current program, significant accomplishments, how to join, and flattering quotes from celebrities. A fact sheet can be typed and mimeographed on paper that will cost about $7 per thousand copies.

A brochure is usually produced on heavier paper, using professional typesetting and design, so it will cost you about $30 per thousand copies. It is perfectly all right to use an obviously low cost, economy-model fact sheet when you start. People will understand that your group is new and small, so they will admire your economy on the fact sheet as long as they get all the facts. When the group is older, larger, and more solvent, spend money on your paper, especially brochures that go to new people you are going to ask for money. It is smart in the long run to invest in professional design and good want to give the image of a successful, effective organization, make up clear, strong, straightforward brochures.*

You can round out your introductory package with a copy of your newsletter, copies of original research reports, copies of complimentary letters (used with permission of the author), and copies of your testimony before government committees. A short letter of introduction from the president, the clippings, and the fact sheet are the minimum you need when you write to ask for an appointment with a potential donor. Use all the written materials to give donors background on who you are, what you do, how you do it, and why you need more money. Do the asking in person.

AUDIO-VISUAL AIDS: In my opinion, audio-visual aids will never replace sincerity and intelligence when you are asking for money. I think most movies, video-tapes and slide shows are just a waste of time in fundraising. However, in fairness it must be said that many successful fundraisers swear by the audio-visual aid. They never ask for money without their props. If you want to use these devices when asking for money, here is how to do it. But you'll probably find you can raise enough money without them.

Slide Show: The simplest, cheapest, quickest, and most flexible way to tell a story about your group is the slide show. If you can get one or more photographers to donate their services, all you need to pay for is the film and the processing. A slide show is an excellent format for showing contrasts; for example, show the luxurious homes of the county board members and then show the humble bungalows the senior citizens will lose because of extortionate property taxes set by these county board members. The advantage of a slide show is that it is easy to revise and update pieces of the show without having to re-do the entire show.

---

*However, don't go overboard. Some of the big hospitals put out hundred-page fancy booklets loaded with photographs and encased in slick embossed covers. The effect produced is: "If they can afford this kind of printing, how can they need my money?" Or "If they are spending all their money on printing, what's left for the patients?" Your goal should be a top quality *short* brochure.

VIDEO-TAPE: The best of all possible publicity pieces is a video-tape of a TV news show featuring your organization. A TV documentary is much better than your self-produced video-tape, especially for an action organization, because the TV news people can usually get access to the people on the other side of the issue. Ironically, the target of an action campaign, especially a corporate target, will often over-react and make your case for you. Even a one-sided news show about the group is excellent because it comes from a believable independent source.

For a local TV station, contact station manager, the news director, the director of public affairs, or a friendly reporter or producer. Tell him or her what exciting events are coming up and why your group is unique. Watch all your local channels to find out which one would most likely be sympathetic to your program. It will take several calls before you sell the director on a feature story on your group, but it is worth the effort. Make an agreement ahead of time to get a copy of the finished story (you will have to supply a video cassette). Finally, if everything works out, do all you can to give the TV crew complete background information and the best possible working conditions.

For a national news or public affairs show, write the producer at his or her office (usually in New York or Los Angeles), and explain your group and your program. Send a copy of your letter to the star of the show. Mention the local importance of your work but emphasize the national implications.

If a station or network chooses to do a feature on your group at its own initiative, try to get a copy of the print as soon as possible. Write the director of broadcasting. Explain that you are a not-for-profit group, and say where and how you plan to use the copy. The TV people should be glad to help as long as you are not planning to re-broadcast the show.

It is also easy to make a video-tape yourself. Make arrangements to borrow equipment from your local university or private school. Anybody can learn to operate video equipment in about an hour, and the tape is ready immediately. Video-tape can be shown on any television set.

Video-tape can also be used in many other ways, especially in training salespeople and leaders. If your local cable TV system has an "access" channel, video-tape is indispensable for making your own shows to get your message to the public. If you know you have the talent and patience to produce the tapes, and outlets to show them, you may choose to buy your own video equipment. Basic equipment will cost about $2,500.

How To Promote An Event

When the organization chooses to do a fundraising event, the publicity people become promoters. Their job is to make the upcoming event the most exciting, unique and sexy occasion happening that weekend. It should be so attractive that people will drive for miles through a blinding snowstorm to attend.

First, think of how you yourself plan a free weekend. Discuss all the ways you personally decide where you are going to go. Rank them in order. If there is one paper or one column that everyone reads first, put most of your effort into getting into that paper or column. After you have listed all the possibilities and put them in order, work systematically from the top down to get your event prominently promoted in each one.

Start early. You will need to send public service announcements to radio and TV stations at least three weeks in advance, and some magazines need copy six weeks in advance of the first of the month in which your event occurs. Ask a veteran for advice on the best people to call and the deadlines for each medium. If you plan to use specialty advertising like buttons or T-shirts you will need to order them at least four weeks in advance.

Here is a list of all the possibilities for free advertising and promotion. In addition, if you have the budget for a big money fundraiser, you can buy advertising space and time. Unless you are spending more than $10,000 to put on your event, stick to free publicity. Remember, even "free" publicity will require an investment for printing, paper, and postage.

PRESS RELEASE—Include description of event, date, goal, celebrities attending, special angles like recipes, chairperson. Send to all local media.

CALENDAR NOTICES—Mail one month ahead to the "What's Happening" calendars in daily and weekly newspapers, and two months or more ahead to monthly magazines.

SIGNS AND MARQUEES ON BUILDINGS—Write the head of the firm that owns the building and ask for free use of the sign.

FEATURE STORIES—Call and write feature department editors of daily papers. Emphasize photo possibilities. Children and animals still appeal.

RADIO-TV PSA's—See "If You Want Air Time" booklet.

FREE CLASSIFIEDS—Offered by some weekly newspapers. Read the rules and send early.

CELEBRITIES—Good for column notes or TV/radio plugs dropped ingenuously on talk shows.

INVITATIONS—To local pastors, politicians and community leaders. It's courteous, and promotes word of mouth publicity.

CHURCH BULLETINS—Mail to pastor two weeks in advance to include in bulletin Sunday before event.

HUGE SIGN—Make and hang over event site two weeks before event.

FLIERS—8½ x 11 inches, printed on bright paper. Tape up on trees and telephone poles around neighborhood, ask other community groups to hand out at their events the weekend before your event, include as stuffers in other programs, and hand out at busy intersections.

POSTERS—11 x 16 inches on heavier, colored paper. Have a team of people hang them up in windows of local merchants, train stations, YWCA, YMCA, and homes near event site. Put up on bulletin boards in schools, churches, bars, theatres, and youth centers.

COUPONS—You can add on coupons to your own newsletter, fliers, letters, or invitations. Offer free entry, free pony ride, per cent discount on merchandise, free glass of wine with dinner, or free dessert.

RADIO SHOW PREMIUMS—Give radio show hosts a quantity of tickets to your sports event, concert or play. Disk jockeys use them as premiums to give away "to the ninth person who calls 555-5789."

COLUMN NOTES—Give an exclusive bit of gossip about a celebrity or unique attraction to a gossip column writer.

OTHER ORGANIZATIONS' NEWSLETTERS—Ask for a paragraph plug on your event in other groups' newsletters. Promise to reciprocate.

YOUR OWN NETWORKS—

Mail to *donors list*.

Feature article, photo, and big ad in your own *newsletter*.

Activate your *telephone chain* to be sure everyone is called.

Build up *word of mouth* promotion with hoopla. Buttons and bumper stickers promote discussion, as do publicity stunts, like milking a cow on the lawn of the city church to promote the "County Fair" bazaar.

Bibliography

BEST FOR THE MECHANICS OF WRITING AND PLACING PRESS RELEASES AND PUBLIC SERVICE ANNOUNCEMENTS:

If You Want Air Time. National Association of Broadcasters, 1771 N St., N.W., Washington, D.C. 20036. 1974. 18 pp. Free. Good, clear how-to for radio and TV; includes six sample public service announcements.

Publicity Handbook: A Guide for Publicity Chairmen. The Sperry and Hutchinson Co., Consumer Services, 2900 W. Seminary Dr., Fort Worth, TX 76133. 1972. 24 pp. 25¢. Clear, simple, thorough how-to. Especially good for the beginner.

WRITTEN FOR SPECIAL GROUPS:

Feminist Organizations:

How to Make the Media Work for You. Catherine Samuels. Women's Action Alliance, 370 Lexington Ave., New York, NY 10017. 1974. 39 pp. $3. Written for women's organizations. Covers both publicity—press conferences, interviews and promotion—brochures, special TV programming.

Minority Organizations:

Public Relations—How to Use It. Scholarship, Education and Defense Fund for Racial Equality (SEDFRE). One Penn Plaza, New York, NY 10001. 1973. 20 pp. $1. Excellent concise explanation written especially for small minority groups.

Electoral Political Organizations:

The How-to Press and PR Handbook, or, I Like Your Song-and-Dance, But Is It News? Barbara Fultz Martinez & Roberta Weiner. National Women's Political Caucus, Third Floor, 1921 Pennsylvania Ave., N.W., Washington, D.C. 20006. 25 pp. $1. Good, with political focus.

Arts Organizations, or groups doing theatrical benefits:

The Publicity Survival Manual for Small Performing Arts Organizations. Yuri Rasovsky, Editor, Chicago Alliance for the Performing Arts, Suite 1810, 176 W. Adams, Chicago, IL 60603. 55 pp. $10. Good general information (valuable for all groups) on press contact, promotion and publicity. Best on bulk mail. (Published annually)

Big budget organizations which buy advertising:

Mediability: A Guide for Nonprofits. Len Biegel and Aileen Lubin. Taft Publications, Inc., Washington, D.C. 1975. 110 pp. $6.50. How-to on all aspects of media use for nonprofit organizations; best on TV and radio.

GENERAL COMMUNICATIONS:

Amy Vanderbilt's Everyday Etiquette. Amy Vanderbilt. Bantam Books, 666 Fifth Avenue, New York, NY 10019. 1974. 290 pp. $1.95. See especially "Correspondence" for the correct way to address letters to clergy, military personnel, and congresspersons. Also business etiquette, especially "telephone courtesy."

The Elements of Style. William Strunk, Jr., and E. B. White. The Macmillan Company, 866 Third Avenue, New York, NY 10022. 1972. 78 pp. $1.25. The best style manual. This book is the model for anything you write: clear, concise, full of memorable examples and good humor.

Help! I Have to Write a Report. Scholarship, Education and Defense Fund for Racial Equality (SEDFRE). One Penn Plaza, New York, NY 10001. 1971. $1. 18 pp. Excellent, clear advice to help everyone from the first-term secretary who has to write up meeting minutes to the president who has to prepare an annual report for the board.

How to Do Leaflets, Newsletters and Newspapers. Nancy Brigham. The New England Free Press, 60 Union Square, Somerville, MA 02143. 1976. 44 pp. $1.25. Wonderful, clear and thorough manual covers start to finish production and editorial work on leaflets, newsletters and newspapers. Indispensable for the novice; valuable for the veteran. Packed with examples.

How to Talk With Practically Anybody About Practically Anything. Barbara Walters. Dell Publishing Co., New York, NY 10017. 1970. 241 pp. $1.50. Excellent practical advice for anyone from the experienced speaker to the person "strangled with panic." Chapter ten includes "The care and handling of a guest speaker" and "Tips for when you're the speaker."

Projecting Your Image. How to produce a slide show. #296. League of Women Voters of the United States, 1730 M Street, N.W., Washington, D.C. 20036. 1977. 4 pp. 30¢. Excellent guide to help you decide when a slide show is the best way to tell your story, and step-by-step advice on putting it together.

Recruiting Volunteers: Views, Techniques and Comments. National Center for Voluntary Action. 1785 Massachusetts Ave., N.W., Washington, D.C. 20036. 1976. 24 pp. $1. How to recruit volunteers from all age and income brackets through the media and special events. What to do with them once they respond.

Chapter 10
Making Book

I recommend that the fundraiser raise funds and leave all the bookkeeping, legal and tax work to the treasurer or bookkeeper. However, the fundraiser still needs to understand the accounting system as well as keep track of the general financial strength of the organization.

The first thing to do is get advice from an experienced bookkeeper and a lawyer. Second, get the books listed at the end of the chapter. Third, try to recruit on-going legal and accounting help from someone in the organization.

Legal and Taxes

Be sure you get started on a firm foundation. In addition to your state incorporation, the organization also needs a federal tax status. The IRS employs people to give you advice. Also ask an experienced lawyer and accountant to help. If you do not already have tax-deductible status under section 501(c)3, of the Internal Revenue Service Code, investigate whether it is to your advantage to do so.

It is very important in many cases to get your charter and federal tax status as soon as possible. Done right, they enable you to apply for exemption from:
1. Social security (FICA) on payroll employees
2. Federal unemployment taxes
3. Some state taxes (each state is different)
4. Local sales taxes
5. Bulk rate postage at "for-profit" rates
6. Local personal property taxes

If your not-for-profit organization is paying these taxes, ask a lawyer how to amend your charter so you can pay the least amount of taxes that is legal.

Accounting

The clearest explanation of how to set up your records and keep track of your money is the *Bookkeeping Handbook for Low-Income*

Citizen Groups prepared by the National Council of Welfare of Canada.

This is a crystal clear, step-by-step outline of how to handle your bookkeeping, explained in words non-accountants can understand. The Handbook committee members have made an enormous contribution to small and new community organizations: They explain everything about bookkeeping without using the words "credit" or "debit." Any group in the U.S. can use this book perfectly well too. The only exception is the discussion of how to do a payroll (the Canadian system is different than the U.S. system). Since payroll requirements are different in every state, the best place to get advice on payroll bookkeeping is from an experienced bookkeeper in your state.

Malvern Gross' *Financial and Accounting Guide for Nonprofit Organizations* is the best reference book on accounting for non-profit organizations and will be very useful for any size group. See the bibliography for other useful books.

Best of all, hire or recruit a competent, conscientious bookkeeper. They can keep the books, pay the bills, and do the reports. Then the fundraiser need only keep track of the overall financial picture.

Ideas from a Non-accountant

In addition to the advice in these books, here are a few suggestions to help you handle money. I am not an accountant, but these are a few ideas I have found from experience to be helpful for those of us without mathematical talent or accounting skills.

1.   Always make a list of your income and expenses from each event and from the fundraising effort as a whole. You should know every week where you stand financially—every day in a tight period. This is your early-warning system to tell you when to step up the work.

2.   Keep track of *all* your money. It can get confusing when you have money in checking accounts, savings accounts, special funds, petty cash and on deposit at the post office for second- and third-class postage. You do not have to adopt a complicated double entry accounting system. (Although the bookkeeper may use one.) Just keep track on a chart where all your money is now (today), whom you owe money, and who owes you money.

Even if you have an outside accounting firm, or a computerized accounting system, it is important that someone in the group keep track of the day-to-day financial picture. The best person to do this is the one who approves expenditures. You need someone to keep a tight rein on your spending. The smaller the budget, the stingier you need to be. Every group needs a Scrooge to say, "No, you can't print two-color posters to help the turnout for next week's meeting. Use the telephone network, for free, instead."

If you have no one who scrutinizes your money from the moment it comes in to the time it is spent, you will spend more money than you need to. You will order too much paper, permit too many long-distance phone calls, and buy too many supplies. All this happens because you are too busy to have someone figuring out how much paper you actually *need,* as opposed to how much you will use if it is delivered to your door. It is human nature to over-project, over-spend and under-utilize what you already have, unless someone controls spending in the context of the yearly and monthly budgets as well as the needs of the moment.

3. Keep all of your bills and receipts from the very first day. Even if you think it will not be necessary to set up books, "because we can win this in three months," keep all your bills *just in case* the fight takes longer, or the group decides to move on to a second fight after winning the first. You can never put enough notes on the bills. Write down the number of the check with which you paid the bill, the date, and what the bill was for: "posters for May 5th rally" or "additional wiring to run mimeograph." Then, if you eventually decide to set up books, you can re-create the past from your bills and receipts. Lots of notes on the bills and checks are also a tremendous help to a future treasurer or fundraiser who needs to research any expenses.

4. Shop for a bank. The law sets interest limits which are the same for every bank. This does not mean that every bank is exactly the same. First, you should look for a bank and a savings and loan that support the community by lending as much money in their primary service area as the people in that community deposit. Ask a bank officer for a report on where the bank gets its money, and where it makes loans. In some states this is public information required of all lending institutions. In other states you have to ask each institution for it. If the bank or S&L will not disclose its lending data, assume they have something to hide and give your business to someone else.

You can always have more than one bank. You may want to use a nearby bank for deposits if you handle a lot of cash every day; for example, from a door-to-door canvassing program, or if you get large amounts of cash from special events. You can still keep most of your money in another bank with a positive lending record and helpful personnel.

You can also deposit your money in more than one kind of financial institution. For example, you may want to keep a limited checking account at a good bank, a savings account at a good savings and loan, and an account in the community credit union which you choose to support for political reasons. Your banker can help you compare the advantages of each type of institution. Of course remember that the fewer accounts you have the easier the bookkeeping will be.

5.   Look for an officer in the bank who will help you. There are lots of services a bank can give you in addition to a checking account. You need to find someone who cares about you and the success of your organization to help you get the most the bank has to offer. A bank can give you:

Advice on the different types of savings accounts and certificates of deposit.

Advice on investments.

Advice on payroll taxes and tax law.

Advice on employee benefits.

Lock box service for the returns from a direct mail program. All the returns are mailed directly to the bank itself. Banks will handle the returns and deposit the checks for a fee per check. This means you do not need a person in the office to handle the checks. It makes it impossible to lose checks or have them stolen from the office. Get competitive bids for lock box services, since there is a wide range in bank charges. Also, get advice from other groups that run big mailing programs to assess the quality of the service.

Advice on establishing a line of credit if you have a lot of money going in and out. This is important for political campaigns where you get big donations and need to make big expenditures quickly.

Advice on borrowing money.

Help on mundane weekly transactions; for example, issuing and redeeming state lottery tickets.

6.   Invest your money so that it makes money for you. If you get any foundation or government grants, your whole annual grant may come in one or two large checks. Many ongoing grass roots fundraising programs have marked seasonal money bulges. Most churches, for example, receive much more money in the winter months than in the summer months; conversely a door-to-door canvassing program often nets a lot more in the summer than in the winter, especially in bad climates.

Try to keep only enough money in your checking account to cover two months' expenses. There are two reasons for this. First, all the rest of your money can be earning interest. Second, you won't be tempted to spend next month's money or to think you are richer than you really are. Your banker or accountant can tell you how to balance your long-term income goals and your short term cash needs.

7. If you need to borrow money, for instance to pay for the postage for your first direct mail campaign, or for advertising in a political campaign, always try first to get an interest-free loan from a friend of the group. This is definitely a case of "people give to people." Since the assets of most new community organizations are some second-hand furniture, rebuilt machines, and a lot of paper, the person who lends you money realizes you have no collateral except your word. It *is* possible to borrow interest-free money if people believe in your personal integrity and your organization's chance for success. In the world of high finance, the wheeler-dealers often raise money simply by trading promises with no collateral other than the stock in a fund they hope will work. In other words, you do not always have to have a lot of collateral to raise money. If people with money respect you and your group, you may be able to get an interest-free loan. At least ask your two or three best prospects for such a loan before you borrow from a bank and pay interest.

If you have to borrow money and pay interest, ask your banker what deal the bank can make. Then research your other possibilities: savings and loans, credit unions, or community co-ops which invest in the neighborhood. Some national organizations will lend affiliate chapters seed money for fundraising. Ask other groups in your area what they would recommend.

8.   Debt is a drag. It is an enormous drain on your time to keep putting off your creditors. It makes all your fundraising much more difficult because you are limited to smaller events. Worst of all, it is terrible for the morale of the entire organization. Try to set up your fundraising prudently at the beginning to avoid debt at any time.

However, there are reasons why you may find yourself in debt. New organizations that have never had a chance to handle money, gauge the risks of fundraising efforts, and predict the seasonal fluctuations of their income may incur a "cash flow problem." This simply means you need to spend more money right now than you have coming in right now. Your goal is to reverse this situation as quickly as possible.

First, step up your fundraising efforts. If you need to cut back on your program to devote more time to fundraising, do it.

Second, cut out all unnecessary spending. If you decide that salaries are necessary, but a Xerox machine is not, send the machine back.

Third, tell your creditors honestly what your situation is now and what your timetable will be for paying them. Some creditors, like the telephone company, will not wait. If you don't pay, it takes your phones away. Others, like printers or suppliers, may wait if you explain that due to extenuating circumstances you are unable to pay them at this time. Explain that you are launching your ad book campaign next week and can assure them of payment in sixty days. As long as they have a specific date to anticipate payment, they should wait. It is in their interest to keep you as a customer in the long run, so they may be patient while you are young and learning.

Fourth, make long-range plans to make your income more predictable. This includes making an annual strategy for fundraising, regularizing your current fundraising, (e.g., dues renewal), and asking your big donors, whether individuals or institutions, to schedule their donations at the best time for you. Obviously the best advice on debt is to make accurate plans so you don't fall into debt in the first place.

Here are just a few other things recommended by veterans:

1. Get a professional audit annually. Although it is expensive, you can ask the auditor to discount or donate the audit. The advantages of an audit are that it gives you an outside professional opinion on your books to show to funding sources, it forces you to get everything completely up-to-date once a year, and it can give you suggestions for improving your system as the organization grows and changes.

2. There will soon be legislation requiring not-for-profit organizations to disclose their fundraising costs. You should ask your accountant or a friendly CPA to keep you posted on pending state and federal legislation so you can comment on the bills in progress and be ready to meet the new requirements when they become law.

3. If your organization is less than eight months old when it applies for its 501(c)3 tax deductible status, it will get a temporary status called an advance ruling. This is good for two years. You have ninety days after the two years are up in which to file for your permanent status called the definitive ruling. If you do not file for a permanent status, you will no longer be able to receive tax deductible funds.

4. Remember that all non-profit organizations receiving more than $5,000 gross receipts in one year must file Form 990 with the Internal Revenue Service within five months after the end of the organization's fiscal year. The only exceptions are churches, missions and religious orders. It is your responsibility to file whether or not the IRS mails you the form.

Taxes Bibliography

All available from: Superintendent of Documents, U.S. Government Printing Office, Washington, D.C. 20402 or, Federal office building in large cities or Free from your Congressperson

FOR NEW GROUPS THAT NEED TO APPLY FOR FEDERAL TAX EXEMPTION:

How to Apply for Recognition of Exemption for an Organization. Publication 557. Internal Revenue Service. 20 pp. 45¢. Published every January. Tells you how to tell which tax exempt category you should apply for (there are 22) and the basic information of how to apply. Collect and understand all the information they ask for *before* you meet with your lawyer, to save yourself time and money.

Having read the above pamphlet and consulted a capable lawyer, you will probably want to apply for exemption as a "charitable, religious, scientific, testing for public safety, literary, education, or prevention of cruelty to children or animals" organization, which fall under section 501(c)3 and are tax-deductible. Ask for Form 1023. Or you may be a "civic league or social welfare organization," which fall under section 501(c)4 and are tax-exempt. Ask for Form 1024. If you are uncertain, ask for both and compare.

TO SUGGEST TO DONORS TO HELP THEM PREPARE THEIR INCOME TAXES:

Income Tax Deduction for Contributions. Publication 526. Internal Revenue Service. 8 pp. 35¢. Explains which organizations are deductible, as well as what amount and type of contributions (cash, property or services) can be deducted.

Valuation of Donated Property. Publication 561. Internal Revenue Service. 12 pp. 35¢. Explains how to determine "fair market value" on non-cash gifts, such as merchandise donated to a thrift shop, or securities such as stocks and bonds.
If you have questions, call the Internal Revenue Service and ask for the Exempt Organizations Branch.

OTHER:
Funding for Social Change: Volume I. Gaining Your Tax Exempt Status and Becoming an Employer. Stella Alvo, Susan Angus, and Kate Shackford. The United Methodist Voluntary Service, 475 Riverside Dr., New York, NY 10025. 1977. $2. 45 pp.

Accounting Bibliography

BEST FOR NON-ACCOUNTANTS AND BEGINNERS:

Bookkeeping Handbook for Low-Income Citizen Groups. The National Council of Welfare. Brooke Claxton Building, Ottawa, Ontario K1A 0K9 CANADA. 1973. 104 pages. Free. Clear, step-by-step instructions to understand getting and spending money. Explanation with samples of opening a checking account, starting journals, reconciling the bank statement, setting up a petty cash fund, preparing financial statements, keeping files, and much more.

BEST FOR ALL-PURPOSE REFERENCE:

Financial and Accounting Guide for Nonprofit Organizations. Malvern J. Gross, Jr., C.P.A. The Ronald Press Co., 79 Madison Avenue, New York, NY 10016. 1974. 572 pp. $16.00. Everything you need—concepts, financial statements, budgeting, control, taxes, books. This is the book that all the other books quote.

OTHER:

Do or Die: Survival for Nonprofits. James C. Lee. Taft Products, Inc., 1000 Vermont Ave., N.W., Washington, D.C. 20005. 1974. 102 pp. $7.50. "How for-profit business methods can be modified for use by the not-for-profit manager."

Financial Management for the Arts—A Guidebook for Arts Organizations. Charles A. Nelson and Frederick J. Turk. Associated Councils of the Arts, 1564 Broadway, New York, NY 10036. 1975. 52 pp. $4.50. This has the best explanation of how to estimate the "personnel cost by program," or how to figure how much each program costs you in terms of the staff's salaries. Since organizations which employ staff spend sixty to ninety per cent of their budgets on salaries, this is the best way to find out if your money is really being spent to accomplish your goals. It also has an excellent clear explanation of planning and budgeting, cash management, fund accounting, general accounting and financial organization. Includes twenty-three examples of budgets, reports and journal pages.

Money and Your Church. How to Raise More . . . How to Manage it Better. Manfred Holck, Jr. Keats Publishing, Inc., 212 Elm St., New Canaan, CT 06840. 1974. 189 pp. $7.95. (The author is both a former pastor and certified public accountant.) Especially good on bookkeeping and clear financial systems for small to medium sized churches. Includes the best chapter on purchasing, "Making Money by Spending Less."

Sylvia Porter's Money Book. How to Earn It, Spend It, Save It, Invest It, Borrow It—And Use It to Better Your Life. Sylvia Porter. Avon Books, 959 Eighth Ave., New York, NY 10019. 1975. $5.95. 1105 pp. Most complete reference book for non-accountants. Explains everything about money in words you can understand. Especially good explanation of investment choices.

Up Your Accountability—How to Up Your Serviceability and Funding Credibility by Upping Your Accountability. Paul Bennett, Taft Products, 1000 Vermont Ave., N.W., Washington, D.C. 20005. 1973. 65 pp. $7.95. Good, clear and useful.

Where Do All the $ Go? What Every Board & Staff Member of a Non-Profit Organization Should Know about Budgeting. Gerald G. Bowe, Jr. The New Hampshire Charitable Fund, One South St., Concord, NH 03301. 1975. 40 pp. $2.50. Covers accounting, bookkeeping and internal control; especially good on clarifying the vocabulary of accounting and introducing double-entry bookkeeping.

You Don't Know What You Got Until You Lose It. An Introduction to Accounting, Budgeting, and Tax Planning for Small, Nonprofit Organizations and Community Groups. Thomas F. Miller and G. R. Orser. The Support Center/The Community Management Center, 1424 16th St., N.W., Washington, D.C. 20036. The Support Center, 27 Maiden Lane, San Francisco, CA 94108. 1976. 32 pp. Free. This is the "Why" rather than the "How to." Includes a partial list of management support organizations.

If you receive grants, see also:

The Bread Game. The Realities of Foundation Fundraising. Herb Allen, Editor. Glide Publications, 330 Ellis St., San Francisco, CA 94102. $3.45. 1975. 96 pp. See especially Chapter 6: "Formation of a Tax-Exempt Organization," Chapter 7: "Suggested Accounting Procedures for Grantees," and Chapter 8: "Reporting on a Grant."

Chapter 11
Appendix

"Grass roots fundraising" is do-it-yourself fundraising. You use your own members and your own resources to raise money for your own organization. This Appendix will give you some suggestions on how to use the members' talents most profitably. Each entry illustrates a general fundraising principle:

1. The goal of your fundraising plan should be to make the most money using the least amount of the members' time. Just as you make long-range goals for the organization's program, make long-range goals for raising money. Use the *calendar* as a guide to help prepare next year's timetable.

2. Break the overall plan into manageable pieces. Divide the work in each activity to attract the most new people, develop the most leadership, and produce the most efficient event. Use the *schedule* for a rummage sale as a model plan to design a popular and profitable fundraiser.

3. Politicians and direct mail professionals have proven that the best people to ask for money are people who have already given you money. Clear, current and complete records make this easy. Use the *donor card* as a model to build a list of people who gave you money.

4. Democratic planning produces the best plans. Your own members will always invent the most workable and popular plan for your group. In addition, use the list of *where to get advice* to find other ideas you can adapt and improve for your own market.

5. It is important to continuously build the morale of the group and the momentum of the campaign. If an unexpected crisis befalls the group, and you lose money on an event, you must take action immediately to save the campaign. Use the advice and the low-overhead events listed in *how to rebound from a fund-loser* to get back on the right track.

6. Consciously work to make the fundraising both profitable for the organization and personally rewarding for each volunteer. Use the *exercises* to get the volunteers thinking about how others do

190

it, why they themselves give, and what new approaches will work. They should find that fundraising is more familiar and less forbidding than they thought.

7. Select books from the *bibliography* to get more information on grass roots fundraising and an introduction to other forms of fundraising such as capital campaigns, government resources and foundation grants.

8. Although this book does not cover grants, they can be an important component of your overall fundraising plan. For the best collection of current information and income tax reports by foundations in your area, use the *Foundation Center Regional Libraries*. They are free libraries with a professional librarian to help you.

9. If you want or need more training for your staff or leaders, consider the list of *training schools* for organizers and leaders. They offer excellent courses in all the skills one needs to build a successful organization.

Last, but not least, decide to have a good time while you raise the budget. Sharing successes, singing songs, and planning parties build the friendships that are the glue of the organization. The fellowship of fundraising festivities is just as important as the income. So have a good time—for fun and profit.

Appendix 1
How to Plan an Annual Fundraising Calendar

The goal of grass roots fundraising is to make the most money in the least time, maximizing the dollar return per member-hour expended. Long-range plans will increase the profits because you can schedule your events when there will be the most help, the best weather, and the least conflict with other events inside or outside the organization. If you plan your big events so they can be repeated every year at the best time, you will be able to make more money each year with less work.

Plan your calendar when you make up your budget for the next year. This would be November if you work on a regular calendar year, or August if you work on an academic year. When you complete the budget and know how much money you want to make from which kinds of events, then you can schedule the events and meetings to make the most money in the least time.

What to do:

1. *Buy a large calendar* with all twelve months on one sheet. It should have the secular and religious holidays printed on it.

2. *Eliminate the times that would be worst for fundraising.* Cross them off the calendar. These include:

    A. All three-day legal holiday week-ends.

    B. All state holidays.

C. All high religious holidays—Good Friday, Yom Kippur, etc.

D. The first and last weeks of school.

E. The week of April 15th (Income tax day).

F. Days of major sports events—Super Bowl Sunday, World Series.

G. In an election year, cross off the week before and the week after the primary and general elections.

(Adapt this for your organization. The Baptist Choir can ignore Yom Kippur; a high school club can ignore the week of April 15th; senior citizens can ignore the school schedule.)

3. Now *write in all the scheduled organizational events,* such as your convention and regular board meetings. Then consider whether you want to combine your fundraising event with the organizational event—for example, print the ad book for the convention— or to concentrate on fundraising when the organizational program is less hectic.

Scheduled organizational events include:

A. Convention.

B. Election of officers; installation of officers.

C. "Birthday"—anniversary of organization's formation.

D. Regular meetings—e.g., second Monday of every month.

4. Now schedule your fundraising events. Think about when you want the event to take place and when the best advance work will get done. Be sure to schedule time for the follow-up paper work. Discuss which events you will want to repeat annually for the next few years. Mark off the total time to prepare, produce, and follow up.

A. Schedule the annual repeatable events first.

B. Schedule your other fundraisers.

C. Schedule one purely social, break-even affair.

D. Schedule four quarterly finance committee meetings.

Sample planning progression

OCTOBER: COMMITTEE BUDGETS

Each committee or coalition sets its goals for the next year, plans the program to achieve those goals, and estimates what it will cost. For example, the property tax committee sets its goals to reform the property tax; it plans to prepare legislation to give senior citizens a refund on their property taxes from the state; it will want to take five busloads of people to the state capital two times to lobby; this will cost $350 per bus times five buses times two trips, or $3,500. Each committee should try to forecast its activities and expenses for the next twelve months.

NOVEMBER: FINAL BUDGET

The finance committee combines and refines all the committees' proposed budgets. They then prepare one over-all organizational budget. This is broken down by income from each source, and expenditure for each expense. The budget is duplicated and mailed to all voting members of the board with written explanation. The chairperson of the finance committee attaches a letter inviting calls for further explanation. The fundraising committee works out the calendar.

A. Schedule annual repeatable events:
Spring—Ad Book. Party to distribute book on April Fool's Day, April 1. Block out February 15 to April 15.
Eight weeks.
Summer—Rummage Sale August 1—five weeks, July 1 to August 7.
Autumn—Halloween Dinner Dance October 31—five weeks, October 1 to November 7.

B. Schedule other fundraisers:
January—launch membership drive—two week push, January 7 to January 21.
Direct Mail—Deliver to post office quarterly, March 1, June 1, September 1, and December 1.
Bingo—Every Friday except Good Friday.

C. Schedule one purely social event:
Plan one event just for the fun of getting together. Should summer be empty, picnics are good for getting people to mingle. Try to choose something for the whole family. In this sample there is nothing scheduled during the winter; we can all go Christmas caroling and have a pot luck supper in mid-December.
Christmas caroling and pot-luck supper—December 15.

D. Schedule four quarterly finance committee meetings: first Monday of the month—February, May, August and November. Committee approves direct mail for following month, supervises membership recruitment, and reviews budget.

DECEMBER: BUDGET APPROVAL

Decision-making board amends and approves budget. Board commits itself to raising the total amount of money needed.

Appendix 2

How to Schedule a Rummage Sale

Schedule each event as precisely and completely as you possibly can. Parkinson's observation (which can be verified whenever you have to do housework or filing) is that work expands to fill the time available. I think people are attracted to political campaigns because they know it will be an exciting, intense, short effort with a definite deadline. Win or lose, after election day, you're through.

In the same way, you can attract people to your fundraising project by making a detailed timetable with a definite deadline. Divide the work into manageable pieces for each person. Make a special effort to get a quick start and be sure to plan enough time at the end to complete all the paperwork.

This is a sample schedule for a sale of used goods. Since all the merchandise is donated your profit should be almost 100 percent. Your only costs are your ads, posters, coffee, photos and mailing. You can call it a garage sale, barn sale, white elephant sale, or something cutesy—Funky Junque, Trash and Treasures. Use this as a sample only—if necessary you could pull off a sale in three weeks instead of four, or get more elaborate and stretch it out over two months. This schedule could also be adapted to any other event which needs little seed money, such as a bake sale or an auction.

Adapt it to your membership and community. People United for Responsible Energy in Madison, Wisconsin held garage sales four weeks in a row—in the north, south, east and west parts of town. The members got around to see the other neighborhoods and PURE made more money each week by forwarding the leftover merchandise to next week's sale.

Groundwork

The fundraising chairperson and staff person have already researched:
1. which members have had experience with successful rummage sales;
2. which community people have run successful sales-type events and can give advice; and
3. which members are hard-working, imaginative people who will be eager to help and contribute ideas for the first meeting.

Now, four weeks before the event, you are ready for your first planning meeting.

Four Weeks Before—First Planning Meeting

First planning meeting. Decide to hold garage sale. Set goal (say $1,000). Determine how much merchandise you will need to reach goal.

Set date. One day or week-end. Check to make sure there are no conflicting events or holidays.

Choose location. Church parking lot, school basement, adjoining garages.

Choose chairperson for sale. He or she will work closely with fundraising chairperson.

Choose person to supervise publicity and hoopla.

Check to see if you need a permit or special insurance.

Ask each committee person to call his or her network to solicit merchandise. Donors need not be limited to members of organization. Learn by role-playing how to ask for merchandise and how to ask for a contribution if someone does not have merchandise to donate. Establish collection point for merchandise.

Decide what you will sell—have an interesting item donated already that callers will be able to mention when they do their calls; e.g., handmade quilt, TV, brass planter.

Set criteria for donations; clothing must be clean, marked for size and purchasable. You don't want garbage.

Decide whether you want to sell other things besides used goods; e.g., plants or baked goods. Decide whether you want to add other low-space, low-seed money fundraising events: face-painting, fortune-telling, raffle for best piece of merchandise.

Set next meeting in one week.

TWO DAYS AFTER FIRST MEETING—CHECK ON A QUICK START.

Sales chairperson calls everyone on committee to see that they have started calls. He or she should have a positive report to give committee members; e.g., "I've got four donations of merchandise and one cash contribution." The chairperson records the results the other committee members have to report.

FOUR DAYS AFTER FIRST MEETING—DOUBLE-CHECK.

Call everyone on committee again. If there are people who have not gotten started yet, it is time to remind them that they will need to report in three days.

Three Weeks Before Event: 2nd Meeting—First Reports

Get reports from everyone on committee. If there is one person who is not working, recruit a new person to "help" him or her.

Approve press releases and fliers for neighborhood. Send releases to local newspapers and bulletin notices to local churches.

Begin collecting and sorting merchandise. Recruit volunteer to pick up donations that cannot be delivered.

Make arrangements with local charity (e.g., Salvation Army) to pick up any left-over merchandise.

Notify police of sale date. Make arrangements to get sawhorses and trash barrels from the appropriate politician. Notify neighbors of sale. Check with closest large public parking lot to okay use on sale day.

Recruit artist to make huge banner to hang on or over sale site week before sale.

Two Weeks Before: 3rd Meeting—Arrangements

Continue calls for merchandise and collection.

Go over prospect list to see if anyone was missed. Assign to your best caller any possible donor who has been skipped.

Make list of what equipment you will need to borrow, where you can get it, who will pick it up and *return* it.

Make a list of what you need to buy. Assign purchasing agent to buy it. (Of course, don't buy anything you can get free.)

Make a plan for the layout for sales day. Involved Citizens Against Crosstown held a garage sale using several garages on the same alley—one for clothing, one for household appliances and utensils, one for children's clothing and toys, one for books and plants, one with free coffee and baked goods for sale. If you anticipate a large turnout, you may also want to assign one area in which to check children, one area in which to check pets, and one area in which to leave "hold" merchandise.

Schedule your personnel: who will put up posters, who will sell, who will handle money, who will supervise coffee, who will arbitrate disputes.

Week Before—Final Preparations

Put up banner over sale site.

Place classified ads in papers. Put fliers around neighborhood.

Assign committee people to announce sale at local church and club meetings.

Sort and price all items.

Collect clothing racks, cash boxes, coffee makers, mirrors, adding machine, any other equipment you need to borrow.

DAY BEFORE—BRIEFING.

Set up merchandise in garage(s).

Prepare clear signs for prices, hours, and parking, and hang them high enough for everyone to see.

Plan timetable and gimmicks; e.g., last two hours all merchandise is half-price. Put arrow signs around neighborhood.

Call all workers to make sure they will show up or send a replacement.

Get cash and receipts.

Walk through the sale as though you were a customer. Be sure everything is clearly marked and you have enough bags.

Check security.

Brief all workers on potential problems. One common trick of garage sale shoppers is to remove price tag and try to bully salesperson into a lower price. Choose *one* person who is patient, firm and tactful to be final arbitrator on all items discovered without prices. Be sure that everyone understands that your arbitrator has final decision-making authority—this is not the time for democracy.

Day of Sale

One hour before sale: all workers arrive. Chairperson and staff person have already prepared coffee and doughnuts. Review sales procedures and be sure everyone knows who to send complaints or questions to—chairperson or arbitrator. Be sure everyone knows location of bathrooms, parking, and fire extinguishers (and how to use fire extinguishers).

Be sure you know how the electrical system works and where fuse box or circuit breakers are.

Start coffee.

Set up cash boxes and ledgers.

THE SALE

Start on time. If you've done your publicity thoroughly, you should have a line at the door.

Salespeople sell, advise, and keep an eye out for thieves.

One person has a table set up with organizational literature, written notice of the next meeting or event, membership cards, current issue of the newsletter, and organizational sales materials—buttons, T-shirts, cookbooks, research reports. He or she should pleasantly explain how the shopper can join or help the organization, but should avoid all ideological disputes.

One person makes sure coffee is ready and coffee area is tidy.

Cashiers handle money. Give a receipt with carbon copy for all purchases over $5 by adults. This will produce a mailing list for the next event. Bagger next to cashier wraps and seals all purchases. Never leave too much cash out. Have one head cashier to approve all checks and large bills. Never cash a stranger's check.

Have a barker, or kids passing out handbills, or a teenager with a sandwich board to bring in more traffic off the street.

Chairperson keeps everyone calm and cheerful, finds replacements for the no-shows, settles all disputes with the neighbors about parking or noise, and makes sure that all jobs are getting done.

Photographer takes black and white photos for newspapers and next newsletter.

Close on time.

AFTER THE SALE—CELEBRATION.

Have small party or special refreshments for workers. Share funny stories. Chairperson personally thanks each person for job well done.

All cash is accounted for and deposited at bank. All merchandise not sold is picked up by charity the group has chosen.

DAY AFTER SALE—WRAP-UP.

All borrowed equipment is cleaned and returned.

Garage is completely cleaned up and contents replaced.

Modest but imaginative gift given to host/hostess.

Thank-you notes sent to: workers, people and organizations who lent equipment, police and politicians who provided services, anyone who gave you a plug in a publication or at a meeting.

Apologies are sent to any neighbors or anyone else who complained.

TWO DAYS AFTER—PRESS FOLLOW-UP.

Press release sent to local media reporting success of event with photo of chairperson or clever news item: Mayor buys antique gavel; local celebrity buys "X" for her famous "Xs" collection, etc. This is good reinforcement for the people who worked hard, and will improve attendance for next event. Done correctly, you can establish that your organization's events are *the* place to see and be seen.

Week After Sale—Reports and Payments.

Sale chairperson prepares report for meeting and fundraising chairperson on gross, expenses, net, number of customers, problems, and suggestions for improvements. Include list with names and telephone numbers of all workers.

Treasurer pays all bills.

Fundraising chairperson and sale chairperson prepare list from receipts of customers. Check against list of current supporters.

Send thank-you and membership application to big purchasers not currently on your supporters list.

Prepare card on all new donors, recording money spent, date, name and address.

Clearly mark and store receipts.

Send report on sale to everyone who donated merchandise or money and thank them for their help.

Prepare story for next organizational newsletter.

ORGANIZATIONAL MEETING AFTER SALE

Chairperson of sale gives report announcing profit, number of new members, positive stories, praise for hard workers. Show clippings of before and after stories.

Fundraising chairperson praises sale chairperson and effort, announces tentative time and type of next event.

Appendix 3

How to Prepare a Donor Card

Smart business people always keep complete records. Discipline yourself to prepare a report promptly after each event, keep up-to-date records on your on-going fundraisers (like the membership drive or direct mail returns), and always keep the books in order. Then you can quickly answer any questions from a donor, officer, or committee member. Include an honest evaluation of mistakes and all the good ideas you always get *after* the event in your reports—they will be a boon to the next person.

One of the simplest but most important records to keep is the information on your donors. In addition to giving a receipt for every donation, you should create a system for keeping track of each donor. This can be as simple as hand-written notes on 4 x 6 inch file cards from the dime store, or as complicated as a computerized program. Choose whatever system will be best for your group.

List on the card name, address, home phone, special interests, employer, office address and phone, and whether the donor wants to be reached at work. Then note each time the donor gives you money (or an in-kind donation) by date, amount and the source of the donation (whether it came in response to direct mail, a newsletter appeal, a TV appearance by your president, etc.). Record each time a member pays his or her dues. Be sure to record which member first recruited the other, so that member can encourage renewal of the other's dues.

It is useful to have a system for retrieving donors' names four ways. 1) By *name,* alphabetically. 2) By *location,* for example zip code or town, so you can notify residents of local events. 3) By *source,* so you can be sure to invite everyone who bought at the last auction to the next auction. 4) By *amount,* so you can ask everyone who gave you, say, $50 or more to become patrons for a special event.

FRIENDS OF THE PARKS DONOR
SAMPLE
Card 1.

OLMSTED, Frederick Law   Phone: 555-6789
102 Main Street
Riverside, IL 60546

Work: Park Designer   Phone: 555-1234
Olmsted, Vaux and Company
42 East Oak Street
Riverside, IL 60546

DATE	AMOUNT	SOURCE
June, 1972	$10.00	Dues (Recruited by Theodore Roosevelt)
Dec. 7, 1972	In Kind	Paper cutter for office (=$30)
June, 1973	$10.00	Dues renewal
Aug. 3, 1973	$25.00	Ad: Annual Meeting Ad Book
June, 1974	$10.00	Dues renewal
Aug. 7, 1974	$25.00	Ad: Shakespeare Festival Program
June, 1975	$10.00	Dues renewal
Sept. 2, 1975	$50.00	Honorarium—speech at U. of I.
April 3, 1976	$ 5.00	Bike maintenance workshop
June, 1976	$15.00	Dues renewal, new rate
Sept. 4, 1976	$25.00	"Save the Elm Trees" mailing
April 2, 1977	$25.00	Patron: Tribute to Duke Ellington
May 7, 1977	In Kind	Rakes for Park Clean Up (=$40)
June, 1977	$15.00	Dues renewal
Sept. 5, 1977	$25.00	Patron: Marathon Run

Appendix 4
Where to Get Advice

1. *Experienced members.* First, and always best, is people in your organization who have run fundraising events before. The longer they have worked and the more money they have raised, the better advice they can give you.

2. *Local talent.* The people in your area who do the best membership fundraising. Find out how they do their fundraising. Father Leonard Dubi proposed the Citizens Action Program's first ad book because his church, St. Daniel the Prophet, had just finished one for its 25th anniversary. CAP's ad book was then copied by Chicago NOW and Women Employed (WE). Bernie Willow set up the Bingo

for Our Lady of Grace school. It is one of the most successful Bingos in Chicago. He has also generously helped set up Bingos for the 16th District Police Sports Program, the CAP Senior Citizens, a drug rehabilitation program, and Steelworkers Fight Back.

3. The best *professionals* in your area. Most large universities and hospitals have professional fundraisers. The president of the women's board of the local large disease association—cancer, heart, multiple sclerosis—often will have more than twenty years experience and is as knowledgeable as the pros. People like that are usually very gracious and willing to talk. Don't be afraid to ask. When Roger Craver was director of development at Common Cause he invented the most successful direct mail membership program in the country. In two years only five people asked him for advice—and he loves to give advice!

4. *Calendar keepers.* In small towns the chamber of commerce often maintains a calendar to clear events so groups won't duplicate dates. The chamber can tell you who else knows the most about the kind of event you are scheduling. In larger cities, often the society editors of daily newspapers serve as the calendar coordinator in lieu of anyone else. They can steer you to helpful people with the right expertise.

5. *National office.* If your group is a chapter of a large national organization, find out what fundraising advice and material tailored for your group the national office offers. For example, National NOW offers interest-free loans to local chapters for seed money; the National Women's Political Caucus produces a T-shirt and poster of Ginny, the courageous Congressional candidate in Gary Trudeau's *Doonesbury*, for sale by local chapters; the League of Women Voters national office prints several good pamphlets for use by local fundraisers.

6. *Similar organizations.* Contact other organizations similar to yours in other parts of the country. Events can be copied from one part of the country to another. The Chicago Junior League began its Paper Peddlers program by flying two women to Texas to learn how the Dallas League did it. Groups in Minnesota, California, and Tennessee adapted the CAP ad book material. You can easily send a letter to another group with the questions you need answered, followed by a phone call to confirm receipt and urge prompt response.

7. *Public relations professionals* often have to "find a charity" for a promotional event—the opening of a theatre or restaurant, a wine-tasting for a gourmet shop, or a showing of new fashions for a department store. If you establish a good relationship with a professional and prove you can deliver the number of people you promise, he or she will enjoy working with you. The Chicago Heart Assn. had not one, but *two* openings of the same restaurant—its original

opening, then the reopening when the first owner bought it back from the second owner. The Heart Assn. made money each time. All you have to do is sell your tickets. It is the PR person and his or her client who have to make everything work.

8. *Continuing education.* Many local colleges or high school adult education classes offer excellent courses in public relations for community groups, sales courses, and good beginning accounting courses. Check the local curriculum. If you will be doing a lot of correspondence without a secretary, you should learn to type.

There are many professional "fundraising," "development," "direct marketing" or "direct mail" seminars for sale. Most are over-priced and aimed at the dinosaurs—huge national charities with many paid staff people. Representatives of small, rural, minority, ethnic, or women's groups almost always feel gypped because the course is useless for them. *Never* sign up for one of these unless it has been personally recommended by someone you know and trust.

9. Order and read the *books* in the bibliography which cover your interest. Ask your library to order them so everyone can use them.

Appendix 5
Exercises

1.   WINNERS
Make a list of every time you gave any person or group money. Include everything from coins in the can for a poppy or a doughnut, to regular dues. Figure out what made you give: cause, asker, habit, guilt, peer group pressure, other. Count the number of ways any one group can get money out of you. For example, your church may get your regular pledge (dues), an extra donation for the seminarian from your parish, another donation for flowers, and a special campaign contribution to protect the stained glass windows; the church may also sell you a calendar, Christmas cards, and numerous small purchases at the Spring Fling and the Fall Fandango.

2.   ALSO-RANS
Make a list of every time a person or group *just missed* getting your money. They moved on too soon, or didn't answer your question, or didn't send the envelope. Make a list of reasons, and solutions.

3.   LOSERS
Make a list of people and groups you would *never* give one cent. Make a list of reasons why.

4.   BEGIN A FILE OF "FUNDRAISING IDEAS"
Clip the society column and the community calendar from the

paper. Send away for free booklets. Write your friends and relatives and ask them what they do in their towns. Go to the library and see what's available there. Ask the library to order books for you.

5. BRAINSTORMING

Get your committee together for an evening of brainstorming. If possible bring in a disinterested outsider to chair. Set two firm rules:

1) All ideas are good ideas.
2) You can only give your idea once.

This is not the time to say "We already tried that and it didn't work," or "We've always done it this way," or "We can't afford it," or "That's not our job; X should do it." This is your chance to stretch the imagination of everyone on the committee.

List all the ideas on big sheets of paper. After the meeting type them up and send them out to all the committee members to consider the possibilities of implementation. Meet again in a month to consider where to go on them.

Sample thought provokers:

"If they find Howard Hughes' will, and we're in it for one million dollars, what should we do with it?"

"What could we do to double the membership and/or the budget in five years?"

"What are the needs of the community which no one is filling now?"

A good one to use is the turned-around question:

"What could we do to put the church (the community congress, the hospital) out of business?"

(This kind of question was used in a brainstorming session at IBM. The question was, "What could you do to slow down your secretary?" They thought of smeary carbon paper, a typewriter with keys that jam together, and indelible ink which could never be corrected. When they turned these around, they came up with the idea for a typewriter with the correcting tape built in—a feature the author personally testifies speeds things up!)

6. BEGIN A FILE OF FUND-APPEAL LETTERS

Keep a file of all the fund-appeal letters you get. Divide them by "membership," "donation," "best" and "worst." Plagiarize freely from the best. Figure out what is especially awful about the worst ones and make yourself a list of "don'ts" to follow.

You can also ask your friends to pass along their letters to you so you can get more examples. Try to get a Republican and a Democrat, a feminist, a public interest law donor, an ecology freak, your dentist, and your minister to forward their mail. You will be amazed by both the variety and the duplication.

7.   SELLING

All fundraising is selling. Learn how the pros sell. This sounds corny, but it works: Go to a Tupperware party (or any kind of "we sell our product in your home" party). See how they use incentives, group pressure, time payment plans, and package deals. Talk to your local Avon lady or anyone who sells cleaning products or greeting cards from his or her home. All of them depend on high sales and repeat customers. Some local chambers of commerce offer seminars on selling; see if you can get a scholarship or a discount to attend for your not-for-profit group. Salespeople love to brag about their successes—ask them.

8.   VOLUNTEER

Volunteer to work on the committee for the next event produced by the best fundraisers in town. Do as much as possible to see how they do it. Tell them honestly that you are the fundraiser for the Carson City Consumers Coalition and want to learn by doing. They should be flattered and glad to spend some extra time with you.

Volunteer to work for a good political candidate. Electoral campaigns are great examples of involving a lot of people for an intense short-term effort with high publicity and a definite deadline. Explain that you want to learn the managerial skills and logistics. Insist on working with the chairpeople and the thinkers. Work hard but don't let them stick you in a corner addressing envelopes. If you can't work with the top fundraising and planning people, don't bother. There will always be other smarter candidates who will let you help where you can learn something.

Appendix 6
Bibliography

Basic; you should have these and know how to use them:
1.   Dictionary—any good paperback.
2.   Thesaurus—any good paperback.
3.   Etiquette—any paperback, e.g., *Amy Vanderbilt's Everyday Etiquette.*
4.   Calendar—one at the office, one at home, and an appointment book to carry with you at all times.
5.   Media Directory—A list of all the working press in your

town: newspapers, radio, and TV. It is usually published by the local publicity club (public relations professionals' association), the telephone company, the Newspaper Guild, or clipping services, such as Luce or Burrelle's.

6. Current postal regulations—Get from main post office.

7. Address book, Rolodex, or card system—an efficient way to organize and retrieve names, addresses, and phone numbers.

8. Telephone books.

9. Subscription to your best daily newspapers and whatever else your members read.

10. A current library card.

11. Local police and fire regulations for crowds. Their emergency telephone numbers.

12. Almanac—any paperback. A handy reference for world facts, such as population, historical notes, and correct spelling of names and places.

General:

Fundraising and Local Community Organizations. Robert Creamer. The Midwest Academy, 600 W. Fullerton Ave., Chicago, IL 60614. one page, 1974. 40¢. How to plan your fundraising to complement your organizing strategy.

Helping NOW Grow—Fundraising. Chicago NOW, 53 W. Jackson, Rm. 1501, Chicago, IL 60604. 20 pp., $2, including ad book. Best on ad books, raffles, canvassing, parties and reports.

The Nonprofit Money Game. Funding Information Service, Junior League of Washington, D.C., 3039 M Street, N.W., Washington, D.C. 20007. 32 pp., $1. Best all-around manual.

Politics (Can be copied for any high-publicity short-term action campaign):

Fund Raising. Democratic National Committee Consultation Program, 1625 Massachusetts Ave., N.W., Washington, D.C. 20036. 1976. 36 pp. $5. Good information on political campaign fund raising. Includes good timetable for ten-week special event.

Tips on Political Fund Raising With Side Trips into Budgeting and Legal Aspects. Campaign Associates, Suite 408, Petroleum Bldg., Wichita, KS 67202. 59 pp. $8.95. Good political wrap-up.

Winning Elections: A Handbook in Participatory Politics. Dick Simpson. The Swallow Press, Inc., Chicago. 1972. 200 pp. $3.95. Best on *coffees* as people- and money-producers. Excellent sample plan for $25,000 campaign and cash budget.

General—Written for Professionals:

The Art of Fund Raising. Irving R. Warner. Harper and Row, New York. 1975. 176 pp. $7.95. Good and most current over-all. Aimed at big-money professionals.

The Complete Fund Raising Guide. Howard R. Mirkin. Public Service Materials Center. 355 Lexington Ave., New York, N.Y. 10017. 1975. 160 pp. $12.50. Overview of professional fundraising —grants, campaigns, deferred giving, and federated funding (United Ways). Good chapter on organizing a house-to-house solicitation.

Designs for Fund-Raising: Principles-Patterns-Techniques. Harold J. Seymour. McGraw-Hill Book Co., New York. 1966. 210 pp. $10. This is "The Bible" for professional big-money fundraisers. (Examples include how to raise $60 million for Princeton's capital campaign.) Written for established groups with leadership with "influence or affluence." Excellent on motivation and human factors.

Giving USA—1976 Annual Report: A Compilation of Facts and Trends on American Philanthropy for the Year 1975. American Association of Fund-Raising Counsel, Inc., 500 Fifth Ave., New York, NY 10036. 52 pp. $5.50. Published annually.

Just for Fun:

Chase's Calendar of Annual Events. Special days, weeks and months in 1977. William D. Chase. Apple Tree Press, Box 1012, Flint, MI 48501. Published annually. $5. 80 pp. All national, state and religious holidays, local agricultural and commercial festivals, plus famous people's birthdays, and more. Great source for party ideas.

Fund Raising for Small Charities and Organizations. H. R. Humphries. David & Charles, Trafalgar Square, North Ponfret, VT 05053. 1972. 124 pp. $5.95. This is how they do it in England. Charming examples—"garden fêtes" and novel gimmicks like the "tombola," which is a sort of roulette raffle.

Give: Who Gets Your Charity Dollar? Harvey Katz. Anchor Books, Garden City, N.Y. 1975. 214 pp. $2.50. (Paperback.) Fascinating scandal stories and how to evaluate where to give *your* money.

Ball. William Wright. Saturday Review Press, New York. 1972. 252 pp. $7.95. Amusing account of a year in the lives of the rich folks who produce and attend the annual "April in Paris" charity ball.

Grants & Government Money:

About Foundations: How to Find the Facts You Need to Get a Grant. Judith B. Margolin. The Foundation Center, 888 Seventh Avenue, New York, NY 10019. 1977. 48 pp. $3 prepaid. Clear, step-by-step instructions for discovering and getting the most out of basic reference books, annual reports, IRS information returns and other resources available at the Foundation Center's national and regional libraries.

The Bread Game: The Realities of Foundation Fundraising. Glide Publications, 330 Ellis St., San Francisco, CA 94102. 1975. 96 pp. $3.45. Introduction to pursuing grants.

Getting Your $hare. An Introduction to Fundraising. Linda Small. Women's Action Alliance. 370 Lexington Avenue, New York, NY 10017. 1976. 36 pp. $2. How to apply for foundation grants, a proposal checklist, a resource list, addresses of the state collection centers of The Foundation Center, and a list of change-oriented foundations.

Grants: How to Find Out About Them and What to Do Next. Virginia P. White. Plenum Press, 227 W. 17th St., New York, NY 10011. 1976. 354 pp. $19.50. Recommended "best" by the *Grantsmanship Center News.* Readable and thorough; covers both federal government grants and private foundation grants.

MAGAZINES:

The Grantsmanship Center News. The Grantsmanship Center, 1015 W. Olympic Blvd., Los Angeles, CA 90015. $15.00/year (six issues). Very readable; best current and comprehensible information on grants and government money. Regularly reviews new books on the grant game. Offers inexpensive reprints of specific grant or government money articles.

Bibliographies (Where to go to get more information on all the not-grass roots kind of funding):

Bibliography of Fundraising and Philanthropy. George T. Holloway, Executive Editor. National Catholic Development Conference, 130 E. 40th St., New York, NY 10016. 1975, with 1976 supplement. $22.50. Books and periodicals in general, plus selected titles by subject such as The Arts, Education, Hospital and Health Care. Eighty-one pages in Bibliography; twenty-three pages in supplement. Ask the library to get this one.

"Basic Grantsmanship Library." The Grantsmanship Center *News,* 1015 W. Olympic Blvd., Los Angeles, CA 90015. Reprint. 1976. 8 pp. 75¢. Essential publications for soliciting foundation grants or federal program funding. (Published annually.)

Sources of Information on Proposal Writing and Possible Funding. U.S. Department of Labor, Employment Standards Administration, Women's Bureau, Washington, D.C. 20210. 1975. 10 pp. Free. Includes bibliography on writing proposals and obtaining grants, private foundation grants and references, and federal grants and sources of information.

Available from the Foundation Center, 888 Seventh Ave., New York, NY 10019. One copy free:

"A Basic Guide to Information on Funding and Other Nonprofit Funding Sources." Lesley Stern, Librarian, 4 pp. 1976.

"Sources of Information for Preparing Foundation Grant Proposals". Lesley Stern, Librarian. 2 pp. 1976.

"Some Sources of Information on Scholarships, Fellowships, and Loans for Individuals." Lesley Stern, Librarian, 8 pp. 1975.

Leadership:

The Effective Voluntary Board of Directors. What It Is and How It Works. William R. Conrad and William E. Glenn. Swallow Press. 811 W. Junior Terrace. Chicago, IL 60613. 1976. 200 pp. $6.95. Two veterans outline how Boards can work most efficiently and effectively. Many useful charts.

How to Be An Effective Board Member. SEDFRE. One Penn Plaza, New York, NY 10001. 1973. 22 pp. $1. Written especially for small minority groups, includes good info on both how to run your own meetings and how to get your voice heard when you are the minority representative to a larger board.

On Being Board, Or, How Not to Be Dead Wood. Rocky Mountain Planned Parenthood, 2030 East 20th Ave., Denver, CO 80205. 1973. 16 pp. 50¢. Written for Planned Parenthood board members, but will serve well for anyone considering a leadership role in a controversial organization. Thorough, clever and very readable. Includes my favorite collection of quotations.

Note: Other helpful books and articles are listed at the end of each chapter and sample event. Check these for more books to order or recommend to your library. See especially the listings at the end of "Publicity" and "Making Book."

Appendix 7
The Foundation Center Regional Libraries

The Foundation Center operates libraries in most states, Puerto Rico and Mexico. Each regional collection is staffed by a professional librarian and is listed in the phone book. All are open to the public at no charge, and some also provide telephone reference service.

THE FOUNDATION CENTER

The Foundation Center, incorporated in 1956 by the Board of Regents of the University of the State of New York, is an independent agency dedicated to the public interest, providing factual information on the philanthropic foundations through its libraries, research activities, and publications.

National Collections

The Foundation Center
888 Seventh Avenue
New York, New York 10019

The Foundation Center
1001 Connecticut Avenue, N.W.
Washington, D.C. 20036

Donors Forum of Chicago
208 South LaSalle Street
Chicago, Illinois 60604

Regional Collections
Geographical Coverage

ALABAMA
Birmingham Public Library
2020 Seventh Avenue, North
Birmingham 35203

Alabama

ARKANSAS
Little Rock Public Library
Reference Department
700 Louisiana Street
Little Rock 72201

Arkansas

CALIFORNIA
University Research Library
Reference Department
University of California
Los Angeles 90024

*Arizona, California,
Colorado, Nevada, Utah*

San Francisco Public Library
Business Branch
530 Kearny Street
San Francisco 94108

*Alaska, California, Colorado,
Hawaii, Idaho, Montana,
Nevada, Oregon, Utah,
Washington, Wyoming*

COLORADO
Denver Public Library
Sociology Division
1357 Broadway
Denver 80203

Colorado

CONNECTICUT
Hartford Public Library
Reference Department
500 Main Street
Hartford 06103

Connecticut,
Massachusetts,
Rhode Island

FLORIDA
Jacksonville Public Library
Business, Science, and Industry
   Department
122 North Ocean Street
Jacksonville 32202

Florida

Miami-Dade Public Library
Florida Collection
One Biscayne Boulevard
Miami 33132

Florida

GEORGIA
Atlanta Public Library
10 Prior Street
Atlanta 30303

Florida, Georgia,
South Carolina, Tennessee

HAWAII
Thomas Hale Hamilton Library
Humanities and Social Sciences
   Division
2550 The Mall
Honolulu 96822

California, Hawaii,
Oregon, Washington

IDAHO
Caldwell Public Library
1010 Dearborn Street
Caldwell 83605

Idaho

INDIANA
Indianapolis - Marion County
   Public Library
40 East St. Clair Street
Indianapolis 46204

Indiana

IOWA
Des Moines Public Library
100 Locust Street
Des Moines 50309

Iowa

KANSAS
Topeka Public Library
Adult Services Department
1515 West Tenth Street
Topeka 66604

Kansas

KENTUCKY
Louisville Free Public Library
Fourth and York Streets
Louisville 40203

Kentucky

LOUISIANA
New Orleans Public Library
Business and Science Division
219 Loyola Avenue
New Orleans 70140

Louisiana

MAINE
University of Maine at Portland-
Gorham
Center for Research and
Advanced Study
246 Deering Avenue
Portland 04102

Maine, New Hampshire,
Vermont

MARYLAND
Enoch Pratt Free Library
Social Science and History
Department
400 Cathedral Street
Baltimore 21201

Maryland

MASSACHUSETTS
Associated Foundation of Greater
Boston
294 Washington Street, Suite 501
Boston 02108

Connecticut,
Massachusetts

Boston Public Library
Copley Square
Boston 02117

Connecticut,
Massachusetts,
Rhode Island

MICHIGAN
Henry Ford Centennial Library
15301 Michigan Avenue
Dearborn 48126

Michigan

Grand Rapids Public Library
Sociology and Education
Department
Library Plaza
Grand Rapids 49502

Michigan

MINNESOTA
Minneapolis Public Library
Sociology Department
300 Nicollet Mall
Minneapolis 55401

Iowa, Minnesota,
North Dakota,
South Dakota

MISSISSIPPI
Jackson Metropolitan Library   *Mississippi*
301 North State Street
Jackson 39201

MISSOURI
Kansas City Public Library   *Kansas, Missouri*
311 East 12th Street
Kansas City 64106

The Danforth Foundation Library   *Illinois, Missouri*
222 South Central Avenue
St. Louis 63105

MONTANA
Eastern Montana College Library   *Montana*
Reference Department
Billings 59101

NEBRASKA
Omaha Public Library   *Nebraska*
1823 Harney Street
Omaha 68102

NEW HAMPSHIRE
The New Hampshire Charitable   *New Hampshire*
   Fund
One South Street
Concord 03301

NEW JERSEY
New Jersey State Library   *New Jersey*
Reference Section
185 West State Street
Trenton 08625

NEW MEXICO
New Mexico State Library   *New Mexico*
300 Don Gaspar Street
Santa Fe 87501

NEW YORK
New York State Library   *New York*
State Education Department
Education Building
Albany 12224

Buffalo and Erie County Public   *New York*
   Library
Lafayette Square
Buffalo 14203

Levittown Public Library   *New York*
Reference Department
One Bluegrass Lane
Levittown 11756

Rochester Public Library   *New York*
Business and Social Sciences Div.
115 South Avenue
Rochester 14604

NORTH CAROLINA
William R. Perkins Library   *North Carolina*
Duke University
Durham 27706

OHIO
The Cleveland Foundation Library   *Ohio*
700 National City Bank Building
Cleveland 44114

OKLAHOMA
Oklahoma City Community   *Oklahoma*
   Foundation
1300 North Broadway
Oklahoma City 73103

Tulsa City-County Library System   *Oklahoma*
400 Civic Center
Tulsa 74103

OREGON
Library Association of Portland   *Alaska, California,*
Education and Psychology Dept.   *Hawaii, Oregon,*
801 S.W. Tenth Avenue   *Washington*
Portland 97205

PENNSYLVANIA
The Free Library of Philadelphia   *Delaware, New Jersey,*
Logan Square   *Pennsylvania*
Philadelphia 19103

Hillman Library   *Pennsylvania*
University of Pittsburgh
Pittsburgh 15213

RHODE ISLAND
Providence Public Library   *Rhode Island*
Reference Department
150 Empire Street
Providence 02903

SOUTH CAROLINA
South Carolina State Library   *South Carolina*
Reader Services Department
1500 Senate Street
Columbia 29211

TENNESSEE
Memphis Public Library   *Tennessee*
1850 Peabody Avenue
Memphis 38104

TEXAS
The Hogg Foundation for Mental   *Arkansas, Louisiana,*
   Health   *New Mexico, Oklahoma,*
The University of Texas   *Texas*
Austin 78712

Dallas Public Library   *Texas*
History and Social Sciences
   Division
1954 Commerce Street
Dallas 75201

UTAH
Salt Lake City Public Library   *Utah*
Information and Adult Services
209 East Fifth Street
Salt Lake City 84111

VERMONT
State of Vermont Department   *New Hampshire,*
   of Libraries   *Vermont*
Reference Services Unit
111 State Street
Montpelier 05602

VIRGINIA
Richmond Public Library   *Virginia*
Business, Science, & Technology
   Department
101 East Franklin Street
Richmond 23219

WASHINGTON
Seattle Public Library   *California, Oregon,*
1000 Fourth Avenue   *Washington*
Seattle 98104

WEST VIRGINIA
Kanawha County Public Library   *West Virginia*
123 Capitol Street
Charleston 25301

WISCONSIN
Marquette University Memorial
  Library
1415 West Wisconsin Avenue
Milwaukee 53233

Illinois, Indiana, Iowa,
Michigan, Minnesota,
Ohio, Wisconsin

WYOMING
Laramie County Community
  College Library
1400 East College Drive
Cheyenne 82001

Wyoming

PUERTO RICO
Consumer Education and Service
  Center
Department of Consumer Affairs
Minillas Central Government
  Building North
Santurce 00908

Selected foundations

MEXICO
Biblioteca Benjamin Franklin
Londres 16
Mexico City 6, D.F.

Selected foundations

Additional Regional Collections Opened in 1977

ARIZONA
Tucson Public Library
200 S. 6th Avenue
Tucson 85701

Arizona

CALIFORNIA
San Diego Public Library
820 E Street
San Diego 92101

California

ILLINOIS
Sangamon State University Library
Shepherd Road
Springfield 62708

Illinois

MICHIGAN
Purdy Library
Wayne State University
Detroit 48202

Michigan

TEXAS
Minnie Stevens Piper Foundation
201 North St. Mary's Street
San Antonio 78205

Texas

Appendix 8
How to Rebound From a Fundloser

> *Murphy's Law: "Anything that can go wrong, will."*
> *Flanagan's Corollary: "Even things that can't go wrong, will."*

My favorite TV show is Julia Child's "French Chef" cooking show on public television. One reason it is so good is that she not only shows you how to do everything right, she shows you what to do if something goes wrong. I have seen her drop a poached salmon on the floor and patch it up with cream cheese frosting, poke a hole in her yule log cake and fill it in with meringue mushrooms, and curdle her hollandaise sauce only to save it with some lemon juice. The idea is that beginning cooks cannot afford to waste anything so there has to be a way to save the ingredients.

The same thing is true in fundraising. Sometimes things go wrong and you have to save the ingredients. In your case the ingredients are the morale of your members and the momentum of your campaign. Fortunately, there are ways to do this.

The best defense, of course, is a good offense, which is plenty of advance planning. You can't be wiped out by the blizzard of the century if you have already pre-sold the tickets for an event. This is why the foundation of your budget must be the dues of the members rather than income from special events.

But let's say you were counting on the income from one event to carry you through one or two months. Crises happen. I have had the cash box stolen from a costume party and had the bartender get drunk and give away all the liquor at a dance. I have helped to throw out 600 pounds of rotten chicken on a hot July day. I have had drunken speakers, stoned bands, and marital fist fights. Believe me, crises happen.

A group in Vermont got a wholesale order of honey that tasted like soy sauce. All the bottles they sold at retail came back. A group in Montana was promised a premier of a big movie only to have the same film open a week earlier across the state line only ten minutes away. A ballet board imported a world-famous French clothes designer to impress big donors ($5,000+) at an expensive dinner. Unfortunately, the designer had a tantrum and refused to attend the dinner because the airport limousine drove off with all his clothes. Remember Flanagan's Corollary: "Even things that can't go wrong, will."

So let's say you planned an event, worked hard, expected to make $300 and lost money. Psychologically, even breaking even is a loss. What do you do?

The first thing to do is discuss it in the committee as soon as possible. Right after the event is best, but if people are too tired, cross or inebriated, schedule a meeting for the next day. The chair-person makes sure the committee members all gather to discuss the crisis. They need to talk about 1) what went wrong 2) what can be done immediately to recoup the money.

The very first thing the chairperson must do is make sure this is not an occasion for pinning the blame on one person. If there were any mistakes of judgment, the chairperson should accept full re-sponsibility. Simply say, "It was my fault." Then you won't debilitate the committee quarreling over who hired the rotten band.

1)   What went wrong? Sometimes, it is a combination of causes that all point toward disharmony on the committee and among the membership as a whole. Fundraising reflects the health of the organi-zation. If people are discouraged, or insult the leadership, or make promises they don't keep, it shows the success of the organization is not very important to them. If the causes are organizational, it is time to reorganize. It then becomes the problem of the executive board, not the fundraising committee.

If the members *are* committed to the group and really tried hard but still didn't make money, there are fundraising reasons and solu-tions. This is the time to discuss what went wrong. Was it that there were only five volunteers killing themselves when there should have been twenty people dividing the work? Was the choice of the event itself wrong—you learned your members really won't buy tickets to a night at the roller rink? Was the price too high or the appeal too low?

Make a list on paper or on a blackboard of what went wrong and what to do differently next time. It is a great psychological re-lief to pin down the precise problem so it doesn't seem like *everything* is a disaster. It is also important that everyone on the committee realizes it is not anybody's "fault" (the chairperson has absorbed that), and that they all agree on what the problems are. This short-circuits the Monday morning quarterback who will want to call everyone to remind them that she never wanted to do a fashion show anyway.

2)   What can be done immediately to recoup the money? The best cure for a defeat is a success. The group needed $300. The event lost $50. So now the group needs $350. Instead of dwelling on the problems, set a meeting in three days to decide what you will do im-mediately to make that $350. Everyone feels better knowing there is a goal in view. Ask each person to collect some ideas for how to raise the $350 right away. The obvious point that will be raised is "We just tried to make $300 and failed; how can we make $350 next week?" The answer is: 1) Next week we will be older and smarter, and 2) it is our responsibility to keep the organization alive. It needs

$350, so we need to raise it. If anyone does not want to see the organization succeed, or refuses to make a commitment to raise the money, it is time for the slacker to get off the committee and make room for someone else who will do the work. The only plus about crises is they are guaranteed to clear the deadwood off your committee in a big hurry! The chairperson should find fresh faces to replace them before the planning meeting.

Emergency fundraisers. Here are a few emergency fundraisers which you can use to raise the money quickly. They are discussed at other places in this book. Depending on your membership, you may have to do two or three to make your goal. They all assume you have no seed money but several willing workers. In addition, there is always the basic level of grass roots fundraising: ask for money. Ask the members who have already given to give again, and ask each of them to ask two other people to give. This will at least keep the phones working until you run your emergency fundraiser.

Emergency fundraisers:
1. Bake sale, p. 100
2. Coffee/tea, p. 65
3. Do-it-yourself cocktail party, p. 115
4. Door-to-door canvassing, member style, p. 165
5. Dutch auction or memorabilia auction, p. 97
6. Membership drive, p. 73
7. Pot luck dinner, p. 86
8. Raffle, p. 89

Appendix 9
Training Schools for Organizers and Leaders

Grass roots fundraising is only one of the challenges for membership organizations. You may want or need more training in all the other skills needed to run a successful organization today, such as planning strategy, choosing tactics, building membership, developing leaders, strengthening leader-staff relationships, dealing with conflict, conducting action research, and maximizing your media campaigns. Fortunately, there are several excellent schools which specialize in training organizers and leaders.

All of them offer training sessions at their own schools, intern-style field placement training, and specialized on-site courses. The courses are taught by experienced professional organizers and veteran leaders of successful membership organizations. All of them also offer on-going consultation under contract. In addition, they can recommend local individuals for personal consultation.

For information on costs, curriculum, criteria for admission, and applications, write:

> Bill Grace
> Director
> Center for Urban Encounter
> 3410 University Ave., S.E.
> Minneapolis, Minn. 55414

> Ed Chambers
> Executive Director
> Industrial Areas Foundation Training Institute
> 12 E. Grand Ave.
> Chicago, Ill. 60611

> Meg Campbell
> Training Director
> The Institute
> 3814 Ross Avenue
> Dallas, Texas 75204
>   or
> Lina Newhauser
> Conference Coordinator
> The Institute
> 523 W. 15th
> Little Rock, Ark. 72202
> (Formerly The Arkansas Institute for Social Justice)

Dave Knotts
Director
Mid-Atlantic Center for Community Concern
554 Bloomfield Ave.
Bloomfield, N.J. 07003

Heather Booth
Director
The Academy
600 W. Fullerton
Chicago, Ill. 60614
(Formerly the Midwest Academy)

Ed Shurna
Director
National Training and Information Center
121 W. Superior St.
Chicago, Ill. 60610

Dave Beckwith
Director
New England Training Center for Community Organizers
19 Davis Street
Providence, R.I. 09208

Mike Miller
Director
Organize, Inc.
814 Mission St.
San Francisco, Cal. 94103

FUTURE GRASS ROOTS
FUNDRAISING INFORMATION

The Youth Project plans to periodically update *The Grass Roots Fundraising Book.* If you are interested in receiving information on future publications concerning the latest advice on "how to raise money in your community," please register with us now.

Fill in the form on the back of this page and mail it to:

Director of Publications
The National Office
The Youth Project
1000 Wisconsin Avenue, NW
Washington, D.C. 20007

Fill in the form below and mail it to:

Director of Publications
The National Office
The Youth Project
1000 Wisconsin Avenue, NW
Washington, D.C. 20007

Please keep me informed about your future fundraising publications.

NAME_____
(Please print)
ORGANIZATION_____
YOUR ADDRESS_____
CITY_____ **STATE**_____ **ZIP**_____

Do you know someone who could use *The Grass Roots Fundraising Book?*

NAME_____
ORGANIZATION_____
HIS OR HER ADDRESS_____
CITY_____ **STATE**_____ **ZIP**_____

NAME_____
ORGANIZATION_____
HIS OR HER ADDRESS_____
CITY_____ **STATE**_____ **ZIP**_____

FUTURE GRASS ROOTS
FUNDRAISING INFORMATION

The Youth Project plans to periodically update *The Grass Roots Fundraising Book.* If you are interested in receiving information on future publications concerning the latest advice on "how to raise money in your community," please register with us now.

Fill in the form on the back of this page and mail it to:

Director of Publications
The National Office
The Youth Project
1000 Wisconsin Avenue, NW
Washington, D.C. 20007

Fill in the form below and mail it to:

Director of Publications
The National Office
The Youth Project
1000 Wisconsin Avenue, NW
Washington, D.C. 20007

Please keep me informed about your future fundraising publications.

NAME_____
(Please print)
ORGANIZATION_____
YOUR ADDRESS_____
CITY_____ **STATE**_____ **ZIP**_____

Do you know someone who could use *The Grass Roots Fundraising Book?*

NAME_____
ORGANIZATION_____
HIS OR HER ADDRESS_____
CITY_____ **STATE**_____ **ZIP**_____

NAME_____
ORGANIZATION_____
HIS OR HER ADDRESS_____
CITY_____ **STATE**_____ **ZIP**_____